THE CONSCIENCE OF CAPITALISM

THE CONSCIENCE OF CAPITALISM

BUSINESS SOCIAL RESPONSIBILITY TO COMMUNITIES

Terry L. Besser

Westport, Connecticut
London

Library of Congress Cataloging-in-Publication Data

Besser, Terry L., 1945–
    The conscience of capitalism : business social responsibility to communities / Terry L. Besser.
        p. cm.
    Includes bibliographical references and index.
    ISBN 0–275–97589–4 (alk. paper)
    1. Social responsibility of business—Iowa.   2. Small business—Iowa.   I. Title.
HD60.5.U52I83   2002
    658.4'08—dc21   2001059098

British Library Cataloguing in Publication Data is available.

Library of Congress Catalog Card Number: 2001059098
ISBN: 0–275–97589–4

First published in 2002

Praeger Publishers, 88 Post Road West, Westport, CT 06881
An imprint of Greenwood Publishing Group, Inc.
www.praeger.com

Printed in the United States of America

∞™

The paper used in this book complies with the
Permanent Paper Standard issued by the National
Information Standards Organization (Z39.48–1984).

10 9 8 7 6 5 4 3 2 1

Contents

Illustrations

CHAPTER 1

Introduction

On a cool Saturday morning in April in the small Iowa town of Socksberg, about 25 people gather in front of City Hall. They are organizing work details to plant flowers and tidy up the downtown area, the parks, and around the town signs that announce "Socksberg, A Town with a Future" along the two highways into town. A group of local business owners and managers planned the work and recruited other business operators, friends, and neighbors to help. A local greenhouse donated the flowers. Tools and materials were provided by local businesses. As the group waits for others to arrive, they eat doughnuts and drink coffee, both donated by the local bakery. Lunch will be provided by the downtown deli and meat market, and served by volunteers from the Jaycees. Among the people standing around City Hall are three downtown retail store owners, two bank officers, a pharmacist who owns and manages the local pharmacy and medical supply store, a realtor, a couple of insurance agents, the owner of a local trucking firm and two of his employees, the agricultural co-op manager, and several retired citizens.

Although the details of the Socksberg spring cleanup project just described are fictitious, the general facts are true. Socksberg business people organize, finance, and staff a spring cleanup every year, plus many other community betterment projects. Yet when *Newsweek* carried the story, "The Good Corporation: RIP" in 1993, the average resident of Socksberg might have agreed with many other Americans that the good corporation is dead, or at least endangered. The disparity between residents' impressions of business social responsibility and the reality in Socksberg highlights the major questions that prompted the research for this book.

Those questions are: What do we mean by good corporate citizenship? Do activities like planting flowers and donating coffee for a community project count? Do expectations about community citizenship differ by size of business? All the businesses in the Socksberg example are small businesses. Is more or less expected of them than giant corporations? What do the operators of small businesses expect of themselves in regard to "corporate citizenship?" Do business operators and citizens agree with some scholars who maintain that the only responsibility of small businesses to society is to make a profit and avoid "social irresponsibility" (Van Auken and Ireland 1982)? Are the resources of small businesses so limited in comparison to large corporations that their contributions to the public welfare don't matter? What role does the industry of the business play in corporate citizenship? For example, do firms that rely on local customers such as retail stores, banks, hospitals, and beauty shops have more responsibility to the community than manufacturers and long distance truckers?

In some of the published studies of the association between communities and businesses, business operators who work for "community betterment" are actually appropriating the term as a disguise for efforts to promote their own personal or business interests. John Logan and Harvey Molotch (1987), created the term "the growth machine" to describe the coalition of business operators who seek their own self-aggrandizement regardless of the consequences to the community, or sometimes with the unexamined conviction that furthering business welfare will always benefit the community. Utilizing the Logan and Molotch perspective, we return to the Socksberg example above and ask, "Are the business people sprucing up Socksberg because they are good citizens or because it will improve their business?" More generally, what are the rewards and costs to business owners and managers who consider themselves to be good citizens and to those who do not contribute to or get involved in community betterment?

I do not intend to discount the numerous instances of business support for "community improvement" that are prompted by personal or business self-interest of some kind. Instead I suggest, and will attempt to show in this book, that the situation is usually more complex than the "growth machine" perspective allows. Findings from interviews conducted for this book support Logan and Molotch's thesis in that business owners and managers reported receiving benefit from their various contributions to the community, even though most noted the difficulty in finding direct evidence of business gain. On the other hand, the majority also recounted incidents when they lost business customers and endured personal threats and insults as a result of their work for the community. Support for controversial community projects such as bond issues for infrastructure improvements, zoning decisions, school reorganization, and building recreation facilities or bike trails seemed to draw the most ire. However, even seemingly innocuous projects like contributing to a pork dinner can be construed as support for a particular livestock production system and result in complaints from customers and threats to "take my business elsewhere."

Some of the rewards and dangers associated with business operators' community involvement require that residents know about and care about what happens in the community. In Socksberg, and many small towns, surveillance of local activities and information dispersal systems are honed to a fine art. As is often said, everybody in town knows everybody else's business within a day of it happening—sometimes sooner. This feature of small-town life leads us to wonder "What is the impact of community size and culture on corporate citizenship?"

The common wisdom today seems to be that communities have very little power to influence businesses. Part of the impetus for *Newsweek*'s focus on corporate citizenship is the prevailing belief that the new global economy has changed the old relationship between businesses and society. Accordingly, in this new highly competitive global economy, businesses cannot afford the luxury of, for example, supporting their communities or giving to the arts. This argument implies that the culture of the local community is no longer important in matters of corporate citizenship (if it ever was) because local businesses are now competing with firms in low-wage, low-tax, low-regulation countries, or more recently with Internet businesses, which do not contribute to the local public welfare in any way except that some have local employees. Another factor contributing to the belief in the demise of corporate citizenship is the consolidation of businesses. The reasoning here is that branch establishments and franchises don't have the same attachment and sense of responsibility to the local community as locally owned businesses. Therefore, they provide less support to the community.

A typical theme in studies of business social responsibility has been the devastation suffered by communities from plant closings and threats of closing, downsizing, demands for tax breaks, infrastructure improvements and other community accommodations to business demands. There is substantial support for the claim that communities, states, and even nations are engaged in an "arms race" to create the most friendly business climate as a way to lure businesses to their area. In these scenarios, communities are hardly in a position to expect anything of businesses besides "avoiding irresponsibility," and even that is subject to variable interpretations.

There is no doubt of the truth of these claims in certain instances. As we proceed in the book, I'll review in detail the relevant research. For now, it is sufficient to say that our knowledge of the interaction of businesses and communities is limited by the difficulty in gathering information from businesses about their level of social responsibility. As a result, in assessing the prevalence of business social responsibility, we often rely on mentally weighing examples of villainous and saintly corporate citizens, and ignore small businesses completely. Simply put, we really do not know much about the level of business social responsibility nor about the impact of communities on business social responsibility. In spite of *Newsweek*'s coverage of this topic, we still do not know how many good corporations have died, how many remain, and whether small businesses are better or worse than big businesses.

The purpose of this book is to elaborate aspects of the mutually intertwining relationship between businesses and communities. In the process I will address the questions raised above. This is an especially pertinent topic today as federal and state governments "outsource" funding to the private sector for programs formerly considered the responsibility of government. Organizations interested in promoting art, education, recreation, youth welfare, community betterment, and assistance to the poor, among many other causes, are forced to seek ways to replace government funding with support from the "thousand points of light"[1] to be located in corporations, businesses, and individuals. Occurring at the same time is what some contend is a qualitative change in the world economy (i.e., economic restructuring). The factors mentioned above, consolidation of businesses and global competition, are considered dimensions of economic restructuring. Given what appear to be contradictory forces, i.e. the heightened need for business support for the public good accompanied by diminished motivation among businesses to be socially responsible, the task of replacing government funding with contributions from business is formidable. Knowledge of business social responsibility and the role of communities takes on a new significance in this climate.

In the research for this book, I paid particular attention to small businesses, those with fewer than 500 employees.[2] They constitute the overwhelming majority of businesses. According to the 1992 Economic Census conducted by the U.S. Census Bureau, 74 percent of all businesses[3] have no employees.[4] Of those with employees, according to the updated 1997 Economic Census, 88 percent have fewer than 500 employees.[5] As a result, in any random sample of businesses (which I used for this research), chances are that the whole sample will be composed of small businesses. Also, since they constitute the majority of business owners and managers in most communities, their numbers dominate business groups involved in community betterment (such as Lions clubs, Chambers of Commerce, community and economic development boards, and Jaycees). Using the 1997 Economic Census, in 1996 more than half of all employees (52 percent) worked in firms with fewer than 500 employees. Those in firms with fewer than 100 employees accounted for 37.7 percent of all employees. In the same year, firms with 500 or fewer employees took in 46.8 percent of all receipts, the smaller employers (fewer than 100 employees) had 33.7 percent of receipts. If that weren't enough, small private businesses accounted for the vast majority of convictions in federal courts for corporate criminal behavior from November 1, 1987 to June 30, 1995, according to the U.S. Sentencing Commission (1995). Only 4.7 percent of convictions during that time period went to businesses with more than 500 employees. Clearly, small businesses represent a significant component of the business-community interchange that deserves more attention than they receive.

The second reason for my focus on small business operators is that in spite of their obvious importance, scholars know very little about their community attitudes and contributions. The subject has not received the research attention it deserves due partly to the challenges involved in finding reliable information about them, but also because of the big-business bias that seems to permeate public media and scholarly discourse alike.

RESEARCH DESIGN OVERVIEW

This book is the culmination of research that started in 1994 with a massive survey of residents of ninety-nine Iowa small communities (500 to 10,000 in population) randomly selected from within each of Iowa's ninety-nine counties. The definition of community used for that study was the telephone exchange area of an incorporated municipality. The same definition is used in the research for this book. In the next chapter, a conceptual definition for the term will be presented. Respondents to the community survey indicated that in their opinion the biggest threat to their respective communities was the demise of small businesses. As a result, in 1995, I led a multidisciplinary research team in a study of "Doing Business in Small Town Iowa."

We went door to door in one of the sample towns, interviewing every available business owner, or when the owner was not involved in the operation of the business, we interviewed the manager. Based on what we learned in those interviews and a perusal of the literature in the field, we developed a survey and contracted with the Computer Assisted Telephone Interview (CATI) Laboratory at the Center for Family Research in Rural Mental Health at Iowa State University to conduct 1,008 telephone interviews with a stratified random sample of business owners and managers in thirty of the original ninety-nine towns. This represented an 87 percent cooperation rate for the contacted business operators. When a business was contacted for the interview, the interviewer asked to talk to the business owner. If that person were not available, an appointment was made to interview him or her at a later time. Only when the owner(s) was not involved in the day-to-day management of the business, was the manager with primary decision-making power interviewed. We defined "business" as a for-profit operation with a listing in the yellow pages or white business pages of the municipality's telephone directory.

In 1997, an additional 670 telephone interviews were conducted with a stratified random sample of business operators in six Iowa cities (10,000 to 50,000 population) and four metropolitan cities (50,000+ population). Among this group, 83 percent of contacted business operators agreed to be interviewed. Details of the research design, sampling strategy, sample representativeness, and the interview questions are located in Appendix A. Summaries and analyses of the telephone interviews are dispersed throughout the book. The next section provides a summary of the characteristics of the sample businesses and respondents.

OVERVIEW OF SAMPLED IOWA BUSINESSES

The statistical details describing the Iowa sample are contained in Appendix C. I present a summary here to provide a context with which to frame the analyses that follow later. The majority of sampled Iowa businesses are sole proprietorships, accounting for 63 percent of all businesses. Size of community does not influence proprietorship characteristics. Almost all Iowa businesses are independent, locally owned businesses or locally owned franchises, although the percentage of local ownership increases slightly as the size of the community decreases. Nine out of ten metropolitan businesses (90.3 percent) are locally owned, while in rural communities the rate is 96 percent.

Using gross sales and number of employees as indicators, the average business in all sizes of communities in Iowa is small. Even so, there are differences between businesses by size of community. Half of the metropolitan businesses had gross sales in 1996 of $500,000 or less. In the small cities, half grossed $320,000 or less, and that figure in small towns was $234,750. Looking at the gross sales figures from a different angle, one in three (33.5 percent) metropolitan businesses topped the $1 million dollar level in 1996, compared to about one in five of both small city and small town businesses. The small size of sampled businesses is reinforced by their employment statistics. In metro communities the average number of employees is 23.9, the median is 6.0, and the range is 0 to 600. The employment statistics for urban businesses are 12.5 for the average number of employees, the median is 4.0, and the range is 501 to 0; for rural businesses, the average number of employees is 8.5, the median equals 3.0, and the range is 0 to 200 employees.

The typical respondent is the owner of the business (78 percent rural, 71.3 percent urban, and 59.4 percent metro) with 19.7 years of business experience, and has lived in his or her community for 27.0 years. Seven of ten respondents (71.1 percent) are men. Respondents in larger communities differ from those in smaller communities in that they reported higher household income, are slightly less likely to be "White," and have more education on average, although the average for respondents in all locations is some postsecondary education.

QUALITATIVE RESEARCH COMPONENT

In spite of my confidence in the findings from the statistical analyses of the interviews, quantitative data leave certain kinds of questions unanswered, particularly "why" and "how" questions. More critically, quantitative data provide limited insight into the human dimension of an issue. To address this weakness, I selected five of the forty communities to visit in the fall of 1999 and the spring of 2000. Communities were chosen for additional study based on their size, level of business social responsibility as measured from the telephone interview data, and dispersal around the state. Two of the chosen communities are rural, two are urban, and one is a metropolitan area. In the non-metro categories, one community in each size category measured high on business social responsibility, and the other was low. In addition, the two rural and two urban communities were closely matched for population size and distance to a metro area.

The county extension director, newspaper editor, public officials, and chamber of commerce executive were contacted in the five selected communities. We (a postdoctoral research assistant worked with me on this phase of the research) gave them background information about the research project. We asked them for the names of business owners or top managers and community leaders who might have insight into the relationship between businesses and the community and who might be willing to talk with us. Approximately twenty-five names were generated in each community. We perused the list and selected those individuals who represented diverse businesses (based on size and SIC [Standard Industrial Code]) and who might have different perspectives on the community. Thus, in each place we interviewed business people, community leaders, a charitable organization director, and a church leader. Additionally, some business interviewees in each community were selected at random. Only two business operators refused to be interviewed; one was a random selection and the other a CEO of a major corporation in the metro community. In total, we interviewed fifty-nine business owners, top managers, and community leaders. The mayors and chamber executives were also asked for a list of local civic organizations and their meeting schedules. In each community we attended meetings of civic organizations and had informal conversations with the business and community people who attended.

All interviews were taped with the permission of the interviewee. Interviewees were assured that we would hold what they told us in strictest confidence and that we would not use their names in reporting our findings. During the first fourth of the interviews, both my assistant and I were present. That allowed us to monitor and critique each other's interviewing style to ensure that we were nonjudgmental and not leading responses. I listened to all interview tapes at least once and many of them twice. In the process of listening, I asked myself "What is the meaning of the information shared?" and "How does this person's account help me understand the dynamics of the community-business interchange?" The information in the tapes was coded, counted, and representative quotes were transcribed.

The identity of the communities selected for visits and that of all interviewees is confidential. In referring to them in the book, fictitious names are used, and all identifying characteristics have been changed. Due to the challenge of assuring the anonymity of interviewees from the smaller towns, I created composites of the interviewees from all five communities. The fictitious names of interviewees, their SIC classification, and community are contained in Appendix B along with a list of the interview questions used in that phase.

THE RELEVANCE OF IOWA DATA

A few comments are in order about the significance of findings derived from a sample of Iowa businesses—representative though they may be of all Iowa businesses—to the situation of businesses and communities in other states and the nation as a whole. First, there are few data sets about this subject that do not contain limitations, some severe enough to compromise their external validity. The majority of studies have one or more of the following problems: nonrandom samples, small samples, low response rates (Arlow and Gannon 1982, Wartick and Cochran 1985, Griffin and Mahon 1997) and/or an exclusive focus on very large companies (Thompson and Smith 1991). In contrast, these data result from a large stratified random sample of all businesses in towns of various sizes and represent a cooperation rate infrequently paralleled in studies of businesses.

Our understanding of corporate social responsibility has been significantly enhanced by studies focused on a particular company or geographic area (Bockelman 2000, Cowie 1999, Burlingame and Kaufman 1995, Useem and Kutner 1986, Galaskiewicz 1985, Baltzell 1979). To illustrate, knowledge about the Twin Cities' culture of good corporate citizenship has been utilized world wide to gain a better understanding of business social responsibility (Bockelman 2000). Minnesota principles and practices provided the basis for the Caux Round Table Principles for Businesses, a standard for good business citizenship adopted by an international consortium of businesses dedicated to global corporate citizenship (Bockelman 2000). Japanese and European business and governmental leaders apparently believe that the lessons learned in the Twin Cities can be generalized, adapted, and employed to increase good corporate citizenship in, for example, Nagasaki and Venice. Even when resources in locales are dissimilar, understanding circumstances and approaches to common problems in one place can be illuminating for people in other settings. It is not the geographic focus of a study that determines the applicability and value of the findings, but rather the quality of the data gathered, the quality of the analyses of that data, and the insight generated from the study.

Nevertheless, the generalizability and usefulness of findings from the Iowa data should not be accepted a priori. As an aid in gauging the external validity of this study, I provide, wherever possible, evidence from other sources to triangulate the conclusions. The outside triangulation points consist of findings from prior research and expectations derived from theory. If the Iowa findings conform to theoretical expectations and/or to the conclusions from prior research, then we can have greater confidence in the applicability of the conclusions to places and businesses outside Iowa. Discrepancies between conclusions from the Iowa study and the other sources should be viewed as opportunities to expand general understanding of the phenomena of corporate social responsibility and represent fertile areas for future research.

PREVIEW

I started this book with an example of business operators demonstrating support for their community. That choice was not an accident. I could just as easily have used an example of businesses harming their community. The headlines in national and Iowa newspapers are replete with accounts of poor business citizenship. However, the more positive picture of business social responsibility portrayed in my analyses of the interview data and in the interviews with community leaders and business operators cannot be ignored.

Business social irresponsibility exists among small businesses and may be the norm among Fortune 500 companies. Likewise, what passes as social responsibility is sometimes undisguised business advertisement and promotion. Even so, my research reveals the untold story of numerous small incidents of socially responsible behavior performed by numerous small business operators throughout Iowa, sometimes in spite of potential risk or actual harm to selves and businesses. I chose to begin with a positive example of business social responsibility to highlight this other story, and to emphasize the complexity of the subject.

Further, I chose the Socksberg spring cleanup example as a way to introduce the importance of the social construction of business social responsibility and as an illustration of the conceptual ambiguity surrounding this subject. The next two chapters are devoted to providing an overview of the extant literature and theories about business social responsibility. This takes us slightly afield from the empirical basis of this book but is necessary to establish a common vocabulary and conceptual framework with which the empirical evidence can be examined.

The relevance of the size, industry, and ownership patterns of businesses has been broached in several questions raised by the Socksberg example. Other features of businesses with consequences for their stance on social responsibility are managerial characteristics and values. These factors are linked with the conceptual orientation developed in Chapter 3 and utilized in the empirical examinations found in the remainder of the book. The focus of Chapter 4 is the relationship of business characteristics and owner/manager features to community support and involvement.

This research underscores the critical significance of other business operators, and the community in general, in influencing business owners and managers to support the community. The spring cleanup is a social event as well as a community betterment project. In the process of planting flowers, participants build relationships and develop trust among one another—a resource that can be tapped for future projects. A successful cleanup project will add to the likely success of future community projects by reinforcing the belief among locals that getting involved can make a difference in the community quality of life. It helps establish the norm that people in this town pitch in and work together for mutual gain and provides an opportunity for organizers to learn how to implement successful projects. Of course, an unsuccessful project will detract from those beliefs and support those who contend that getting involved won't make any difference. Political scientist Robert Putnam (1993) refers to the resource created by relationships, trust, and norms that support working together for the common good as social capital. In his study of democracy in Italy, he found a relationship between social capital, government effectiveness, and economic development—with social capital existing prior to the other two variables. His work catapulted social capital into the public policy and academic discourse of the late 1990s. The social capital conceptual framework is presented in Chapter 5 and applied to the question of whether communities influence business citizenship. Also bringing social capital concepts to the study of business social responsibility helps us understand and assess the strategies that communities use to spur good citizenship among local businesses, the topic of the last chapter.

The costs and benefits of business social responsibility to the success of the business and the personal well being of the owner/manager are considered in chapter 6. We learn from interviewees the complicated calculus of figuring out whether business was gained or lost from supporting the community. Frequently, these businesspersons are forced to rely more on faith than cost accounting in determining the net return from good citizenship. Also, a summary of the considerable body of prior research devoted to this issue and a statistical examination of the Iowa data will be covered in chapter 6 to help ascertain whether doing good is good for business. In the final chapter, I present an overview of the strategies communities have developed to enhance business citizenship, and I examine the implications of globalization for business social responsibility. According to some scholars, and common wisdom, globalization represents a grave threat to conscientious capitalism and, therefore, deserves serious consideration in a book on the subject.

THE CONSCIENCE OF CAPITALISM

Before proceeding, I would like to explain the title of this book. Herbert G. Gutman in his book *Work, Culture and Society in Industrializing America* (1976) effectively debunks what he calls the misleading generalization that "from the start, industrialists had the social and political power and prestige to match their economic force, and they controlled the towns." In fact, Gutman provides convincing evidence that small business people and professionals frequently did not support nor defer to the large capitalists and that laborers were not passive and alienated victims of all-powerful industrialists. He describes the industrial history of Paterson, New York, to illustrate his claim.

Between 1850 and 1870 the population of Paterson tripled, mostly from an influx of immigrant workers lured by jobs in plants manufacturing locomotives, machinery, iron goods, silk and other textiles. By 1876 the silk factories alone employed 8,000 employees. Two thirds of the silk employees were women and one of every four was under sixteen years of age. In 1877 the silk workers went on strike to protest a 20 percent wage cut and other conditions of work. The strike lasted ten weeks, idled the plants, and was successfully resolved from the workers' point of view with a restoration of wages to pre-cut levels.

In effect, the "docile" women and child workers won wage concessions during an economic depression. Gutman maintains that the community support for the strikers tipped the scales in their favor. The community refused to sanction and support the mill owners. The mayor and the Board of Aldermen, independent skilled workmen, and shop owners gave the manufacturers a great deal of trouble. Local merchants provided goods and credit to strikers. Although critical of strikers, the two daily newspapers did not support the mill owners either, and they scolded the mill owners to "put conscience as well as capital into their enterprises" (p. 243).

The editors' call for capitalism with a conscience could have come straight from contemporary newspapers. The theme parallels *Newsweek*'s concern about the demise of good corporate citizenship. I used a variation of the Paterson newspapers' scolding in the title of this book to emphasize that capitalists without consciences are not new. Sometimes in this era of consolidations and global competition, we think the changes in how business is conducted are so significant that current problems are qualitatively different from anything experienced in the past. In regard to business social responsibility, at least, an examination of history should disabuse us of that belief. I selected the title, also, as a way to highlight Gutman's contention that there is a history of small-business people displaying more loyalty to their community than to the capitalist principle of profit maximization. Even in the 1800s, the interests of big businesses did not necessarily coincide with the values and interests of small businesses and community residents.

In the preceding pages I used several terms interchangeably to refer to business social responsibility. Add to my terms, "corporate social responsiveness" and "corporate social performance," two more that frequently appear in the literature, and it becomes clear that the place to begin this account is with an elaboration of definitions and theoretical perspectives. Chapter 2 addresses the question "What do we mean by corporate social responsibility?"

NOTES

1. This is a term used by President George Bush to refer to his administration's emphasis on privatizing government programs meant to address a wide array of social problems. Since then, an organization, "The Thousand Points of Light," has been formed to encourage corporate and individual philanthropy and volunteerism.

2. According to the Small Business Administration a small business is one with fewer than 500 employees (Our 1992 State Profile, 1993).

3. The U.S. Census Bureau distinguishes between firms and establishments. Firms are for-profit entities that may own and operate many other for-profit entities located at diverse sites. Establishments are physically unique, for-profit entities, regardless of legal ownership. As such, General Motors is a firm. The manufacturing plants, corporate headquarters, R&D facilities, credit organizations, and other for-profit entities owned by GM are each separate establishments if they have separate addresses in different locations. The figures reported here are for establishments. In this book, "business" refers to establishments. Those businesses owned by other entities will be separated from independently owned businesses for some analyses.

4. 1992 Economic Census, *Enterprise Statistics*. Table 1 "Employers and Nonemployers." Available online at www.census.gov.epcd.www/smallbus.html#empsize.

5. 1997 Economic Census, United States: The Number of Firms, Establishments, Employment, Annual Payroll, and Estimated Receipts by Industrial Division and Enterprise Employment Size for 1996. Available online at www.census.gov/epcd/ssel_tabs/view/tab3_99b.html#tot.

CHAPTER 2

More than Making a Profit

"Businesses have no social responsibility . . . but there's no question that they have an obligation to their community."
                Lance Butterfield, a business owner in Socksberg, Iowa.

Butterfield isn't alone in holding conflicting views about what businesses owe society. The first question I asked everyone I interviewed was "Do you think businesses have any responsibility to society?" and then I asked them to elaborate. The question appeared to be troubling for some. So I rephrased it, substituting the word "obligation" for "responsibility." That was no better. If interviewees did not mention community support or leadership in their response to the first question, I asked them next if businesses had any obligation to the community in which they operated. There was no hesitation in answering this question. Given the fact that most interviewees were selected for their insight into the community business interface, their attitudes toward business's obligation to community came as no surprise. What was unexpected was that several business owners and community leaders who declared that businesses had no social responsibility, or only the responsibility to be ethical in making a profit, expressed the conviction that businesses should contribute to the welfare of the community. Why the difference? Are the terms "social" and "society" too abstract, too broad, compared to "community?" Does the term "responsibility" to society imply a threat to business freedom, i.e., more restrictions, regulations, and requirements that "community obligation" does not? The definition of responsibility found in *Merriam-Webster's Collegiate Dictionary* (2000) supports the regulatory connotation. *Merriam-Webster's* defines responsible as "liable to be called to account as the primary cause, motive or agent; liable to legal review or in case of fault, to penalities; able to answer for one's conduct and obligations: trustworthy."

Additional levels of complexity are added by confusion between descriptions and prescriptions of social responsibility, between what is and what ought to be, and between moral obligation and legal obligation. This was most obvious later in the interviews, when I asked about differences in social responsibility based on various business features, like size, industry, and ownership. A couple of interviewees were clearly uncomfortable in specifying any expectations that they thought might be translated into legal obligations. This seemed to be the sentiment of Christine Bernstein, the owner of a manufacturing plant in Caizan, when she said, "I don't feel I owe a whole lot to anybody. We do support the community, but I'm not obligated to do it."

Whatever the explanation for the difficulty in responding to the social responsibility question, it underscores the ambiguity and misunderstanding of the terms and conceptual frameworks employed to describe, elaborate, and explain the relationship between businesses and society. My interviews demonstrate the problem in common parlance, but some of the same confusion exists in the academic literature. During the last three decades, scholars have labored to refine and more clearly specify the subject. In this chapter, I briefly chronicle their work and elaborate the conceptual definitions that are the basis for this book. My goal is to clarify the meaning of terms, help us think about the internal processes used to turn values about business social responsibility into action, and identify tangible indicators of that action. Ultimately, this will help us better understand, explain, and predict aspects of the interaction between business and society. As much as possible, I leave the presentation of the normative positions about what should be the social responsibility of business for the next chapter.

DEFINITIONS OF CORPORATE SOCIAL RESPONSIBILITY

The relationship between business and society has been the subject of social scientists and philosophers at least since the industrial revolution. In fact, one could argue that the impact of businesses on society at the beginning of the industrial revolution was a principal factor in the development of the social sciences. The works of Marx, Comte, Durkheim, Weber, Toennies, Spencer, along with many others, were prompted by the authors' desire to explain the societal antecedents and consequences of the forces of capitalism. However, not until the 1950s was the subject of business social responsibility per se addressed in any systematic way. The social unrest of the 1960s and economic turmoil of the 1970s in the United States led to heightened interest in, and critical examination of, business's role in society. The resulting foment generated a period of productive conceptual work, which has significantly refined the analytical tools available for the study of business social responsibility.

Among those calling for a reexamination of business's role in society was a consortium of business leaders, academics, consultants, and government leaders called the Research and Policy Committee of the Committee for Economic Development (CED). Their original mission was to study how businesses could better serve society's economic objectives. During the course of the committee's work, however, the mission changed to determining how business could help ameliorate existing social problems. Their report *Social Responsibilities of Business Corporations* was published in 1971. A key assumption of their work was that "[b]usiness functions by public consent, and its basic purpose is to serve constructively the needs of society—to the satisfaction of society" (1971:11). In their view, businesses have a social contract with society that extends beyond their economic role.

According to the CED, businesses have a responsibility to meet society's expectations in three concentric circles of responsibility. The inner circle includes business's clear economic responsibilities such as product quality and safety and the provision of jobs and services. The intermediate circle expands the responsibility of businesses to make their policies and practices consistent with societal values in such matters as fair employment practices and a benign environmental impact. The third and outlying circle calls for businesses to work actively to improve the social environment. The rationale for the last circle of business responsibility was that the public expects the vast financial and human resources possessed by businesses to be utilized to help solve social problems. Additionally, the CED, citing the growing negative public sentiment toward business evident in the 1960s, argued that if businesses do not become more socially responsible, they will face heightened regulation, taxation, and public animosity.

Lee Preston and James Post in their 1975 book *Private Management and Public Policy: The Principle of Public Responsibility*, rejected the CED's concentric-circle classification schema. Public responsibility, in their thinking, consists of two areas of social involvement. (They preferred to use the term "social involvement" instead of "social responsibility," as they believed it was more ethically neutral.) The primary area of social involvement relates to any interaction businesses have with society in order to fulfill their economic function (i.e., pay taxes, purchase supplies, hire employees, sell products). The secondary area of social involvement consists of activities to address the consequences to society caused by businesses in fulfilling their economic function. Thus, product safety, environmental impacts of production, and the ramifications of production processes on the health of workers would each be considered matters of secondary social involvement.

Guidance about the nature of businesses' public responsibility in the two social involvement domains comes from the market in the first domain and public policy in the second. According to Preston and Post, businesses have public responsibility only in these two domains of social involvement. However, business owners and managers as private citizens may assume responsibility for other problems in society, such as the CEO of Boeing providing leadership for a national drive to raise money for medical research to cure childhood leukemia. The distinction between the public responsibility of businesses and the responsibility of the individuals who own and work in businesses is an important one that we will encounter repeatedly in our examination of business social responsibility.

Preston and Post differ from the CED and others in the field, whose position is articulated by William Frederick. Frederick claims that "[t]he fundamental idea embedded in corporate social responsibility is that business corporations have an obligation to work for social betterment" (1978, 1994:151). Preston and Post's public responsibility conceptualization is a response to the critics of the social betterment position in that it attempts to define and limit the scope of business penetration in and responsibility for society. Actually, the limitations imposed by primary and secondary social involvement are not as clear and Preston and Post had hoped. For example, Boeing's image as a "good corporate citizen" would be enhanced among potential employees, government officials, bank lenders, etc. by the CEO's involvement in the children's leukemia cause. Who could be opposed to helping children with cancer and who would not think more positively of a company whose CEO helped critically ill children? Additionally, Boeing's CEO, in supporting a national drive to raise funds for leukemia research, would no doubt be using the networks and prestige available to him or her as the CEO of Boeing in the support of this "private cause," even if no monetary or in-kind Boeing resources were used. Hence, what appears at first glance to be completely out of Boeing's area of primary or secondary social involvement can, upon closer scrutiny, be classified as public relations and fall in the primary social involvement arena. The public responsibility conceptualization turns out to be as ambiguous in specifying areas of business responsibility to society as is the admonition to work for social betterment.

Both Preston and Post's and Frederick's definitions are prescriptions indicating what the social responsibility of business ought to be. Frederick recognized that normative prescriptions are problematic in that the moral underpinnings of business responsibility to society are difficult to establish, open to disagreement, and a questionable foundation for scientific discourse and research. Thus, he notes that by 1978 there had been a shift away from concern about social responsibility to a focus on social responsiveness. This term refers to "the capacity of a corporation to respond to social pressures" (1978; 1994:154). Social responsiveness is preferred by its advocates because it is more tangible, less normative, and able to capture changing societal circumstances.

Corporate social responsiveness has its own problems and has been frequently criticized in the literature. Steve Wartick and Philip Cochran summarize the criticisms in their 1985 article. They argue that if social responsiveness replaces social responsibility as a charge to managers, companies could ignore absolute or normative standards of good citizenship and instead be concerned only about those matters that produce a public outcry. Responding to public outcries translates into scattered, disparate activities that are subject to frequent change, depending upon the public concern of the day. It offers no guidance to managers who are forced to chose between opposing public outcries or who must decide how to respond to an extremely vocal minority in the face of a silent majority with a likely opposing view.

Due to these shortcomings, in 1986, Frederick called for the return to the normative based definition of businesses' interaction with society. He challenged the field to replace what he called CSR (corporate social responsibility) and CSR2 (corporate social responsiveness) with CSR3 (corporate social rectitude). According to Frederick, "In viewing the social performance of corporations, we look for more than mere responsibility and more than mere responsiveness. We want corporations to act with rectitude, to refer their policies and plans to a culture of ethics that embraces the most fundamental moral principles of humankind" (1986, 136). In spite of his catchy terminology, corporate social rectitude has not caught on among researchers.

Instead of eschewing social responsiveness, Archie Carroll (1979) included it in his multifaceted, three-dimensional framework of corporate social performance (CSP). The other two dimensions are an elaboration of the categories of business social responsibility and social issue areas that reflect current, and thus ever changing, public concerns. Carroll's categories of social responsibility are, in order of importance: economic, legal, ethical, and discretionary responsibilities. In this schema, businesses' first and foremost responsibility is economic, i.e., to produce and distribute goods and services for economic exchange. The legal category specifies that in the process of producing and distributing goods and services, businesses must abide by the laws of society. Though less well defined, the third area of business responsibility requires businesses to conduct their affairs in an ethical manner. Generally, this translates into expectations that businesses comply with the spirit of society's laws and with the normative base that under girds them. The fourth category deals with what Carroll calls discretionary responsibilities. Social betterment activities like philanthropy and community leadership are examples of discretionary responsibility. In Carroll's account, society expects businesses to do something beyond their economic, legal, and ethical responsibilities. However, businesses may choose, or have discretion regarding, the area of societal betterment they will support.

For the social responsiveness dimension, Carroll combined McAdam's (1973) and Wilson's (1974) compatible typologies of the philosophical stances businesses can take to their social responsibility. Those stances are: 1) fight all the way (reaction philosophy); 2) do only what is required (defense philosophy); 3) be progressive (accommodation philosophy); and 4) lead the industry (proaction philosophy).[1] Completing the corporate social performance framework is the dimension of social issues. By this, Carroll meant the social issues or topical areas to which corporate social responsibility can be applied. These issues change over time and vary by type of industry. Included at any given time might be social issue topics such as environmental quality and teen pregnancy.

In Carroll's corporate social performance model, the CED's circles of business responsibility are more clearly specified and the business responses to those responsibilities and specific social topics to which they apply are added. To illustrate the usefulness of Carroll's CSP model, let's consider the social issue of the recreational infrastructure within a given community. For some businesses, this social issue is in the category of economic social responsibility. Examples would be construction companies who have a shot at building the facilities, development companies who own potential sites, and hospitality businesses adjacent to the planned infrastructure. If enhanced local recreation facilities assist businesses to attract and retain employees, they would be categorized as related to economic social responsibility. Where none of these circumstances apply, then business involvement in the provision of community recreational infrastructure would be a discretionary social responsibility. For this particular social issue, the legal and ethical responsibilities would not apply.

Whether an economic or a discretionary responsibility, businesses can theoretically respond with any of the four response philosophies. In truth, the response philosophies are meaningful when recreational infrastructure is categorized as an economic responsibility, but less so if it is a discretionary responsibility. Any one particular business cannot be expected to accommodate or be proactive on all social issues falling in the discretionary category. However, does that make their stance reactive or defensive? Identifying the appropriate response philosophy for social issues that are discretionary responsibilities is problematic. Carroll's social responsiveness categories are intended to be generalized philosophical orientations that businesses can take to social responsibility. They are less helpful for understanding a business's specific response to a particular social issue. Thus even though Carroll's corporate social performance model was a step forward, more work remained.

At the same time that Carroll's conceptualization was published, S. Prakash Sethi (1979) published a different social responsibility framework.

Sethi argued that businesses must respond to market and nonmarket social expectations to maintain legitimacy and survive. Business behavior in response to nonmarket societal expectations falls into three categories: social obligations, social responsibility, and social responsiveness. Social obligations consist of corporate actions to meet businesses' economic and legal obligations. Social responsibility implies that the behavior of companies should comply with prevailing societal values and norms, even though not codified into law. Firms have a social responsibility to mitigate the negative impacts they impose on society. The last category is social responsiveness. Business behavior here is aimed at promoting positive change.

Implicit in Sethi's framework is the notion that the kind of response exhibited by, and expected of, businesses depends on the area of responsibility. Response categories are not the same for all kinds of responsibilities. Instead Sethi's categories incorporate both the area of responsibility and the response expected. The social obligation category admonishes companies to *do what is required* in the areas of economic and legal responsibilities. Social responsibility instructs businesses to *do no harm*. It roughly coincides with Carroll's legal and ethical social responsibilities and Preston and Post's secondary area of social involvement. Sethi's social responsiveness category deals with Carroll's discretionary social responsibility, but recognizes that the only business action that appropriately falls in this category is proaction.

Social responsiveness was an unfortunate and confusing title for Sethi's proactive, discretionary responsibility category. By the time of Sethi's writing, the term had come to mean something entirely different in the literature. The term usually meant business's reaction to societal expectations, not their proaction in achieving positive change. Or alternately, it suggested the processes of responding to social expectations. Sethi's ideas have had a profound impact on the business social responsibility literature, but his terminology has been infrequently used. Instead Carroll's corporate social performance model has had more staying power, evolving through the work of three sets of researchers. (See Figure 2.1 for an overview of the evolution of Carroll's CSP model.) I will present each iteration in turn below.

Steven Wartick and Philip Cochran (1985) build upon Carroll's CSP model by replacing social issue topics with social issues management. Social issues management is a set of techniques consisting of issue identification, issue analysis, and response development, created to help businesses deal with uncertainty. The addition of social issues management, Wartick and Cochran argue, equips the CSP model with specific techniques with which businesses and analysts can understand the nature of business responsibilities and develop appropriate responses.

In a 1991 article, Donna Wood further improves the corporate social performance model. She addresses what she considers to be the weaknesses of the model: its normative overtones, its less-than-clear responsiveness cate-

Figure 2.1
Evolution of the Corporate Social Performance Model

	Social Responsibility	Social Responsiveness	Social Issues
Carroll - 1979	Economic Ethical Legal Discretionary	Fight Be progressive Minimal action Lead industry	Environmental quality, teen pregnancy, e.g.

	Social Responsibility	Social Responsiveness	Social Issues
Wartick & Cochran - 1985	Same as Carroll	Same as Carroll	Set of techniques - identification, analysis, and response development

	Social Responsibility	Social Responsiveness	Outcomes
Wood - 1991	Legitimacy, public responsibility, managerial discretion	Issues management Environmental assessment Stakeholder management	Social impacts, programs, policies

	Social Responsibility	Corporate Culture	Social Impacts
Swanson - 1995	Macro level duties/principles Economizing & ecologizing Micro level (manager) duties/principles Decision making process to economize & ecologize Personal values Limit power seeking	Decision making Personal values → Social responsiveness Environmental assessment Stakeholder management Issues management Social programs, policies	Increases or decreases in economizing, ecologizing, and power seeking

gories, and the absence of an outcome component. In her rendition, CSP is defined as "a business organization's configuration of principles of social responsibility, processes of social responsiveness, and policies, programs, and observable outcomes as they relate to the firm's societal relationships" (1991:693). She replaces Carroll's categories of social responsibility—(economic, legal, ethical, and discretionary—with three principles of social responsibility: legitimacy, public responsibility, and managerial discretion.

The principle of legitimacy states that society and businesses have an implicit social contract. Society grants legitimacy and power to business so that they can produce and distribute goods and services. In return, society expects them to use their power and wealth to further the common good. Therefore, if business power and resources are not used to further the common good, legitimacy will be rescinded. The principle of public responsibility states that businesses are responsible for the societal outcomes related to their primary and secondary areas of social involvement as defined by Preston and Post (1975). Finally, the principle of managerial discretion specifies that managers are moral actors in society who are expected to be ethical and engaged citizens working for the common good. Wood's principles are, in fact, overlapping normative bases for business social responsibility.

Wood judged that social issues management, Wartick and Cochran's final dimension of CSP, was a process to be utilized as a response to social responsibility and, therefore, should be classified as a technique of social responsiveness, not as an outcome. Wood's categories of social responsiveness include environmental assessment and stakeholder management along with social issues management. Environmental assessment is a strategy that keeps businesses apprised of societal circumstances, trends, and potential impacts.

Stakeholders, a concept developed by R. Edward Freeman (1984), are all those who have a "stake" in a business, including owners, employees, residents of the communities where it operates, consumers, and pertinent government bodies. By building stakeholder management into the social responsiveness dimension of the CSP model, Wood draws attention to the considerable literature that instructs managers in the mechanics of handling stakeholder relations. These three—social issues management, environmental assessment, and stakeholder management—represent processes that businesses can use to respond to society and craft their social performance positions.

Wood's third dimension of CSP is outcomes, defined as social impacts, programs, and policies. She argues that outcomes are an essential third dimension of corporate social performance. They are the only observable aspect of CSP and, as such, can capture the actuality of a business's social performance, not just the rhetoric employed to create an image. This is a critical consideration as we attempt to find ways to measure CSP.

The latest contribution to Carroll's model was presented by Diane Swanson (1995). Swanson maintains that corporations are so powerful that they can alter public policy, the basis for public responsibility, to suite their own interests. Therefore, if business social responsibility consists of conforming to society's interests as specified in public policy, in fact, it requires little more of businesses than to follow their self-interests. She argues, like Frederick, that there has to be a normative foundation undergirding social responsibility. In the model she proposes, the social responsibility of business is divided into the macro level (the responsibility of the business as an institution and an organization) and the micro level (the responsibility of the managers as individuals). Businesses have a responsibility to economize (i.e., enhance social good by producing good and services as efficiently as possible), and to ecologize, or forge cooperative and collaborative links with society to adapt production to life-sustaining social needs. Correspondingly, managers have a responsibility to use their decision-making power to move the business to achieve its economizing and ecologizing goals, to act according to their personal values, and to limit power seeking.

Swanson recognizes the importance of individuals in organizations and the social processes that occur within organizations that mold individual interests and views into a corporate culture. By adding managers, decision-making processes and personal values, she draws attention to the fact that businesses are composed of people. Moreover, Swanson's social responsiveness dimension is entitled "corporate culture" to highlight the significance of the internal social processes that transform individuals into a group and ideas into action. Within the corporate culture category, she retains Wood's environmental assessment, stakeholder management, and issue management, but adds decision making, personal values, and social programs and policies. Wood's outcome dimension is renamed "social impacts," defined as increases or decreases in economizing, ecologizing, and power seeking.

To my thinking, Carroll's elaboration of the categories of social responsibility—economic, legal, ethical, and discretionary—is simpler, clearer, and more useful than Wood's principles or Swanson's macro- and micro-level duties and principles. Additionally, it conforms more closely to the way business people and community leaders think about business social responsibility. Consider, for example, the recent court finding that State Farm Insurance required claimants with a loss to replace their damaged auto parts with substandard, cheaper parts (France and Osterland 1999). How shall we think about this, using Wood's principles? The firm risks losing social legitimacy since it is using its power and resources in a way that harms the public good. At the same time, it is violating its public responsibility in its secondary area of social involvement due to the negative consequences to customers who drive cars with substandard parts. Furthermore, some

managers have violated all known articulations of personal moral rectitude. It is difficult to think of a situation where a known violation of the primary or secondary area of social involvement would not result in a
challenge to a business's social legitimacy. Have the principles clarified our
thinking about State Farm's social responsibility transgression?

It is not immediately apparent how State Farm's action fits into
Swanson's dimensions of social responsibility. Their social irresponsibility
does not pertain to macro-level economizing principles and duties as State
Farm continues to provide services and jobs and pay suppliers, etc. Then, it
must relate to a failure to ecologize at both the macro and micro level. It is
difficult to move from Swanson's abstract principle of ecologizing to the
concrete example of State Farm Insurance. Swanson's model is more instructive in leading us to consider the management values, decisions, and
goals that precipitated the action and how those values were supported
and promulgated throughout the business via the corporate culture.

In Carroll's conceptualization of social responsibility, State Farm Insurance's actions pertain to the categories of legal and ethical responsibilities.
The company was providing a service, making a profit, creating jobs, paying taxes, and adding to society's wealth. It was meeting its economic responsibilities. There is a place in the economy for low-cost providers.
Apparently, however, State Farm led customers to believe that they would
receive top-quality replacement parts. The act of irresponsibility, then, is in
the breach of contract between consumer and business, a legal infraction.
While not all legal violations are necessarily ethical violations, this one appears to be. I find Carroll's framework more helpful in illuminating the social responsibility ramifications of State Farm's actions than Wood's
principles or Swanson's macro/micro-level duties and principles.

In spite of these shortcomings, Wood's and Swanson's contributions are
substantial. Wood's CSP model draws our attention to the need for measurable outcomes. Swanson reminds us that businesses are made up of individuals with personal values and strengthens Wood's social
responsiveness dimension to force us to think about how values become
policies and programs and how personal values and organizational social
processes combine in a corporate culture of good or poor citizenship.

THE BUSINESS SOCIAL PERFORMANCE FRAMEWORK

I build on the previously described versions of the CSP model to create a
business social performance framework with what I think is greater ex-
planatory power than the others possess. We expect a conceptual framework to classify, describe, show the relationship between concepts, and
address the "how" and "why" questions about a topic. My goal is to provide a CSP model that meets these expectations. Breaking with tradition, I
entitle it the business social performance (BSP) model. Corporations are a

subset of businesses. The terms "corporate social performance" and "corporate social responsibility" eliminate or trivialize matters related to noncorporate businesses. Therefore, I use the word "business" instead of "corporation" to cover all for-profit entities. I choose to retain the term "social performance" as it is less normatively charged than "social responsibility" and can encompass social responsibility and other dimensions of social performance.

Like Wood's CSP models, the BSP model contains three dimensions: social responsibility, social responsiveness, and outcomes (see Figure 2.2). However, I revert back to Carroll's categories of social responsibility: economic, legal, ethical, and discretionary for reasons specified above. The BSP social responsiveness dimension is composed of processes through which businesses actualize their various social responsibilities. This dimension is suggested by Swanson's work but is expanded to apply to small businesses as well as large corporations. It is organized hierarchically with the first component being managerial/owner discretion. In addition to Swanson, a number of studies (Useem and Kutner 1986, Thompson, Smith, and Hood 1993, Buchholtz, Amason, and Rutherford 1999, Miller and Besser 2000) have demonstrated that the belief system, values, and moral orientation of the owners or top management of a business set the tone for the organizational policies and procedures that determine the business's stance toward society. Likewise, my interviewees consistently identified the values of top management as the critical determining factor in a business's support of the community.

If the business is very small, or not professionally managed, manager discretion may be the extent of internal processes defining the business' social performance (Thompson, Smith, and Hood 1993). The owner/manager decides, based on a personal code, peer or community influences, or serendipity, how his or her business is run and what causes will be supported. In professionally managed companies, there will likely be systematic processes in place for strategic planning, i.e., mechanisms for transforming organizational goals into work plans, job descriptions, policies, programs, and, ultimately, goal-oriented action. Top management (whether owner/manager or nonowner managers) determines how open the process is and who is involved in decision making and planning. Through this mechanism, the organizational vision, mission, and guiding principles are determined. These decisions guide the business regarding what market strategy to pursue for economic success, how employees and customers will be treated, what image the company wants to project, how involved it will be in the community, and so on. In other words, it is this process that turns the business's view of its social responsibility (derived from top management with input from others at their discretion) into policies, programs, job descriptions, and company culture.

Figure 2.2
Business Social Performance Model

SOCIAL RESPONSIBILITY	SOCIAL RESPONSIVENESS	OUTPUTS/OUTCOMES	
Economic	**Internal articulation of business social responsibility**	**Economic social responsibility**	*Measurement techniques*
Produce and distribute goods and services for market exchange	Owner/top management discretion (personal values)	*Outcomes* Profit, survival, market share, return on investment	• Accounting procedures • Independent CPA's and/or internal accountants
Legal	Top management, alone or with others, using a systematic procedure like strategic planning or a "seat of the pants" procedure determines:	**Legal social responsibility** *Outcomes* No findings of legal culpability Compliance with U.S. sentencing commission standards	*Measurement techniques* • Perusal of court records • Review of internal program
Abide by the law of society			
Ethical	vision mission guiding principles programs policies procedures positions culture and reward system to actualize internal articulation.	**Ethical & discretionary social responsibility** *Outputs* Existence of a set of articulated ethical and/or social betterment vision, principles, and policies.	*Measurement techniques* Social audit
Abide by the spirit of the law and conform to the normative base that undergirds the law.			• Independent auditors • Stakeholder input • Review & revision of internal articulation based on audit findings
Discretionary		Congruence of business practices with articulated standards, or with societal normative standards.	
Contribute to social betterment			Existence & extent of outputs • Stakeholder assessment • Absence of harmful impact on employee, environment, & community • Observation by analysts and/or reports from management
		Company sponsored employee involvement in social betterment causes.	
		In-kind and/or financial business contributions to social betterment causes.	

As a result of this process, management may decide to implement the suggestions of the U.S. Sentencing Commission. Congress charged this commission with establishing consistent sentencing regulations for individuals and other entities (e.g. corporations, proprietorships, partnerships, nonprofits) who are found guilty of violating federal law. The commission reported in 1995 that the severity of penalty for businesses found guilty of a crime will depend upon, among other things, whether the business can show that it attempted to be a good citizen. Evidence to support a business's claim of good citizenship consists of having standards and procedures in place to prevent criminal conduct, oversight by top-level personnel, and disciplinary mechanisms to deter criminal activity among employees. Implementing a compliance program is an example of the use of internal procedures to actualize the businesses legal social responsibilities.

Likewise, top management may decide to implement a version of "ethics-based" management. If so, they have available to them a number of ethics-based management packages for sale from consultants, or they can utilize business ethics centers at colleges and universities. Examples of ethics packages on the market are Stephen Covey's 7 *Principles of Effective Management*, Peter Block's stewardship approach, and Michael Josephson's *Five Pillars of Ethical Management*.

Based on decisions made at the top-management level, and/or contained in the strategic plan, some businesses may create positions specifically charged with implementing the business's policies regarding its legal, ethical, and discretionary social responsibility. These positions include human resources specialists, public relations specialists, legal experts, community relations specialists, corporate giving specialists, environmental (the "birds and trees" environment) specialists. The U.S Sentencing Commission recommends that "good citizen" businesses create compliance positions and/or ethics officers. They could be modeled after the inspector general positions developed in the U.S. Department of Defense. Their role would be to actualize top management's view of the business's legal and ethical responsibilities, and incidentally, also signal to the outside world (especially the federal courts) that the business has made a good-faith effort to deter crime and be good. However, later in the Sentencing Commission report, businesses are warned that good citizenship and ethics programs will not be effective if line managers (those with direct responsibility for the business's performance) feel that ethics is the solely the responsibility of the staff (not in the hierarchy of decision making) position (430–31). For big businesses, creating a specially designated position may be a necessary prerequisite for exemplary legal and ethical social responsibility, but it is not sufficient.

Part of the task of these specialists is to ascertain the business's vision of itself and its social responsibility and to use their professional expertise to translate that vision into programs and policies and, ultimately, into actions that conform with the vision. Human resource specialists, as an example, soon learn if the business views its social responsibility to employees as economic only, economic and legal only, or involving ethical and discretionary considerations. The mere existence of a community relations position indicates that the business recognizes some ethical and discretionary social responsibility to the community. Finally, some businesses implement their discretionary social responsibility through an independent foundation established to administer their philanthropic activity.

The specific tools used by management, its social responsibility specialists, and/or foundation employees might involve environmental assessment, issues management, and stakeholder management. In the BSP model, however, the scanning and evaluating tools are focused by managerial discretion and strategic planning, and are not the centerpieces of the social responsiveness dimension. Michael Useem and Stephen Kutner (1986), and Useem (1988) showed that when business social responsibility is actualized by designated professionals, its form and outcomes are influenced by the norms and practices common in the relevant professional disciplines. Useem and Kutner maintained that this explains why big corporations with social responsibility professionals are more similar in their criterion for gift giving and the causes they support than are businesses without such professionals.

The business social performance model is completed with an outcomes dimension. Outcomes are defined as measurable indicators of ultimate goals. Thus, a management team that decides to engage workers as full partners in the production process of the business may utilize the "sociotechnical system," a specific, participative team-based approach, to actualize their decision. However, implementing the sociotechnical system is not the outcome. In the lexicon of program evaluators, implementing the sociotechnical system is an "output," not an outcome. Instead, the outcomes are measures of workers' perception of the extent of their partnership with management and their perception of involvement in the production process. Ideally, the perceptions would be gauged before and after implementation of the new system and substantiated with accounts by knowledgeable, outside observers. If the ultimate goal of implementing the sociotechnical system was to decrease the time it takes to make a car or reduce the cost of production waste, then the change in those measures, before and after implementation, would be the outcomes. The appropriate outcome indicator depends on the ultimate goal of the actor in instigating the action. Therefore, the same action (program, policy, donation) may have different outcome indicators if the goals of the actors differ.

While outcomes are the optimum indicators of social performance, sometimes less rigorous performance measures are acceptable, and even appropriate. Hence, an office supply business that provides an annual college scholarship for a local high school student may have as an ultimate goal improving the level of educational achievement among graduates from the local district. The scholarship is a motivational mechanism educators can use to encourage hard work and study. Nevertheless, it would be unreasonable, and invalid, to use local educational achievement as an indicator of the business's discretionary social responsibility. Too many other factors, over which the business has no control, are involved in determining students' educational achievement. Therefore in this instance, offering the scholarship is sufficient evidence that the office supply business is proactive and contributing positively to society. More generally, outputs (programs and policies) may be acceptable indicators of discretionary social responsibility under certain circumstances.

Outcome indicators vary according to the category of social responsibility being considered. Very sophisticated accounting mechanisms measure the outcomes related to the economic category of social responsibility. In public companies, the economic outcomes are validated by public accounting firms and reported to the public in annual reports and in Securities and Exchange Commission filings. Public and private companies must report economic outcome data to state and federal government for tax purposes.

In the legal category of social responsibility, outcome indicators rely on findings of culpability in violations of law. The number of instances of getting caught at illegal behavior is the measure of legal responsibility. The problem with this measure is that it may encourage businesses to avoid getting caught instead of avoiding illegal activities. Nevertheless, compared to outcome indicators in the last two categories, it is easily understood, comparable between businesses, relatively consistent across time, available to the public, and generally accepted as a valid measure.

As businesses respond to the U.S. Sentencing Commission's 1995 standards for measuring criminal culpability, they will set in place steps to comply with the law and not simply avoid detection. Their degree of conformity with the standards represents a way for businesses to internally measure their legal social responsibility outcomes. Information about the degree of compliance will probably not be available to outsiders, however, except for businesses found guilty of a crime.

I utilize the considerable work in the field of social auditing to address outcome indicators in the ethical and discretionary categories of social responsibility. The term "social auditing" was originally proposed by Howard R. Bowen in 1953 and was picked up by John Corson and George Steiner writing for the Committee for Economic Development in 1975. However, what follows was drawn from the work of Peter Pruzan and Simon Zadek (1997). They are part of a team from the Copenhagen Business School and the New Economics Foundation in London that, in conjunction with a Danish bank (Sbn Bank), developed a social auditing methodology utilized by businesses in Europe, Canada, Japan, South Africa, and the

United States (e.g., The Body Shop and Ben and Jerry's Homemade Ice Cream).

The purpose of the social audit is to determine whether internal social performance goals have been realized. It makes stakeholder input available to management so that policies and procedures can be assessed and adjusted to better accomplish the goals. Additionally, it encourages management to reevaluate the goals to reflect changing circumstances and better information. In this way, it is also a mechanism of social responsiveness, i.e., a process for effective achievement of social performance goals.

Pruzan and Zadek recommend that the social audit begin with the identification of stakeholders and with clear statements of business social performance goals and implementation policies and procedures. Next, independent auditors, through surveys and focus groups, gather input from samples of stakeholder groups about company performance and stakeholder expectations. The findings are compiled, analyzed, compared to the business's goals, and reported back to management. The social audit measures a combination of outputs and outcomes, depending upon the scope and time frame of the goals. Usually, the results are not made public. In fact, internal audits are not privileged information in the legal sense and can be subpoenaed and used against the businesses in civil and criminal proceedings. Naturally, this may discourage businesses from conducting audits of their legal and ethical social responsibility. Even so, examples are available for public perusal. Vancity, a Canadian credit union, has made its social audit available to the public at the company's internet web site.

Businesses, especially those with social responsibility professionals, may compile less comprehensive internal reports documenting the expenditures, programs, and achievements of their social responsibility efforts. Even the smallest businesses add up their contributions to charitable causes each year for tax purposes. They may use this information to adjust the amount, or the recipients, of future contributions. While these have value for internal management purposes, without outside auditors and, limited if any, stakeholders' feedback, their accuracy as measures of social performance outcomes is dubious.

For businesses that are serious about social responsibility, the social audit is an ideal outcome measurement methodology and implementation mechanism. Due to the potentially incriminating nature of social audits, even universal business usage would not inform the public and researchers about business social performance outcomes in general. Researchers have been forced, as a result, to use creative, but less than optimal, measures. As we begin to examine the empirical evidence about levels of business social performance in chapter 4, I will present an overview of the measures used in the past by researchers, as well as those generated from the data collected in this research.

In closing this chapter, it's only fair to submit the BSP model to the same scrutiny that I applied to the previous CSP models. In other words, how does it help us understand real-life examples of business social responsibility and irresponsibility? I will use two examples, one relating to a small business and the other, a large corporation. The first example comes from an article published in the *Des Moines Register* (Santiago and Beaumont, December 14, 1999) about a lawsuit brought against Iowa Beef Packing Inc. (IBP). If there is one company everyone in Iowa loves to hate, it is IBP. The company is seen as the archtypical bad corporate citizen in the same way that Deere and Co. is the archtypical good corporate citizen. IBP is the largest meatpacking business in the United States today, with plants throughout the Midwest, mostly located in small, rural communities. As of this writing, IBP is negotiating a purchase by Tyson Foods.

The article reported that a former manager of medical care at the IBP plant in Perry, Iowa, accused the plant manager of ignoring serious injuries among workers hurt on the job, delaying or refusing treatment for those injuries, and forcing the medical manager to quit because she would not comply with his orders. Supposedly, the plant manager's motivation for orders to ignore workers' injuries and refuse them treatment is that his bonus is tied to the plant's safety record. The more injuries treated, the more must be officially reported, and then, the lower the plant manager's bonus.

According to the article, IBP "strongly denies the allegations" (1999, 10S). However, for illustrative purposes, let us assume they are true. How does the BSP model inform our thinking about the situation? The safety of workers clearly falls under legal and ethical categories of social responsibility. Creating or not remedying unsafe work situations are violations of state and federal occupational safety and health laws. Failure to report job-related injuries is also a legal violation. Furthermore, it is hard to imagine a code of ethics that does not prohibit causing harm to others.

With regard to economic social responsibilities, IBP's Perry safety situation is less clear. Marketplace logic would tell us that if the safety of workers is sufficiently imperiled, the employer will have difficulty attracting and retaining employees and employees will be demoralized, leading to their decreased economic productivity, maybe even to industrial sabotage. The cost of fines for violating the law and the heightened health and liability insurance expenses would add to IBP's cost of doing business. Thus, all of the economic consequences of poor workplace safety should make IBP less profitable, and thereby, make the safety situation a violation of their economic responsibility. However, if IBP can cover up the safety hazards, it will not suffer economic hardships in the form of fines and heightened insurance costs. In IBP's case, since the state subsidizes the cost of training new employees and the company relies on immigrants for new employees, even the costs of high turnover may be less than the cost of improving the safety of the workplace. Therefore, it is quite likely that IBP is not violating its economic social responsibilities. Notice that, in this train of reasoning, I have used cost/benefit logic of the kind one would expect in an assessment of achievement of economic goals. That is, I have considered how the economic outcomes of this situation might be measured by IBP's top management, independent auditors, and investors.

Again assuming the charges are correct, how did it happen that an IBP plant manager would institute policies and unwritten rules that communicated to his staff that workers' injuries should be ignored, that, in effect, said that the official appearance of a safe workplace was more important than the reality? Where did he ever get the idea that that kind of policy was congruent with corporate policy? These are critical questions, the answers to which are key to understanding how social responsibility is actualized by businesses, or, in other words, to understanding their social responsiveness.

The BSP model forces us to think about questions like "How did it happen?" We're given a hint to the possible answers in this case by the report that the manager's bonus is tied to the plant's safety record and its profitability. On the face of it, the reward system seems to show that top management is as concerned about workers' welfare as it is about profits. IBP has plant positions whose function is to ensure the safety of workers (the medical manager). Why did this manager get the signals mixed up and think that profit was more important and that the appearance of safety would be adequate to satisfy corporate headquarters?

These questions require us to consider IBP's corporate culture, past history, and its actual reward and sanctioning systems for answers. If IBP's top management is serious about worker safety, they will find ways to measure it (not just official reports of injuries) and ways to reward managers for promoting it. They will insist on policies and procedures that result in worker safety. They will hire and promote management staff who share their values about worker safety. The end result of poor workplace safety, unless the Perry plant is uniquely different than other IBP plants, causes us to doubt the commitment of top management to workplace safety. At this point, the argument incriminating IBP's top management is based on inference from a few observations reported by employees. Access to IBP's internal operations would be necessary to definitively answer our questions about the company's social responsiveness. The BSP model has focused our attention on the identification of the kinds of social responsibility involved in the IBP situation, consideration of the management values that resulted in the situation, the policies and programs that actualized those values, and the outcome indicators that management and interested outsiders can use to assess the situation.

For the second example, I take you to a small town bank housed in a beautifully restored old Victorian building. Dark, worn, well-polished wood desks, floors and banisters; rich, upholstered antique furniture; thick, plush, dark-red carpets and drapes; displays of the works of local and renowned artists; a vine covered brick patio furnished with wicker furniture for employee breaks; and a meeting room in a library with old leather-bound books, and a real wood fire in the fireplace describe the physical structure of the bank. It is hard to believe that this building is a bank—in a small town—where farmers, occasionally with manure on their boots, come in regularly to do business. In small Iowa towns, such an ostentatious display of wealth is usually not well received by local residents. "Putting on airs" they call it. Sometimes a great show of wealth will lead residents to conclude that the business is too profitable (meaning customers are being taken advantage of) or that the business person is spending more than she or he should on frivolous display—causing residents to wonder about the fiscal health of the business.

This bank gets away with violating the norms for many reasons. Principal among them is that it has aligned its display of grandeur with the health of the community. Historically, the family that owned the bank believed that the bank's economic success and the health of the community were inseparable. The current president, a scion of the founding family, continues in that belief. Employees are told that they are expected to participate in the community. The major responsibility of one of the vice presidents is community development, and another bank officer serves in a local elected office. The officers are given released time from work to attend to their community responsibilities. Representatives of the bank are included in downtown beautification efforts, new business attraction programs, business retention programs, school reorganization and improvement programs, community recreation planning, and many others. In addition, the bank provides a substantial amount of funding for many of these projects.

The bank's grand building fits into their community betterment vision since as a prominent downtown feature, it provides a focal point for community pride. It sets an example of downtown beautification that has encouraged other downtown businesses to spruce up. It makes the downtown a pleasant destination, luring residents and visitors to come downtown to shop and for entertainment. Finally, it's grandeur should make the downtown more appealing to new businesses looking for a place to locate.

The bank's community betterment efforts are manifestations of ethical and discretionary social responsibility. These efforts are also viewed by the bank as a way to fulfill its economic social responsibilities. The bank's top management reasons that more prosperous, happy residents and businesses in town will mean more business and more profit for the bank. This logic is not universally accepted, however. The top management of some other banks strictly limit their staff and monetary contributions to local community betterment. Their definition of economic social responsibility demands a shorter term return on investment, a larger profit margin, more lucrative management salaries and benefits, or alterations in other variables that change the economic calculus altogether. In this thinking, contributions to community betterment would be equated with economic irresponsibility.

It is necessary to consider the outcome measurements corresponding with each category of social responsibility to understand how the bank viewed community betterment. Moreover, examining how the bank's owner and top management transformed their vision of the bank's social responsibility through the mechanisms of physical renovation, organizational policies, corporate culture, and job descriptions into action for community betterment is, in my opinion, very illuminating. Of course, the IBP and the Socksberg bank examples do not "prove" the BSP theory. It is not my purpose to prove the theory, even if it were scientifically possible to do so. Rather, I offer these examples to demonstrate the utility of the BSP model and to highlight the questions I asked and the factors I considered in this research.

Henceforth, in the chapters that follow, business social responsibility will mean discretionary social responsibility. The Iowa study was focused on the contributions businesses make to community betterment, a further refinement of discretionary social responsibility. However, where appropriate, evidence from research about other or unidentified kinds of discretionary social responsibility will be discussed also. Community betterment refers to contributions to the quality of life in a defined geographical location. A notion that will be developed in the next chapter is that community betterment shares many characteristics with the economic concept of public goods—which helps explain the difficulty in measuring outcomes.

The influence of managerial discretion on a business's level of discretionary social responsibility will be investigated with findings from the literature and from analyses of the Iowa data. The weight of the evidence provided later in the book supports the significance of managerial discretion in determining how businesses interact with society. While it is not possible with the current data to consider the societal outcomes of business social responsibility, I will explore the ramifications of businesses social responsibility to the business and the business operator.

NOTE

1. The terms in parentheses are Wilson's and the colloquial expressions are McAdam's.

CHAPTER 3

Stealing from Owners and Giving Back to the Community

Do businesses have any responsibility to society or not? Before addressing the question directly, I thought it was important to establish some common terminology. Thus in the last chapter, I attempted to cover only the definitions, leaving normative positions for this chapter. The fact that I was not completely successful in dividing definitions from normative views underscores the artificiality of, and challenge involved in, approaching a subject about responsibility without referring to "shoulds" and "ought tos." In this chapter I will confront the more interesting debate about the role of businesses in society. To that end, I will examine the case for and against business social responsibility utilizing the terms established in the last chapter, arguments contained in the literature, and rationales expressed to me by interviewees.

BUSINESSES HAVE ECONOMIC AND LEGAL SOCIAL RESPONSIBILITIES

Reverend McCaffery, a community leader in the small Iowa city of Manasis, told me that "businesses have no responsibility other than to fulfill their economic function." I'm sure that if he thought a little more about it, he would have added that they also must obey the law. Even the staunchest opponents of business social responsibility agree with the principle that businesses have economic and legal social responsibilities. They differ from the proponents of broader responsibilities for businesses, as

McCaffery's comment implies, in that they do not define economic and legal responsibilities as social responsibilities. Economic and legal responsibilities may not seem like social responsibilities due to the controlling mechanisms engaged when they are violated. Businesses are supposed to be subject to the discipline of the market in meeting their economic responsibilities and of the courts for their legal responsibilities. Disagreement over terminology, however, masks substantive agreement that businesses have economic and legal social responsibilities.

BUSINESSES DO NOT HAVE ETHICAL AND DISCRETIONARY SOCIAL RESPONSIBILITIES

The social responsibilities in dispute are the ethical and, especially, the discretionary categories. The most often cited opponent of business social responsibility is Milton Friedman. He represents the opposition to discretionary social responsibility on the right but is joined by opponents on the left who make the same argument for different reasons. Friedman's position is elaborated in his 1962 book *Capitalism and Freedom* and succinctly stated in a 1971 article. To Friedman the reason for the general rise in the quality of life in the West is that capitalists have been allowed relative freedom to pursue profit maximization. He believes that the common good is best served by businesspeople focusing on the financial return on capital investment. When they channel business resources, including their time and expertise, into nonbusiness, discretionary social responsibility areas, they fail to fulfill their primary responsibility to society. If they are business managers, in addition to their irresponsibility to society, Friedman claims they are neglecting their duty to the business owners. In effect, managers who contribute business resources to social causes are taxing the business owners without their consent—or to put it more bluntly, they are stealing from owners. As Friedman sees it, managers are bound by an implicit contract to use business resources for profit maximization purposes only. Beyond economic responsibilities, managers must obey the law and do business by the rules of the free enterprise system, e.g. free competition and fair pricing. This later summarizes the ethical responsibilities of businesses in Friedman's perspective.

Friedman makes another point in his argument against discretionary social responsibility for businesses. On this item, he is joined by Richard Abrams (1979), an opponent of business discretionary social responsibility on the left. Both sides concur that managers do not have the inclination, education, or skills to address social problems. Abrams is particularly concerned that businesses have at their disposal tremendous resources and power, yet are not accountable to the public for action they take regarding social issues. He cites an entry in the Celanese annual report stating that the company is "taking leadership in supporting citizens' groups dedicated to maintaining law and order" (1979: 50) as a disturbing example of what can happen when businesses assume discretionary social responsibility. Theodore Levitt (1958) goes so far as to describe business social responsibility as a threat to democracy itself. Abrams doesn't trust businesses to put their self-interest aside and work for the common good. He believes that surplus business resources should be available for the solution of social problems, but through the auspices of governmental institutions that are accountable to the public. This must be accompanied, in his thinking, by fuller corporate disclosure of operational information. Levitt, Friedman, and Abrams agree that the only responsibility of business should be business.

The views represented by Friedman and Abrams against discretionary business social responsibility are founded in ideologies. Neoclassical economics, popularly depicted as the invisible hand guiding profit maximization into the greatest good for all, is the basis for Friedman's call for businesses to be unfettered by social responsibilities. Abrams's distrust of business, especially large corporations, stems from the Marxian contention that capitalism is ultimately antithetical to the common good. Recently, a more pragmatic argument against businesses having discretionary social responsibility has been articulated. It claims to be based on facts and not ideologies and, hence, appears harder to refute. Statements of this position appear frequently in newspapers as businesses attempt to justify closing plants and laying off workers, and a similar approach was the basis of Samuelson's obituary for the good corporation in *Newsweek* (1993).

An articulation of this position in academic literature is presented by Edward Stendardi, Jr. (1992). He maintains that businesses are no longer able to be as philanthropic as they were previously. Now, discretionary contributions must be guided by the discipline of "social investing"—meaning that businesses must be able to show a return in business profit for contributions they make to social causes. Social investing is undisguised advertising or profit making piggybacked on a charitable cause. Examples include Pizza Hut giving discount coupons to school kids who offer them as an incentive to encourage people to donate money to the high school athletic program and, on a national scale, Coca-Cola's support of the Atlanta Olympic Games.

The reasons for this change are, according to Stendardi, fourfold. First, increased global competition has lessened corporate profit, decreasing the amount of money available for philanthropic giving. Second, the passage of the Tax Reform Act of 1986 reduced the maximum marginal tax rate of corporations from 46 percent to 34 percent. Since corporate charitable contributions up to a certain percent of profit, and under certain circumstances, are tax deductible, reducing the tax rate means that taxpayers reimburse companies less (through reduced taxes) for each charitable dollar contributed. Stendardi reasons that companies will consequently lower their charitable contributions. Third, Wall Street has taken an increasingly short-term view of company performance. Under these circumstances it becomes very difficult for business executives to justify expenditures that do not show a quick return on investment. Lastly, one of the enforcers of the short-term horizon is the specter of corporate raiding. Companies with undervalued stock are prime targets for predatory takeovers. Corporate executives who do not meet quarterly profit goals are disciplined by a drop in their company stock prices . . . and this could draw the interest of corporate raiders who see the stock as a bargain relative to company assets. Stendardi believes these factors singly and together portend a future drop in corporate philanthropic activity, with companies substituting social investing in its place.

According to S. Prakash Sethi (1996), other behavior of good corporate citizenship is similarly affected by the events Stendardi describes. Sethi characterizes the situation thus: "It would seem that our previously socially responsible corporations are no longer able to provide the wages that permit a good life to their various constituencies as they go through the wrenching experiences of downsizing to meet the new realities of international markets. The radical paradigm shift in our competitive environment, brought about by global competition, changing technologies, and a communication revolution, compels corporations either to alter their behavior drastically in order to adapt or risk obliteration" (1996: 84).

So powerful is this argument that it has been used as a rationale by some businesses to void all social responsibilities, even economic and legal ones. U.S. Steel (now USX) and Chrysler (now Daimler-Chrysler) claimed that, due to foreign competition, they could no longer pay their bills, pay property taxes, and vest their employee pension funds—economic and legal responsibilities. They argued that unless they received taxpayer funded loans and grants, forgiveness of debts, and tax holidays, they would not be able to make steel or cars—undisputed economic responsibilities. Corporation executives frequently claim that meeting the highest safety and environmental standards is not feasible because their foreign competitors do not have to bear the costs of meeting the standards. The car manufacturers made this argument back when Ralph Nader first petitioned them to use safety glass in windshields and when asked to switch automobiles to unleaded gasoline. Translated into the terms used here, these executives were saying that competition constrained them from fulfilling their ethical social responsibilities. The issues of competition, global and within industries, and industry consolidation are so important to business social responsibility that we will see reference to it frequently in this book. I will examine in depth the validity of the global competition argument against business social performance in the closing chapter.

A different and equally provocative argument against business social responsibility is presented by Henry Mintzberg in a 1983 overview of the pros and cons of business social responsibility. Mintzberg cites several research studies describing the internal structural features of large organizations that encourage managers to give priority to the goals of efficiency and profit over ethical and social goals. Accordingly, even the CEO at headquarters will find it difficult to implement social goals (like a "family friendly" workplace) with the divisional structure and a financial reporting system that don't allow consideration of proactive ethical or socially responsible behavior. Mintzberg concludes that machine bureaucracy and the "very concept of management itself" may be antithetical to social responsibility (1983:11). His reasoning is that managers are professionals hired to design and implement efficient ways to achieve the goals determined by the owners. Their expertise is the implementation of goals, not vision or critique. In spite of his gloomy prognosis for business social performance, Mintzberg ends his article by suggesting ways that businesses can become more socially responsible.

To summarize, the points in the argument that businesses should have no ethical and discretionary social responsibility are:

1. The responsibility of business is to maximize profit through the production and distribution of goods and services in a market exchange.
2. Using business resources (capital or labor) for other purposes lessens the amount available for the business's economic mission and is thus an act of irresponsibility to society.
3. Business managers who divert business resources from profit maximization are stealing from owners and not fulfilling their duty to them.
4. Business managers lack the inclination, education, and skills to understand social issues and propose solutions to social problems.
5. Businesses are not accountable to the public for their intrusion in social, essentially public, affairs.
6. If the vast resources and power of businesses were used to implement business's solutions to social problems, it would represent a major threat to democracy.
7. Global and industry competition make ethical and discretionary social responsibilities luxuries that businesses can no longer afford.
8. The drive for short-term profits makes it difficult or impossible for businesses to be responsible for anything other than economic and legal areas.
9. The machine structure of large corporations discourages businesspeople from acting in ethical and socially responsible ways.

I bring two elements of this overview to the reader's attention before we proceed. First, the Manasis community leader I quoted above made it clear to me that he was referring to businesses as institutions when he said they had no responsibility other than their economic functions. In contrast, he believes that businesspeople do have ethical and discretionary social responsibilities. This is the same distinction made by Preston and Post (1975) in their articulation of business public responsibility and a major tenet of the neoclassical school of economics. In items 1 through 8 above, the referent is certainly the institution of business. The ethical, civic, and social responsibilities of the people who own, manage, and work in the businesses are not considered. The distinction is less clear in item 9.

I suggest that distinguishing between the social responsibilities of businesses and business people is theoretically plausible, but tricky, in real life. The approval of Hans Becherer, former chairman and CEO of Deere and Co., given in support of a social cause is described by one interviewee as "the kiss of life." Nonprofit fund raisers in Iowa study Becherer's idiosyncrasies and know what causes and values are important to him as a person. Nevertheless, the "kiss of life" has nothing to do with Becherer as a person, and everything to do with his position at the time of the interviews as Deere's chairman and CEO, and with the prestige and resources represented by Deere in Iowa. How can the characteristics of the person and the power of the position be disentangled for those who advise Becherer on his social responsibilities or those who try to recruit his support for a local public art display? If the distinction is problematic with big companies, it is even more challenging for the veterinarian who runs a small animal hospital, the furniture store owner with thirty employees, and other small businesses (and businesspeople).

That brings me to the second point. It is obvious that the focus of these thinkers is big business. Their assumption is that business is conducted in public corporations with stock owners, large management staffs, machine bureaucracies, and vast resources. Points 3, 4, 5, 6, 8, and 9 do not apply to nonpublic, owner-managed small businesses. As I indicated in the introduction, small businesses constitute the overwhelming majority of businesses, employ the majority of workers, and take in slightly less than half of all receipts. Even though these facts apply to all small businesses and not just those that are owner managed and nonpublic, the professionally managed, public, small business is probably more like other small businesses than the megacorporations envisioned as the standard. I do not question the importance of big, publicly owned businesses. My concern is that the big-business bias leads to propositions that purport to apply to all businesses when they obviously do not. We will see the same bias in the arguments for business social responsibility.

BUSINESSES DO HAVE ETHICAL AND DISCRETIONARY SOCIAL RESPONSIBILITIES

Power and Wealth = Responsibility

Let's start with a familiar name. As I hinted above, Mintzberg concludes his overview of the pros and cons of discretionary social responsibility by siding with the pros. He contends that no matter what the argument against business social responsibility, the fact is that, in fulfilling their economic functions, businesses impinge on all other areas of society and must be held responsible for the mayhem and destruction they cause. He says, "Size alone makes economic decisions social." (1983:12) An apt metaphor to summarize Mintzberg's view of the relationship of businesses and society is the elephant in the living room. It's all well and good to say that the elephant's only responsibility is to survive and do the work assigned it, when the truth is that, regardless of restricted claims of responsibility, every move she makes critically impacts the welfare of the rest of the household. Following Mintzberg's logic, it's purely an intellectual exercise to pretend that businesses' economic activities can be walled off from other domains of society. Like Preston and Post (1975), however, Mintzberg believes businesses' responsibility to society is limited to primary and secondary areas of social involvement. In short, their social responsibility is to rectify the damage they cause in the course of fulfilling economic functions and to act proactively to ensure positive social outcomes from business activity in accordance with society's standards determined through public policy processes.

From another point of view, Mintzberg is making a familiar argument for business's social responsibility. He implies that other entities have a valid claim on business surplus resources in addition to the owners. These entities are Freeman's stakeholders: workers, communities, and consumers, as discussed in the last chapter. William Evan and R. Edward Freeman (1988) make the case that managers have a responsibility to the welfare of stakeholders that is as compelling as their responsibility to owners.

The notion that business's vast resources require commensurate responsibility was popular in the 1960s and 1970s. Keith Davis and Robert L. Blomstrom, writing in 1971, called it the Iron Law of Responsibility: "In the long run those who do not use power in a manner which society considers responsible will tend to lose it" (1971: 95). In other words, society has allowed businesses to amass great fortunes and power. If those businesses do not ultimately serve the interests of society, society will take the resources away from them. The way the "iron law" is enforced is through the loss of business or through government regulation. Consider first the loss of business. On the national level, consumer boycotts have been organized to punish businesses for acts of social irresponsibility. Famous examples are boycotts of Nestle's products over infant formula marketing in third-world countries, boycotts of tuna from firms using non-dolphin-safe fishing techniques, and boycotts of retail stores that buy clothes made with child labor.

Ian Deese, who owns and manages a thriving retail and business service establishment in Manasis, explained how the public sanctions irresponsible businesses at the local level. "The bottom line is if you don't support the community, they won't support you." Keith Runciman, a real estate business owner in Caizan, echoed Deese's comment when telling me why he supported various community causes. "Because they'll get you if you don't," he said. This sentiment was mentioned by over half the interviewees. It closely resembles tenets of the enlightened self-interest position to be presented below.

Both at the national and the local levels, monitoring and consumer sanctioning of businesses can be effective in encouraging businesses to act responsively.

Complexity is added, however, when one realizes that the definition of responsible behavior enforced through boycotts depends on the values of the agitated consumer. Consumer boycotts have become a powerful weapon in the arsenal of special interest groups, whether it is conservative Christians who want Disney to rescind gay-friendly employee benefit packages, animal rights groups who want all sales of fur products stopped, or local groups opposed to the closing of a school. The danger is that these groups may not be acting in the interest of the common good. Further, consumer ire encourages social responsiveness, with all the associated problems noted in the last chapter, and not necessarily performance corresponding to ethical and discretionary responsibility.

Turning now to the possibility of regulation as a means of enforcing the social contract, we confront an entirely different situation. Whereas the last thirty years has witnessed greater reliance on, and perfecting of, consumer sanctions as a mechanism to change business behavior, the opposite has happened with regard to regulation. Looking at this aspect of business social responsibility (BSR) takes us back to another era and what seems like a foreign country. Thirty years ago, the stick of regulation was a very real prod in motivating businesses to attend to their image of social responsibility. To give you a sense of the discourse at that time, consider an article written by Melvin Anshen in 1970 for the *Columbia Journal of World Business*, a periodical written for a management audience. In the article, he describes what he calls a redefinition of the social contract between society and business, wherein business is expected to assume ethical and discretionary social responsibility. He advises "businessmen" to put aside their "raw emotional revulsion" (1970:7) at the prospect and get involved in the public discussion of the nature of those responsibilities. Otherwise, he warns, people who know nothing about business will impose regulations that are likely to constrain business, "emasculate incentives," and, in general, create conditions unfriendly to vigorous economic and social progress. Become involved they did.

The previously mentioned Committee for Economic Development (a consortium of business people, academics and government officials) was organized in the late 1960s for the purposes identified by Anshen. In their 1971 publication of the social responsibilities of businesses, they admonish the business community to become more socially responsible with these words: "Insensitivity to changing demands of society sooner or later results in public pressures for governmental intervention and regulation to require business to do what it was reluctant or unable to do voluntarily" (28).

I have presented the stick of regulation as a weakened weapon because it has lost much of its power in contemporary United States. The near-universal acceptance of the belief in the efficacy and goodness of unfettered business and the corresponding belief in the inefficacy and badness of government are so much a part of unquestioned common knowledge today that they resemble ideological mantras.[1] In this climate of downsizing government and deregulation of business, support for new government regulation of business is extremely unlikely.

The Social Contract

The Iron Law of Responsibility is sometimes called a formulation of the social contract, but it does not capture many of the nuances of the social contract between business and society. A more complete statement is expressed by Tom Cannon in a 1994 business textbook written for college students. Cannon describes the social contract this way.

There exists an implicit or explicit contract between business and the community in which it operates. Business is expected to create wealth; supply markets; generate employment; innovate and produce a sufficient surplus to sustain its activities and improve its competitiveness while contributing to the maintenance of the community in which it operates. Society is expected to provide an environment in which business can develop and prosper, allowing investors to earn returns while ensuring that the stakeholders and their dependents can enjoy the benefits of their involvement without fear of arbitrary or unjust action. (32)

Contributing to the maintenance of the community implies discretionary social responsibility. The environment provided by society includes, among other things, protecting patents and property rights, contract regulation, monetary stability, national defense, infrastructure availability, and the education of workers. An extremely important benefit provided by society to businesses is the rights and protections granted through incorporation. Incorporation creates a fictive legal entity with more rights than human beings. In 1999 the United Publishing Corporation sued the state of California over a violation of its first amendment rights when the state refused to provide the corporation with a list of the names and addresses of arrestees that it intended to sell to subscribers. At issue was whether the corporation should be allowed to make money from public information, not whether the corporation had a first amendment right to the information. That corporations have first amendment rights is obviously accepted without question.

Another important feature of incorporation is that it legally separates the institution of business from the people of the business. It protects owners from personal liability for corporate illegal activities and debts, including tax liabilities. Owners can lose the capital they have invested in the corporation, but incur no risk beyond that. Imagine trying to sell stock to people if owners were held responsible for the legal and fiscal activities of corporations. Added to the already listed benefits of incorporation, today's corporations are relatively immortal when compared with the lifespan of the humans who own and work in them.

Richard L. Grossman and Frank T. Adams (1996) briefly review the history of incorporation in an edited book called *The Case Against the Global Economy*. They report that, originally, businesses were granted the privileges of incorporation in order to serve the public good in some specific way and were considered quasi public corporations. The East India Company and the Hudson Bay Company were early incorporated businesses, established with limited charters to undertake the risky business of exploiting the colonies for the crown of England. In the first century of United States history, state legislatures were careful to limit the number of companies to be chartered and to limit the lifespan and power of chartered companies. In other countries at the time, the right to charter businesses rested in the monarchy. By placing chartering rights in state legislators, the colonial government wanted to ensure that citizens would have power over corporations. Given the United States disdain for the Hudson Bay Company, and centralized power of any kind, this stance is understandable. Grossman and Adams (p. 378–379) illustrate the prevailing sentiments toward chartering: "The Supreme Court of Virginia reasoned in 1809, 'If the [business] applicants' object is merely private or selfish; if it is detrimental to, or not promotive of, the public good, they have no adequate claim upon the legislature for the privileges [of chartering].' The Pennsylvania legislature stated in 1834, 'A corporation in law is just what the incorporating act makes it. It is the creature of the law and may be molded to any shape or any purpose that the Legislature may deem most conducive for the general good.' "

Beginning in the late 1880s, the situation changed. States started competing with each other to attract industries and corporate headquarters. Consequently, they watered down the stipulations, originally contained in chartering legislation and accepted practice, that incorporated businesses should serve the public good. Also at this time, states started granting charters to businesses that lasted essentially forever without procedures for citizen review or oversight. So changed has the common thinking become, most have forgotten that the ultimate legal source of U.S. corporations' power rests with citizens through their legislatures. In a very real sense, corporations, and the benefits realized by their owners, exist at the indulgence of society. Kuttner (1996) and Grossman and Adams (1996) believe that refamiliarizing citizens with these facts and reinvigorating corporate charter oversight could create an actual, as opposed to a tacit, social contract between society and business.

How is the social contract articulated at the local level? John Crowell, the owner of a manufacturing firm in Gatlin City, is a particularly articulate advocate of business's ethical and discretionary social responsibilities. His logic begins with his belief that:

"Businesses are no more than a collection of people. For that reason, we should serve society. That's us. In effect, we 'is' society." Later he put it slightly differently when he said, "Businesses are part of the fabric of society, so we have a duty to the rest of the rug."

A restaurant owner in Gatlin City, Maggie Nock, said it this way: "This may sound trite, but without society there would be no need for business. Service and retail businesses must be especially involved in supporting society."

Also, from Bryant Gear, an independent insurance agent in Caizan: "People and business often do not realize that their mutual interests are intertwined."

Hildeth Haubrich, a Chamber executive in Pikeville, put it even more strongly: "Businesses absolutely have an obligation to their community. It's not an option. Communities and businesses need each other."

Crowell, Nock, and Gear are describing the social contract from the vantage point of small businesses. In this account, the social contract is more a sense of a shared fate, a commonality of interests, between businesses and the rest of society than a contractual arrangement. Small businesses, even when incorporated, do not (cannot) create a world separate from and above the rest of society. Large corporations, on the other hand, can, and do, create their own worlds. They develop their own culture, history, language and—for management—a worldview that extends beyond the community in which it operates. This is intentional in some corporations as they move management staff from place to place for the purpose of assimilating them to the organizational culture and loosening their ties to any one geographic community. The owners and managers of small businesses live in the same local world that the rest of us experience. No wonder they feel that business is part of the fabric of society.

It's the Right Thing To Do

There is more to Crowell's and Nock's comments than a formulation of the small-business social contract, however. In addition, they are conveying the notion of the inseparability of personal moral responsibilities and business social responsibilities. My interviewees, even if their business was incorporated, found it hard to distinguish between business and society and between the people who own and run businesses and business as an institution. After all, what is business if not a collection of people? Many interviewees conflated the responsibilities they felt as citizens and human beings with the social responsibilities of their businesses. Reverand McCaffrey was the only interviewee who expressed a dissenting view. Below are some of the responses to two of my questions: 1) Please elaborate why you think businesses do or do not have social responsibilities? and 2) If you were trying to convince another business owner to get involved in the community, what would you say?

Business people have a responsibility to take their turn at providing leadership in the community. (Bryant Gear, independent insurance agent in Caizan.)

As a citizen we have a responsibility to get involved. Many people don't do it. We owe something to the community we live in whether we know it or not. (Michael Palmer, veterinarian in Manasis.)

I support the community, because I want to give something back. It's important to make the community a better place to live. (Walter Klazowski, owner of a public relations firm in Gatlin City.)

I'm not so sure businesspeople get involved to support the community because they're in business. It's more that they have an ethic of involvement in the first place. (Robert Markus, manufacturer in Socksberg.)

We should give back to the community. Give until it hurts. (Derek McIntyre, owner of a car dealership in Caizan.)

Businesses need to give back to the community. (Aaron Rosenberg, retail store owner in Gatlin City.)

It's what people should do . . . take care of children and community. (Nick Grafton, a banker in Socksberg.)

I could go on with similar comments, but this is sufficient to convey their meaning. The comments express the sense of personal moral obligation that prompts some businesspeople to work to improve the common good or to display discretionary social responsibility. Giving back to the community was an especially popular theme.

Some researchers suggest that the use of moral justifications for business social responsibility is not just a characteristic of some small businesses. Rather, they stress the significance of the identification of the business owner/manager with the local community. Joseph Galaskiewicz's influential 1985 book about the grants economy of the Twin City area, Robert and Helen Lynd's classic 1937 study of Muncie, Indiana, and E. Bigby Baltzell's 1979 description of the upper class of Boston portray communities with upper-class capitalists who possess a strong sense of noblisse oblige, or the feeling that they have a responsibility to work for the general welfare of the community. David Kamen's (1985) term for this upper-class group is "family capitalists." Due to the exceptional nature of this group, he created a special section in his theory of corporate giving just to explain their civic activity. Kamen believes that integration into the community sets this group of business owners apart from those who are less responsible and from those motivated for other reasons.

Craig Smith (1994a) (more below on his ideas) calls this view the "old responsibility paradigm" of business social responsibility. He is cynical toward this position, claiming that businesspeople are merely wrapping self-serving behavior in the guise of altruism and moral obligation to curry favor with society (and probably also to look good in the eyes of the researchers). In contrast, in the new paradigm of social investing, businesspeople are forthright in admitting that they engage in philanthropy for business gain of some kind.

Stendardi (1992) and Smith contend that the sentiment among business people that social responsibility is the right thing to do, if ever more than a ruse, is now a thing of the past. However, Galaskiewicz (1997) found an increase in moral vs. economic rationales among the local capitalists of the Twin City area when he restudied them in 1989. "Sixty-eight percent said in 1989 that companies, because of their citizenship rights and privileges, have a moral obligation to share their wealth and help the less fortunate in society, as opposed to 50 percent in 1981" (1997:458). Similarly, researchers Gary Weaver, Linda Klebe Trevino, and Philip Cochran examined the impact of top management's personal moral commitment on company ethics programs in large industrial and service businesses. In two reports, both published in 1999, they conclude that when top executives are morally committed, the scope and efficacy of company ethics programs are substantially greater than when they are not morally committed. Moreover, they add, researchers' focus on the relationship of good corporate citizenship to company success does a disservice to managers who implement ethics programs because they think it's the right thing to do, rather than for the additional profit it might bring their business.

Smith's (1994a) criticism of the "do gooder" rationale forces us to closely scrutinize what business people tell us about their motives for socially responsible behavior, including scrutinizing the rationales that claim that philanthropic acts are self-serving. Given the ideological climate today, businesspeople might be equally likely to hide moral rationales for their socially responsible acts and disguise them as profit seeking. Without proof to the contrary, I think that businesspeople understand the motivation for their behavior better than I do, that they will not purposefully lie about it, and, therefore, that some businesspeople do guide their behavior by moral principles. Unless there are inconsistencies in what they say, or between what they say and do, on what basis can analysts dismiss the validity of what people tell them?

A different interpretation of the prevailing belief in the decrease in moral justifications for business social responsibility is presented by the Gatlin City manufacturer, John Crowell. He said, "I'm involved because I think it's the right thing to do, but I would convince another businessperson to get involved with an economic rationale. I'd talk about the contribution it makes to employee attraction and retention." As Crowell suggests, given the resonance of economic rationality today, moral justifications for business social responsibility are likely to be couched in terms of cost/benefit analyses and contributions to the bottom line. Let us turn now to the economic rationales, or what in the literature is called the enlightened self-interest rationale.

The Enlightened Self-Interest Rationale

Sole owners of businesses don't need an enlightened self-interest rationale to justify their social responsibility. They are not required to account to others for their use of business resources. However, like Crowell, they are probably familiar with it and may resort to it to justify to other people, especially business people, why they provide leadership and support for social causes. Managers, on the other hand, do not have the option of relying on moral justifications in explaining to owners, boards of directors, and stock owners at large why they gave company dollars to charity or loaned an executive to the United Way campaign for a year.

Milton Friedman (1962) argued that corporate charitable contributions are theft by managers from owners. Indeed, in 1953, stock owners of A.P. Smith Manufacturing challenged in a New Jersey court management's right to give company resources to charitable causes that do not show a direct benefit to owners. The court ruled that management had the discretion to use charitable contributions as a way to promote the corporation's interests. The U.S. Supreme Court refused to review the case, establishing management's right to engage in discretionary social responsibility—so long as, in management's judgment, it served the corporation's interests. The Smith Manufacturing ruling codified what was already accepted practice at the time.

Beginning in the 1980s, however, prevailing beliefs about social problems and the culpability of business changed, and stock owners are again challenging management's right to distribute company resources for charitable purposes. Stendardi (1992) reported that shareholders in some corporations have brought suit against their management. In other instances, they wage proxy battles to force management to reduce philanthropic activity. For example, some shareholders of Dayton-Hudson, a company that contributes 5 percent of its pre-tax income to charity, have filed resolutions to force management to reduce contributions or eliminate them all together. Without a doubt, there is a continuing need for managers committed to discretionary social responsibility and representatives of communities and social causes who solicit the support of owners and managers to construct an economic rationale for their discretionary social responsibility.

The enlightened self-interest rationale states that businesses that do good will realize economic benefits as a result. The economic justifications, and the evidence necessary to support the justifications, vary depending upon the type of BSR being considered. Thus the economic rationale for creating outstanding customer service, an economic social responsibility, requires a particular logic and evidentiary set that differs from the economic rationales utilized for discretionary social responsibility. All of the economic rationales are worthy of consideration, but my focus will be the economic justifications for discretionary social responsibility.

Following Gerald Keim (1978), John Aram (1989) and Michelle Sinclair and Joseph Galaskiewicz's (1997) lead, I use the concept of public goods to elaborate enlightened self-interest rationales. James Buchanan (1968) defined public goods as those goods and services that possess two unique characteristics: consumer satisfaction with the good is not diminished by others' consumption of it, and once the good is made available, people cannot be excluded from enjoying it. There are very few pure public goods. Clean air and community beautification, however, come close. Your enjoyment of clean air or community beautification does not diminish my enjoyment of them, and there is no legal or moral way to exclude someone from enjoying community beautification or clean air once they are created. Pure private goods, such as food and gasoline, are goods that cannot be shared infinitely without some lessening of consumptive enjoyment and are commodities for which access can be denied. Many goods fall on a continuum between pure private goods and pure public goods and may change their position on the continuum depending upon the social context. One person's enjoyment of fine art does not diminish another person's, but if the art is in the form of a painting, it can be owned by one person who can deny access to others or charge them a fee for enjoying it. In that instance, the art is a private good. It could be a public good, however, if everyone were allowed to see the art without cost—as would happen with outdoor building murals or billboards in public places. Then again, murals and billboards in public places can be private goods if they are privately owned and display a privatized message like advertising.

By their very nature, public goods encourage free riders, that is, people who realize the benefit of the good without paying the cost of its creation or maintenance. The scene I portrayed in the introduction of this book of people in Socksberg who contributed their equipment, their money, their time, and their energy to beautify the town with flowers and spring cleaning were creating a public good. Everyone in Socksberg, and everyone visiting the town, can enjoy it without lessening the enjoyment of it to any one person. There is no way to charge admission to recapture the expense of creating this public good. Thus the return on investment for this activity is an enhancement in local community pride, praise from residents and visitors, and a sense of personal accomplishment. The economic gain, if any, would result from general enhancement of the community and would be very difficult to measure. Free riders are those people and businesses that enjoy the flowers, and whatever business gain might result, without bearing the cost of providing them.

Using the logic of neoclassical rational choice theory, free-rider businesses will be in a better competitive position than those that do not incur the cost of providing public goods, i.e., lower costs plus same revenue equal more profit. Rational choice economists like Russell Hardin (1982) conclude that contributions to public goods are irrational. Businesses that make them will be less competitive than the free riders and will not survive in the long run. As S. Prakash Sethi maintains, in this climate of fierce competition and free-rider problems, companies that do good, just because it is the moral thing to do, will not succeed (1996: 86). However, the evidence to support Sethi and others who make this case is less than convincing. A sizable number of research studies have attempted to test the relationship between doing good and business success with mixed results. (Refer to Peter Arlow and Martin Gannon (1982), Steve Wartick and Philip Cochran (1985), and Jennifer Griffin and John Mahon (1997) for comprehensive reviews of the literature.) The consensus of these reviewers is that not only are the findings on this subject inconclusive but the scholarship has been plagued by problems in defining and measuring key concepts (business social responsibility and business success), relying on small, nonrandom samples, controlling for industry and economy effects, and factoring in time-lag considerations. Given the lack of consensus in the empirical evidence, businesses that contribute to public goods use various logical arguments to justify those contributions.

I suggest that enlightened self-interest rationales can be distinguished by the nature of the business gain expected from the socially responsible action and the ability of the responsible businesses to capture the gain. An important consideration, which will be addressed shortly, is whether a public good is still a public good when it is effectively harnessed to produce private profit. Figure 3.1 contains a visual depiction of the relationship between different rationales and public goods. The vertical axis is the amount of measurable, exclusive economic gain expected from the action. The horizontal axis shows the placement of various rationales based on the nature of economic gain described in the rationale, the ability of the business to capture exclusive gain from the action, and the measurability of that gain.

On the far left side of Figure 3.1 is the "shared fate" rationale. The tone of the shared-fate rationale is captured by Al Matsumoto, a Pikeville banker: "We can't succeed as a business if society and employees aren't successful. If all you have are businesses that take out of communities, then that place is going to wither and die." Melvin Timm, a contractor, also from Pikeville, said it this way:

Businesses have an obligation to society, but it's not codified. It's in their self interest to contribute. It helps business if the community is strong.

Figure 3.1
Enlightened Self-Interest Rationales and Captured Economic Gain

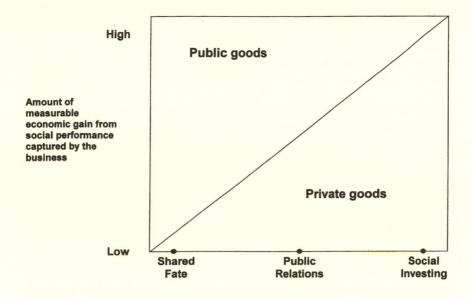

Acts exhibiting discretionary social responsibility that might fall in this category are those undertaken to improve the quality of life in the community. Support for programs to provide low-income housing, lower teen pregnancy, and improve recreation, education, and feelings of safety might fall in this category. The defining element in the shared-fate rationale is that the justification for the largesse is the mutuality-of-interests argument made by one of the business owners: "We is society." If society gains, business gains too. In the long run, businesses will prosper when the community is strong and healthy. There is no consideration in the rationale of the problem of free riders, and it is accepted that the gains cannot be precisely measured. Since the economic gains are illusive and essentially are taken on faith, it is necessary to bolster this position with the social contract logic and/or moral justifications. Another dimension to this rationale is suggested when business owners and top managers live in the community where their business operates. If their kids attend the local schools, play in the public parks, and participate in Little League, and if the parents become concerned about safety and property values, the shared-fate rationale has more salience than it might for absentee owners.

Belief in the shared-fate rationale is common among Iowa business owners and managers, as indicated in their response to a question in the telephone interviews. Interviewees were asked to evaluate the importance of fifteen different strategies to the success of their business. Among that list of strategies was "working to strengthen the local community." Since operators in different sizes of communities varied significantly from each other in their responses, frequency distributions were calculated separately for each community-size category. Roughly, three of every four surveyed rural business operators (74.8 percent), diminishing to still well over half of business operators in the metro communities (urban–71.0 percent, metro–61.5 percent), believe that working to strengthen their communities is important to the success of their business.

Returning to the enlightened self-interest rationales displayed in Figure 3.1, we see in the middle of the continuum the rationale wherein the socially responsible business captures an exclusive economic gain for its philanthropy through enhanced public image. I use Sinclair and Galaskiewicz's term for this variant of enlightened self interest—"public relations." The business contributions and the public goods provided here may be indistinguishable from those provided under the shared-fate rationale. The difference is that the business justifies the action by contending that economic gain will result from the boost to the business public image associated with providing the public good.

Deere and Company's contribution to downtown renovation in Moline, Ill., and the McIntyre car dealership's support of the Caizan community playhouse are examples of the kinds of business actions that might be categorized under the public relations rationale. Deere's name is all over the new Moline downtown public space. It may not directly lead to farmers buying Deere tractors instead of Case tractors, but, since it heightens Deere's prestige and improves the quality of life in the area, it may help in recruiting and retaining employees—especially technical and managerial employees. In fact, in a study published in 1997, Daniel Turban and Daniel Greening find evidence to support the proposition that companies that have reputations for doing good are more attractive to new entrants to the job market. Additionally, enhanced prestige may encourage regulators to give Deere the benefit of the doubt and legislators and financiers to help it overcome a vexing trade problem. Businesses like the McIntyre car dealership that support local arts will gain the goodwill of potential car buyers who appreciate the arts and perhaps local government entities as they decide where to purchase public cars or as they determine which streets should be plowed first after a snowstorm.

On the national level, economic rewards for discretionary social responsibility are favorable treatment by social investors (not to be confused with Stendardi's (1992) social investing by businesses). People who consider themselves social investors base their investment choices on the social responsibility of companies, thus partially countering the impact of short-term investors whose only concern in making investment decisions is quarterly profit statements. The Kinder, Lydenberg, and Domini scale of corporate social responsibility (1990) was developed to assist them to make informed choices. In addition to individual investors, large pension funds are more likely to invest in socially responsible companies. Richard Johnson and Daniel Greening in a study published in 1999 discovered that pension fund investors actively encourage socially responsible behavior in businesses in which they own stock.

Another economic benefit from business philanthropy is explained by Walter Klazowski, a business owner in Gatlin City: "I give support in order to build my practice, so that other business people become familiar with me—as a way to network." Klazowski's motivation for BSP is echoed by comments from the Twin Cities business people interviewed by Galaskiewicz for his 1985 study of the Twin City local capitalists, and in the 1989 revisit. He concludes that heightened prestige and the opportunity to network with important elites in the Cities is a central motivation spurring businesses to assist in the provision of public goods. In the five communities I examined in depth, networking with other businesspeople provided a strong incentive in encouraging local businesses to provide public goods.

The economic returns available to a business with a reputation for "good works" from other businesses can take the form of access to capital from local bankers, being treated fairly by suppliers, professional vendors (accountants, engineers), and enhanced opportunities to join lucrative joint ventures. Brian Uzzi (1999) demonstrated that networking with bankers provides businesses easier access to capital at favorable rates. In an earlier research study, Uzzi (1997) revealed the positive business returns associated with networking among business people in the garment industry in New York. It is only fair to mention that, in addition to rewards to businesses perceived to be good citizens, there may be punishment for those judged to be "free riders." I will elaborate this aspect of free-rider damage control in the chapter on the impact of local culture on BSP. For now, it's sufficient to recall the realtor Keith Runciman's words: "I support the community because they'll get you if you don't."

David Kamens, in a 1985 article explaining his theory of corporate civic giving, identifies another explanation for public relations philanthropy. Managers, he argues, give to charitable causes in order to legitimize their power as managers, and the power of their corporation, to the local community, government, and others. They use philanthropy to shape public thinking and manage local dependencies. Usha Haley (1991) suggests that businesses, through philanthropy, have cultivated the public's belief in the value of corporate growth and stability, as well as belief in the negative consequences of government regulation. Also, he adds that philanthropy can be a tool to help businesses form alliances with critical special interest groups, such as consumer or environmental organizations. In so doing, the company hopes to influence and moderate the group's position with regard to the company, or at the very least, be privy to the concerns, arguments, and likely strategies of the group. Haley's term for this kind of social responsibility is "managerial masques."

Belief in the value of improving the business's image in the community is very common among the operators of the small Iowa businesses sampled. Returning to the set of questions about strategies for business success cited previously, 79 percent of business operators identified improving business image as an important strategy for the success of their business. There is no significant difference between businesses in different sized towns on this question. Metro business operators valued their image in the community as much as their rural counterparts.

While there is considerable overlap in the kinds of philanthropy that are justified under the shared-fate and the public relations rationales, the justifications themselves are quite unique. Even so, companies may use both to justify an act of philanthropy. In the public relations rationale, public recognition for philanthropy has facilitated a partial transformation of a public good so that exclusive gain can accrue to some businesses and not others. The transformation is not complete because the economic gain is still difficult to measure precisely. Nevertheless, the free-rider problem has been partially addressed. The public relations rationale is aptly summed up by Ian Deese, the Manasis business owner, when he said, "What we do (for the community) is 50 percent altruistic, 50 percent advertising. It will come back to us."

To the far right of the continuum of direct economic gain expected from the contributions falling under the discretionary social responsibility category is social investing as described by Stendardi (1992). The same phenomenon is called "strategic philanthropy" by Sandra Waddock and Mary Ellen Boyle (1995) and "cause marketing" in Clark Smith's writing (1994). The economic return to the business for acts that are justified as social investing are captured and measured. When Caizan's downtown retail businesses support the yearly sweet corn festival, they do so to help build community spirit—that's a public good. Nevertheless, their enthusiastic support would almost surely be less if they didn't experience a substantial increase in sales over the festival weekend. The festival is a local business promotion activity as well as a celebration of community heritage. Both the community and the businesses gain. The difference between social investing and the other rationales is the fact that the economic gain to the business is short term, direct, and measurable. In Caizan, informal mechanisms developed by involved business operators monitor contributions and sanction free riders, thereby encouraging less "public spirited" businesses to contribute. Free riders are still possible, however.

Smith (1994) heralds social investing as the new "opportunity paradigm" as opposed to the old "responsibility paradigm." In the old paradigm, business philanthropists viewed donations as a way to give back to the community. Now, they understand that philanthropy is a business opportunity. Credit card companies get new cardholders and increased use of their cards by tying the cards to a social cause. I have a Master Card with a Greenpeace logo on it. Greenpeace is supposed to get a fraction of a percent of all the purchases I charge to the card. The bank that underwrites my Greenpeace credit card is using a mechanism that completely eliminates the risk of free riders. The question is, however, are they practicing discretionary social responsibility?

Let us not forget that all legal economic activity is supposed to provide gain for society and profit for businesses. Providing gain for society doesn't make a business activity philanthropic. Is a defense contractor engaging in philanthropy when it manufacturers tanks to be used to defend the nation against its enemies? How about the pharmaceutical company that comes up with a cure for cancer? Both of these business activities contribute greatly to the common good and make a profit for the businesses. If the recipient of the gain is a nonprofit organization instead of individuals or the nation as a whole, is the arrangement magically transmuted into philanthropy? I think not. We would all agree that national defense and a cure for cancer are in the public's best interests. We certainly would not all agree that contributions to Greenpeace serve the public's best interests. According to the BSP framework developed in the last chapter, social investing is economic social responsibility with a creative twist. Supporting my contention, most companies fund social-investing activities from advertising budgets and not from budget lines dedicated to philanthropy or community relations (Varadarajan and Menon 1988).

In fairness to Smith's position, he contends that social investing is a way for businesses to make internal operations consistent with the social causes supported by their philanthropy. Some companies who use this strategy (Smith cites AT&T as an example) bring all their organizational resources to the table in support of their philanthropic causes. While introducing philanthropic causes into the mainstream of business decision making sounds good, the power exchange is uneven. That is, profit making and marketing paradigms are much stronger than philanthropic paradigms to most business managers. The conquest of philanthropy by the marketing forces is much more likely than the opposite.

Movement from left to right on the continuum of enlightened self-interest rationales pictured in Figure 3.1 doesn't mean that the public value gained from business activities decreases. What changes is that rationales on the right are premised on direct, short-term, measurable business gain resulting from their action. In the middle, mechanisms to publicize socially responsible behavior and to reward good business citizens help to limit the negative impact of free riders. The gain from discretionary activities justified with the shared-fate rationale on the left cannot be measured and free riders can share in the gain.

Pulling together the arguments for business social responsibility, we have the following list.

Society has a legitimate claim on business resources because:

Power + wealth = responsibility

- In fulfilling their economic responsibilities, businesses (especially big businesses) impact all areas of society. They can cause tremendous harm to people and communities. Therefore they must assume responsibility in ethical and discretionary areas of social responsibility. Economic social responsibility cannot be separated from other social responsibilities.

- Those given great power and resources are expected to use it for the common good or it will be taken away—The Iron Law of Responsibility.

There is a social contract between business and society such that

- society provides enormous benefits that contribute to business success and in return expects business to work for social betterment.

- those granted the privilege of incorporation by society are expected to be responsible corporate citizens.

It's the right thing to do.

- Businesses are a collection of people, therefore it has the same moral responsibility as individuals have to treat people with respect, conduct affairs with integrity, give back to society, and work for social betterment.

Doing good will contribute to business success, also known as the enlightened self-interest rationales.

a. The shared fate rationale: If society gains, business gains.

b. The public relations rationale: An improved business image will:

- facilitate the attraction and retention of employees.

- increase customer loyalty.

- provide networking opportunities with business elites.

- encourage regulators and other government officials to be more helpful and willing to give the responsible businesses the benefit of the doubt.

- provide easier access to capital at favorable rates (better reputation with local bankers and social investors).

- positively change the public's view about the legitimacy of business power and about other issues important to business.

c. The social investing rationale: Philanthropy is a business opportunity.

The reader should know that I am convinced by the arguments on the pro side. I think businesses have a responsibility to society beyond fulfilling economic functions and complying with the law in the same way that individuals do. In my mind, it is a moral obligation based on social contract premises. The primary purpose of business is to fulfill economic responsibilities in an ethical manner. Over and above their primary responsibility, some part of resource slack, financial or human, resulting from businesses' economic activities should be used for social betterment. Some argue that contributions to social betterment are strategies to enhance economic success. If businesses can make more profit by doing good, that's great. However, in my opinion, business gain should be a byproduct of social responsibility, not the driving motivation. When business gain is the primary motivation for business social responsibility, I fear it will be abandoned whenever gain can be secured more easily or cheaply through unethical, exploitative, or sinister means.

As for the contention that business people do not have sufficient expertise to tinker in social and community causes, as a country, we have never disallowed citizen involvement in solving social problems in deference to experts—quite the contrary. Businesspeople have as much or more knowledge of these matters as the average citizen, and perhaps as much as the average new legislator. Why should businesspeople be excluded for lack of expertise on policy and social issues? The objective should be to ensure an open and equal exchange of ideas between groups in society, in spite of the greater power of big businesses, not to bar businesses from the table when social betterment is the topic. It is true that businesses are only indirectly accountable to the public (through the marketplace) for their activities in the areas of ethical and discretionary social responsibility. Nevertheless, the issue should be devising ways to create more public accountability of businesses' social performance, not absolving them of these responsibilities.

The first three chapters of this book served to establish a common vocabulary and conceptual framework about business social performance. With this background, we now have a context within which to examine the details of the subject. In the next chapter, I consider the firm level characteristics associated with business social performance. These include features of a business like size and ownership location, and features of the top decision maker, whether the owner or manager (such as values, place of residence, and education). In chapter 5, I will look at the role of environmental (non-firm) factors. Of particular interest here is the impact of community characteristics on business social performance.

NOTE

1. See Robert Kuttner's book *Everything For Sale* (1996) for an exposition of the ideology.

CHAPTER 4

Most Likely to Help

The building was constructed in 1910. In the *Gatlin City Gazette*, the reporter who covered the opening night gala raved about the luxurious green velvet carpeting and the green silk curtains. It was Gatlin City's site for live entertainment, including vaudeville acts, touring musical and acting troops, and the Gatlin City theater group. At the time, it was the center of Gatlin City's thriving cultural and commercial life—a grand facility.

In spite of its promising start, it became clear after a few years that the theater could not survive with live entertainment alone. Fortuitously for Gatlin City, a Universal Picture's employee visited the theater to take photographs. He was so enamored with the facility that in 1918 he moved to Gatlin City from California, purchased the theater, and transformed it into a movie house. It was the first movie theater in Iowa to show talking films. For more than half a century, the theater showed films with stars like Errol Flynn, Betty Grable, Mickey Rooney, Rock Hudson, and Liz Taylor. Like many downtown theaters, however, it was allowed to deteriorate in the 1970s and 80s. You would never know it had endured a period of neglect by looking at it now.

The theater has been restored to its former magnificence; plus, the infrastructure has been updated to meet current fire and accessibility codes, as well as modern expectations about rest room facilities, concessions, and so on. It seats an audience of 500 for events such as invited guest speakers, foreign film showings, and five or six annual productions of the local theater club. Sylvia Mahoney, a proud Gatlin City official, told me a great deal about the theater and the renovation project. She claimed that the restored theater contributes to the upbeat cultural ambiance the community is aiming for and is a source of great community pride. Located downtown, the theater's restoration adds momentum to other beautification work already completed or under construction. With a diverse range of restaurants, specialty stores, coffee shops, bars, and upscale renovated apartments on the second and third levels of the stores, and now the theater, local residents, and nonresidents are drawn back downtown for entertainment and shopping. In the lingo of developers, the downtown is again becoming a "destination."

The renovations cost $1 million, consumed uncounted hours of volunteer time and in-kind contributions, and took two years of planning, fund raising, and construction work. I asked Mahoney how Gatlin City managed to find and marshal the resources to achieve such a feat. Briefly, here's what she told me: Wendy Aitchison, who headed the community theater club, got the idea for the restoration. She convinced others in the club to take on the project. They talked about it with downtown merchants, Chamber of Commerce members, civic organizations, family, friends, and the city to assess possible support and gain information about what would be involved in the renovation. The core group recruited local business people with the skills that would be needed for the project and who were known for their community spirit. Especially critical were people with expertise in law, engineering, construction, architecture, and those with knowledge of and connections to local sources of funds.

After getting organized and preparing the specifics of the plan, the committee approached the big businesses in the area for support. Their logic was that one big gift of money would make the whole effort much simpler. Also, if they could point to support from the biggest businesses, securing the remainder of the contributions should be easier—sort of the bandwagon effect. At the same time, members of the committee who personally knew local wealthy families contacted them to get input and solicit support.

Needless to say, while they garnered support and some major donations from this group, it wasn't enough. It wasn't to be that easy. Next, they targeted the downtown retail and service businesses, since this group would benefit directly from the increased attractiveness of the downtown. Mahoney pointed out that assistance from one Gatlin City bank and the Gatlin City public utility was invaluable in this effort.

A campaign to solicit help from the general public was then launched. The committee sold room plaques and other forms of recognition, and held money-raising events. According to Mahoney, some donations came from business owners and managers as individuals, making it difficult to separate individual from business contributions. Support from local residents and businesses, assistance from the city, and the organizational skills and commitment of the core committee combined for a successful renovation of the Gatlin City theater. The restored theater was only the most obvious achievement of this committee. Additionally, they learned how to complete a massive volunteer project effectively. This knowledge, accompanied by the relationships generated through this project, will be available for future community betterment endeavors.

Mahoney's account of the Gatlin City theater renovation is a textbook example of how to do effective community development. More importantly for my purposes, it illustrates the main focus of this chapter: the features of businesses that are associated with high levels of discretionary social performance. The renovation committee mentally surveyed the local business community, gauging the likely support of individual businesses and crafted their work plan accordingly. They considered business size, ownership (local vs nonlocal), industry (e.g., consumer based retail and service firms), and the personality and values of the owner. In a nutshell, these are the business features that have been identified in the literature as key factors associated with business social performance (BSP). In this chapter, I will review what past research has to say about the relationship between business features and BSP, bring in findings from the telephone interviews of Iowa business operators, and illuminate those two sources of information with accounts from my interviewees.

THE IMPACT OF BUSINESS SIZE

As with other topics discussed in this book, the first task we face is distinguishing between what people believe should be and what actually is. The perspective among some analysts, either explicitly or implicitly, has been that small businesses should have less discretionary social responsibility than big businesses. Philip Van Auken and R. Duane Ireland (1982) claim that the only social responsibility of small businesses is to deliver to society quality products and services. Or put differently, they contend "the real challenge for small business lies not so much with embracing political social responsibility as it does with steadfastly avoiding social irresponsibility" (p. 2). The great majority of research publications, however, are silent when it comes to the social responsibility of small businesses, or are based on a truncated measure of size such that a small business is one in the bottom fourth of the Fortune 500. The implication is that small businesses either have no discretionary social responsibility or they are too insignificant to bother with.

Of the small group of published analyses dealing with small business social performance, a sizable portion focus on the economic, legal, and ethical dimensions of social responsibility. This research reveals that small business people and the public alike agree that small businesses have a responsibility for product quality, customer relations, profitability, fair wages, and compliance with the law (See Chrisman and Archer 1984, and Wilson 1980).

In an examination of ethical social responsibility, Justin Longenecker, Joseph McKinney, and Carlos Moore (1989) reported that people from big and small businesses were similar in their acceptance of unethical behavior, although they differed with regard to which unethical behaviors were deemed to be acceptable.

Our concern, however, is whether less is expected of small businesses in discretionary social responsibility. Insight into the relative responsibility of big and small businesses in this domain is provided by James Chrisman and Fred Fry (1982). They asked small business owners/managers about their expectations of the BSP of big business vs. small business. The researchers summed up the answers they received in these words: "Most small businesspersons, on the other hand, did not feel their size excused them from any of the obligations that a larger firm should have" (1982, p. 23).

Among my interviewees, only Jim Thomas, the mayor of Socksberg (a retired business owner), believed that big businesses should have more responsibility than small ones. He said, "Big businesses should have more responsibility. They're taking a lot more resources from your community." He qualified that by adding that he expected more personal involvement from the businesses around the square, all of whom are small. The minister from Manasis, Jeff McCaffrey, told me that businesses, regardless of size, don't have discretionary social responsibility. Still, he noted, "You must get big businesses involved in community projects. They have the resources and expertise to make the projects successful." Likewise, Walter Klazowski (another Manasis interviewee) believes big and small businesses have equal responsibility, "even though the contributions of all the small businesses in town combined probably don't equal what one big business can give." To put the issue in a slightly different context, Vince Barker, the director of a charitable organization in Gatlin City, commented, "Small businesses generally don't help us. Their employees are more likely to be recipients of our services, rather than benefactors."

Five interviewees were top managers or CEOs of large corporations in Pikeville. All in this group believed that businesses of all sizes have a social responsibility, but since large companies have more resources, they should carry a larger share of the financial burden for social betterment than small companies. Bill Mannes's comment is representative of their views:

Whether or not big businesses would benefit the most from community improvement, the burden is left to them. Financial size is more important than number of employees, however. One reason I've been able to be involved as much as I have is that I'm the CEO of a company that's large enough to feed my habit.

With an opposing view is the Gatlin City manufacturer John Crowell, who claimed that "small businesses have more responsibility than large businesses, because they are more dependent on the community. They have to project a good profile for good employees." The most common sentiment, however, was that small businesses have proportionately equal responsibility to big businesses. Two caveats were expressed: Denise Basset, an architect in Gatlin City, responded that "bigger businesses were more likely to give money and small businesses more likely to give personal time and involvement." And, "Size doesn't matter, except for those who don't have the resources to spare. Around here, some contribute when I know they probably can't afford it" (Mitch Eisenstadt, Socksberg attorney).

These views seem to be reflected in polls that compare public opinion about small vs. big businesses. Since 1973, the Gallup Poll organization has asked the public how much confidence they have in a variety of institutions including big business. In 1997 and 1998, they added small business to the list. Consistently since 1973, between 20 percent to 30 percent of the public indicated that they have a great deal, or quite a lot of, confidence in big business. In contrast, 63 percent (1997) and 56 percent (1998) of respondents reported that they have a great deal, or quite a lot of, confidence in small businesses. If we interpret having confidence in someone to mean that he or she can be trusted to do what is expected, or trusted to do what is right, then the Gallup Poll findings show that two to three times as many people trust small business to do what is expected and right than trust big business. It would be hazardous to extrapolate the public's greater confidence in small business beyond economic, legal, and ethical responsibilities. Still, it suggests an expectation of discretionary social responsibility for small businesses at least in proportion to their resources.

To summarize, the prevailing opinion of businesspeople and the public is that size shouldn't matter in relation to social responsibility. Either all businesses have discretionary social responsibility, or none do. This principle is modified to take into account differences in organizational resources; that is, those that have more are expected to give more, and to reflect differences in the kind of support, time vs. money, provided by businesses for social betterment.

Now we can turn to the second part of our examination of the effect of business size on social performance—research findings. I leave out of consideration all the studies that looked at the impact of size, but did not have small businesses (less than five hundred employees or $5 million in gross sales) in their sample. Fred Fry and Robert Hock (1976) analyzed the annual reports of 135 firms ranging from $2 million to $1 billion in sales. Their measure of business social performance was the amount of space in the annual report that was devoted to social issues. They discovered that the larger the company, the more space they devoted to social responsibility. Due to the limitations of their measure of BSP, however, the finding could have various meanings. It could mean that big companies can afford more skilled public relations staff and writers to construct an annual report more likely to appeal to all segments of the public. Given the public's greater distrust of big business compared to small businesses, it could be that big businesses realize they have to work harder than small businesses to present an image of positive social responsibility. Hence, they devote more space in annual reports to crafting a "good corporate citizen" image. Or it could mean that bigger companies are truly more socially responsible than smaller companies.

Using a different measure of BSP, tax deductible charitable contributions reported to the IRS as a percent of pretax net income, Benwardi Kedia and Edwin Kuntz reported in 1981 that contributions were highly correlated with pretax net income. The bigger the business, the larger the percentage of pretax net income donated to charity. Katherine Maddox McElroy and John Siegfried conducted a similar analysis in 1985, with the same results. However, more current data about corporate giving in Indiana finds small businesses give a higher percent of their pretax net income to charity (Burlingame and Kaufmann 1995). IRS data are a valuable source of information about business income and charitable tax deductions due to the fact that a significant percentage of businesses will not divulge this information to researchers or the public. Unfortunately for analysts, in order to protect the confidentiality of businesses, the IRS only releases the tax information in industry and size categories.

The majority of small firms claim no deductions for charitable contributions, bringing down the average in that category. In his 1985 analysis of Canadian small businesses, S.A. Martin included only businesses that actually made contributions and found that contributing small businesses donated more than contributing big businesses as a percent of pretax income. Also, charitable deductions underestimate actual contributions because small firms are more likely to give time than money.

Judith Thompson, Howard Smith, and Jacqueline Hood (1993) overcame some of the problems with the IRS data by surveying 420 small businesses (15 to 100 employees) in one metro area, asking them to report their annual gross sales, contribution dollars, employee time donation, and other relevant information. One hundred and fifty-seven businesses returned surveys complete with gross sales figures. Their results showed that within this group of small businesses, number of employees, but not gross sales, was positively associated with monetary donations. The donation of employee time was not related to either of the business size measures. Moreover, they found that small businesses are not likely to have formal policies about charitable giving, and 85 percent provide gifts to charity that are not claimed as tax deductions.

The attention accorded to small businesses by my interviewees decreased perceptibly as the size of their community increased. No doubt this is due to the fact that few small towns have a really big business (a Fortune 500 company) operating within their boundaries and even fewer are headquarters for a Fortune 500 company. As a result, community leaders in those small towns must focus on the resident small businesses. However, when very large companies are present, community betterment strategies seem to change. Even though the owners/managers of small businesses are still involved, the magnitude of the money necessary for the larger scale projects makes it essential to find major donors. Naturally then, more time and energy is devoted to finding and appealing to the people who command great wealth. This is exemplified by Reid Schmidt's (a Pikeville charitable organization director) comment about his latest money-raising endeavor:

To be effective, we must have the public endorsement and active support of at least some of the CEOs of the big businesses in town. It's true, however, small businesses are headed by local entrepreneurs who may have more personal wealth and community commitment than the CEOs of the major corporations located here. Many of them have been very generous. Just the same, without big business buy-in, the project won't succeed.

The focus on large donors was echoed by Pikeville business leader Jerome Rossides when he recounted how a recent project was implemented:

We needed an additional two million dollars for a downtown project we were working on. So I tried to think of business people who we had not tapped in the past and who might be persuaded to be a donor. It came to me that (a very successful Iowa businessman) had not contributed to any Pikeville renovation projects. After some meetings with him and mutually agreeable changes in the project, he agreed to donate the full amount.

In the Iowa telephone interview data, the two indicators of size used by Thompson and her associates are available—number of employees and gross sales. Since the distributions of both gross sales and number of employees are highly skewed, I used the logs of gross sales and number of employees in the statistical analyses to determine the relationship of size and business social performance. To measure discretionary social responsibility, I asked questions about how frequently businesses provided various kinds of support to their communities and the involvement of the owner or manager in community affairs. The distinguishing feature of these measures of business social performance is the community focus. Whereas other measures of discretionary social responsibility focus on particular social causes (e.g., education, health care, environment) or the tax status of the recipient. Tables 4.1 and 4.2 show the specific questions used to assess the community involvement and support reported by business owners/managers.

Throughout this book, I group the findings from the analyses by community size unless there is no significant statistical difference in the independent factor under consideration for the three size categories. Therefore, if there had been no significant statistical difference between the average size of businesses in the three community categories, I would conduct a single analysis. Since business size (measured both by gross sales and number of employees) is significantly different for the three categories of communities (See Appendix A), the relationship between business size and support for and involvement in the community will be analyzed separately for each community category. Pooling the responses from the three communities together would distort the overall findings when there is a significant statistical difference between them, giving undue weight to the rural businesses.

Let us first consider the findings displayed in Table 4.1. I employed the chi square likelihood ratio to test whether responses to the questions differed by community size category. The likelihood ratio for each question is significant, indicating that business operators in small towns reported significantly greater involvement than their city colleagues reported. Especially remarkable is the comparatively large percentage of small town business operators who have held local elected public office and the greater involvement of metro business operators as compared to small city operators in all but non-organization-sponsored community activities.

Since the involvement questions are categorical variables and the measures of size are interval variables, I used analysis of variance (anova) to evaluate the relationship between them. Anova is a statistical calculation that tells us, in this instance, whether the average number of employees (log) and average gross sales (log) are significantly different for those who

Table 4.1
Frequencies of Community Involvement and Anovas with Business Size for Different Sizes of Communities

	RURAL 500 - 9,999 pop N = 1008 (731) **		URBAN 10,000 - 49,999 pop N = 262 (175) **		METRO 50,000 + pop N = 410 (284) **	
Held elected local office since becoming an owner/manager	Log Sales $F = 24.07^*$	Log Employees $F = 5.3^*$	Log Sales $F = .84$	Log Employees $F = 1.18$	Log Sales $F = .00$	Log Employees $F = 2.12$
Yes		21.5%		6.4%		6.8%
No		78.5%		93.6%		93.2%
Held leadership position in local civic organization or church since becoming owner/manager	$F = 23.25^*$	$F = 7.88^*$	$F = 7.07^*$	$F = 0.50$	$F = .60$	$F = 0.22$
Yes		48.0%		41.7%		45.4%
No		52.0%		58.3%		54.6%
Been active in civic organizations or church without holding leadership role since becoming owner/manager	$F = 13.78^*$	$F = 4.52^*$	$F = 2.69$	$F = 0.01$	$F = 3.16$	$F = 0.12$
Yes		71.9%		63.6%		67.1%
No		28.1%		36.4%		32.9%
Been active in community activities not associated with an organization since becoming owner/manager	$F = 21.77^*$	$F = 28.65^*$	$F = .41$	$F = .00$	$F = .01$	$F = 0.01$
Yes		68.3%		57.6%		52.2%
No		31.7%		42.4%		47.8%

*Indicates significant difference $p < .05$
**Number answering the gross sales question

answered "yes" to the involvement questions compared to the averages for those who answered "no" in each community size category. I reported only the F score for the anova for each question and whether it is significant at the p .05 level. In each case where the anova is significant, the average for the "yes" category is greater than the average for the "no" category.

According to the statistical analyses, size of business does not matter when it comes to community involvement in small cities and metropolitan areas, except for providing leadership in local civic and church organizations in small cities. In that case, owners and managers of businesses with higher gross sales are more likely to be involved. In small towns, both measures of size are significantly related to every measure of involvement. The owners and managers of businesses with more employees and higher gross sales are more involved in the community than owner/managers of smaller businesses. The positive impact of business size seen in small towns may be countermanded in urban and metro areas if there is a greater propensity for bigger businesses in those locations to be managed by professional managers instead of owners. There may also be something about the culture of small towns that encourages the owners of bigger businesses to get involved. The role of local culture and personal qualities of owners/managers will be considered later. Sufficient to say here that none of these dimensions acts in isolation to influence a business's social performance even though this kind of analysis may give that impression.

We see in Table 4.2 a similar configuration of significantly higher levels of business social performance reported by business operators in small towns compared to those in cities. It would be a mistake, however, to disregard the substantial amount of support reported by city business operators, even though less than the amount reported by small town business operators. Since responses to the support questions are ordinal rather than categorical, I used Pearson's correlation (r) to measure whether there is a statistically significant relationship between responses to the question and gross sales (log) and number of employees (log). Results show that the relationship of business size (both gross sales and number of employees) with support is more pronounced than its relationship to involvement. The larger the business, the more likely its operator is to report providing support in all three community sizes. This corroborates the views of interviewees and makes intuitive sense. Support requires some amount of extra revenue and not solely the time and energy of the business operator. The exceptions are that size doesn't matter in metro communities when it comes to support for bond issues, and in urban communities, for youth programs. Again, in small towns, bigger businesses are more likely to report providing support in all categories than smaller businesses.

Particularly revealing is the amount of support for local bond issues reported by businesspeople. Bond issues can be extremely controversial in communities and, according to my interviewees, supporting them can be

Table 4.2

Frequencies of Community Support and Correlations with Business Size for Different Sizes of Communities

	RURAL 500 - 9,999 pop N = 1008 (731) **		URBAN 10,000 - 49,999 pop N = 262 (175) **		METRO 50,000 + pop N = 410 (284) **	
	Log Sales	Log Employees	Log Sales	Log Employees	Log Sales	Log Employees
Technical and financial assistance in community development or planning	r= .28*	r= .20*	r= .28*	r= .14*	r= .12*	r= .11*
Very Often		9.2%		3.5%		6.2%
Often		27.1%		17.4%		13.7%
Sometimes		26.5%		24.3%		27.4%
Seldom		17.7%		20.1%		21.4%
Never		19.5%		34.7%		31.2%
Support for local youth programs (Little League, Girl Scouts)	r=. 26*	r= .21*	r=.14	r= .08	r= .12*	r= .07
Very Often		17.4%		11%		13.0%
Often		43.8%		30.3%		26.7%
Sometimes		24.4%		33.7%		29.8%
Seldom		7.8%		12.9%		15.9%
Never		6.6%		12.1%		14.7%
Financial donations to local schools	r=.24*	r= .18*	r=.21*	r= .15*	r= .13*	r= .16*
Very Often		16.5%		8.8%		12.1%
Often		36.3%		27.3%		20.7%
Sometimes		21.6%		27.3%		21.2%
Seldom		13.4%		13.5%		16.5%
Never		12.1%		23.1%		29.4%
Support for local bond issues to finance community improvement projects	r= .11*	r= .07	r= .21*	r= .02	r= .07	r= .02
Very Often		9.6%		5.5%		4.8%
Often		25.3%		15.0%		14.9%
Sometimes		17.9%		21.7%		16.9%
Seldom		18.3%		18.2%		18.9%
Never		29.0%		39.5%		44.4%

The items above are ways businesses support the community. How often has your business assisted the local community? Would you say you have provided support never, seldom, sometimes, often or very often?
*Sig at p < .05
**Number answering the gross sales question

costly to business and personal welfare. Given the risk involved, I think it is remarkable that approximately one of every three business operators in small towns, and one of five in the cities, report that they have provided support for local bond issues often, or very often, in the past.

According to prior research and findings from the Iowa study, businesses with more employees and those with more financial resources as measured by gross sales, or pretax net income, do give more in charitable contributions and in support for their community than smaller businesses. In small towns, size is also positively related to the community involvement of the business owner/manager. It seems safe to conclude that size, variously measured by financial resources or number of employees, is an important predictor of discretionary social responsibility, even among relatively small businesses, and especially in small towns. However, in small cities and metro areas, the owners and managers of small businesses are equally likely to be personally active in community affairs as are those from big businesses. Since Gatlin City is an urban community, Wendy

Aitchison's committee was right on the mark when its members sought time, expertise, and smaller donations from the owners of smaller businesses, professionals, and downtown merchants and solicited the big businesses for financial donations.

THE ROLE OF INDUSTRY TYPE

Why should the product or service offered by a business affect its discretionary social responsibility? To understand the reasoning, return for a moment to the conceptual framework I presented in chapter 3 to elaborate the enlightened self-interest rationales—the one where expected economic gain from contributions is paired with types of rationales. In that framework, the public relations variant posits that part of the cost incurred in contributing to public goods can be partially captured by businesses through enhanced public image. The application of that logic to industry differences in BSP is that businesses delivering a product or service directly to the public should be more concerned about their public images, and, as a result, more willing to contribute to the public good. In this thinking, individual consumers are more easily swayed by a company's public image when they buy toothpaste or open a checking account than is a manufacturer when it purchases machine tools or contracts with a janitorial service.

A list of the general categories of industries, as defined in the Standard Industrial Classification system, is displayed in Figure 4.1 below. Mining is a major industrial sector missing from the Figure 4.1 list because there were no mining firms sampled in the Iowa study. The label FIRE, contained in the list, is an acronym often used to refer to the finance, insurance, and real estate sector. I bring to your attention the fact that classifying all businesses into nine major industrial sectors masks the immense diversity between

Figure 4.1
Distribution of Businesses by Standard Industrial Classification Code in Community Size Categories

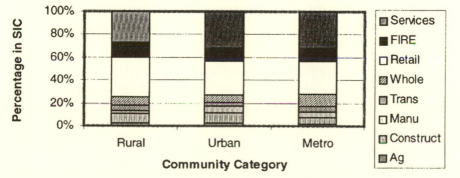

businesses within sectors. The sector I have abbreviated as transportation, for example, includes utilities and communication businesses as well as transportation companies. So Baby Bells, rural electric cooperatives, and long-distance truckers are all together in this category. The service sector is even more diverse, containing medical clinics, business consultants, and janitorial businesses all lumped together. For this reason and others, the industrial classification system is currently undergoing major changes. The new North American Industrial Classification System (NAICS) will soon be completely elaborated and available. For now, however, we continue to use the SIC codes.

By definition, retail businesses sell directly to the public, and wholesale businesses sell to other organizational entities for resale to the public. Businesses in the mining sector rarely sell directly to the public. Other industrial sectors contain a mix of businesses differentiated by customer type and/or with varying percentages of customer type. For example, consulting engineers and software programming companies are service businesses that infrequently sell to households; physicians, funeral parlors, and hairdressers are service businesses that sell almost exclusively to households. Manufacturers of automobile seats, machine tools, and industrial chemicals do not sell to households. But newspapers, which are categorized as manufacturers, and disposable diaper manufacturers sell primarily to households (through retail channels). If it is true that creating a good image influences individuals as consumers, but not organizational consumers, then newspaper publishers, auto manufacturers, retail stores, for-profit hospitals, and local beauty shops should provide more support for social causes than consulting engineers, machine tool manufacturers, long-distance trucking firms, and wholesalers.

Supporting this line of reasoning are several studies. One group shows that a significant correlation exists between the amount of money businesses spent on advertising and charitable donations (see Navarro 1988, and Fry, Keim, and Meiners 1982). The correlation is interpreted to mean that businesses view charitable donations as advertising to improve their public image. More direct evidence of the link between industry and discretionary social responsibility is provided by Ron Burt (1983) and Linda Lerner and Gerald Fryxell (1988). Both studies concluded that industries that have a higher proportion of consumer products (Lerner and Fryxell 1988) or those with a higher percent of sales to households (Burt 1983) contribute more to charity than businesses in other industries.

Industry wide data, however, may not be the best predictor of the behavior of individual businesses. Joseph Galaskiewicz's (1997) study of the Twin Cities grants economy found that, when comparing firms (not industries), percent sales to households was not related to giving. Also Judith Thompson, Howard Smith, and Jacqueline Hood (1993), in their study of small businesses, discovered no significant difference in charitable contributions or employee time donations between manufacturers, retailers, and service firms. Another factor in this equation is business competition. If the medical clinic, grocery store, and cable TV company have no realistic competition in the local market, then public image may matter less to them than it does to highly competitive auto manufacturers, even though they all market their products directly to households.

A variation on the logic that firms that sell to the public should look like good citizens is the claim that labor-intensive businesses, especially those requiring highly skilled employees should look good too. The argument is that firms with a good public image will be more successful at attracting and retaining employees than companies with a poor reputation. The research reported by Louis Fry and his colleagues (1982) and Peter Navarro (1988) concluded that labor intensities are positively related to marginal changes in contributions. When McElroy and Siegfried (1985) asked CEOs why they donated to charitable causes, approximately 80 percent indicated that they believed it improved their ability to attract and retain employees. Daniel Turban and Daniel Greening (1997) surveyed a small sample of college students about their willingness to be employed by a variety of businesses. Those businesses with the best reputations, as measured by the Kinder, Lydenberg, and Domini (KLD; 1990) scale of business social responsibility, rated highest among the students as their choice for future employers.

Three of the manufacturers I interviewed mentioned their employees as one reason why they support community betterment. Craig Gerdes, who owns a manufacturing firm in Socksberg, said, "If you don't give to the community, people will tell potential employees, 'you don't want to work there.' Image isn't so much of a problem in a big city as it is in a small town." John Crowell from Gatlin City and Christine Bernstein, a manufacturing owner in Caizan, were also concerned about employee attraction and retention, but, in addition, they expressed a feeling of responsibility to help improve the quality of life of their employees. "Even if all my customers were on the coasts, it's important to help the community. It's where my employees live. I have an obligation to the environment and my workers, but not to the community, per se," Bernstein said. Crowell expressed it this way: "There is a certain self-serving aspect to it (community support). It supplies you with workers, and so you have a duty to help improve the education and safety of your community as a service to your employees."

I do not want to give the impression that manufacturing firms have consistently high labor intensities, nor that they, exclusively, have high labor intensities. Some highly automated manufacturers, like chemical processors, have low labor intensities. Conversely, many service businesses like architectural firms, hospitals, and colleges, have high labor intensities. In some businesses, labor intensities coincide with the public as customers to create what should be a double reason for management to be concerned about the business's public image. In others, like wholesale and transportation businesses, neither labor intensity nor the general public as customers are present to motivate owners and managers to be good citizens. And then there are the many businesses with either public customers or labor intensity, but not both.

In the main, my interviewees didn't see the relevance of industry sector to social performance, except for a few statements indicating that downtown merchants have more responsibility for downtown beautification and promotion than other businesses. Also, physicians and teachers were singled out by a couple of interviewees as professions (although physicians are also usually business owners) that never get involved in the community. More salient to them than industry factors as an explanation for the differences in business social performance were ownership patterns and the personality and values of the owner/manager. I will address these factors below.

The evidence presented thus far is mixed about the role of industry type in business social responsibility. Analyses of data from the Iowa study support the argument that discretionary social performance varies by type of business. We see in Figure 4.1 the distribution of sample businesses by industry type in the three community categories. The differences in the SIC distributions are not statistically significant (Chi sq likelihood ratio = 22.89, p = .06). Therefore, the comparison of community involvement and support by industry type will be conducted for the sample as a whole.

To simplify the analyses, I combined the responses to the questions that measure involvement and those that measure support into two scales. The involvement scale was created by summing the values of the responses to the four questions listed in Table 4.1 and dividing the sum by four.[1] The same procedure was used to create a support scale[2] from the questions in Table 4.2.

Figure 4.2 displays the average value on the support scale for businesses by industry type. The amount of support reported by business operators is significantly different for different industries (Anova, F = 5.79, p = .00). The FIRE, retail, and agriculture sectors have the highest support scores, with wholesale and services ranking the lowest. When I examine the relationship within each community type separately (not shown), the same pattern is revealed. FIRE and retail industries are the highest in the three community categories. Wholesale businesses are the lowest, with the service sector coming in second to last. Only in metropolitan communities is the service sector pushed out of that position (second to last) by construction businesses.

Turn now to Figure 4.3 to evaluate how industries vary when it comes to involvement in the community. Statistically, there is a significant difference between the industries on the involvement scale (Anova, F = 7.77, p = .00), but the difference is due to the relatively high score of FIRE businesses com-

Figure 4.2
Support by Standard Industrial Classification Code, All Communities

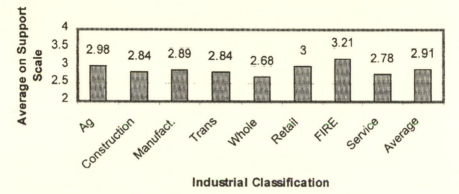

Industrial Classification

Figure 4.3
Involvement by Standard Industrial Classification Code, All Communities

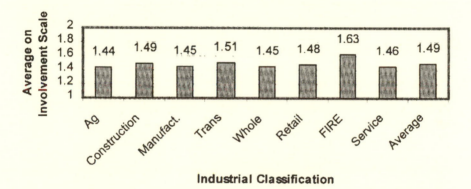

Industrial Classification

pared to all the rest. The remaining sectors display little variation from each other. When the three community categories are examined separately (not shown), the spike for FIRE involvement is similarly surrounded by averages in the other sectors that differ little from each other.

The message from the analyses of support and involvement by industry seems clear. When planning a community betterment project, be sure to seek the support and involvement of the financial (the bank), insurance, and real estate businesses. The next stop should be the retail and agriculture businesses. Extra effort will be necessary to solicit involvement and support from the wholesalers and service businesses. This pattern follows the predictions derived from the logic outlined at the beginning of this section—with one big exception. The unexpectedly low ranking of the service sector should give us pause. Validating the low support and involvement ranking of the service sector is the fact that the businesses least willing to cooperate in the telephone interview portion of the Iowa research were physicians, beauty shops, and auto repair shops, all service businesses. The findings from the analysis seem to indicate that improvement in public image, whether to attract and retain customers or employees, is an insufficient explanation for business support for community betterment at least for some kinds of businesses.

Since the measures of discretionary social responsibility used in the Iowa study are measures of community outputs, the Iowa results may also be explained by the shared-fate rationale. That is, FIRE, retail, and agricultural businesses may be more likely than other business types to ascribe to the proposition that their business success rises and falls with the fate of the local community. Further, inasmuch as manufacturers are more labor intensive than wholesalers, the power of the shared-fate credo in encouraging community support should be almost as effective with them as it is with FIRE businesses. This presents us with another way of thinking about the low levels of support and involvement reported by service businesses. Perhaps, the shared-fate credo has less resonance with them than with FIRE, retail, agricultural, and manufacturing firms.

The shared-fate rationale is premised on local ownership. When Sara Lee closed its processing and bakery facility in New Hampton, Iowa, in 2000, idling over six hundred workers, they demonstrated how the fate of the Sara Lee company is independent from the fate of its New Hampton employees and their community. This is my way of introducing the next firm-level factor that may impact business social performance, the location of ownership.

LOCAL VS. NONLOCAL OWNERSHIP

Nothing evoked as much passion from my interviewees as complaints about the lack of community support provided by the likes of chain stores, branch banks, and convenience stores.

Roger de la Renta, a local retail store manager from Manasis, declared, "The problem with chains and branches is that they suck the economy in one place dry and move the money to the headquarter's city."

Doug Avala, who owns an insurance business in Socksberg, agreed: "Kum & Go and Casey's (convenience stores that are ubiquitous in Iowa) don't do anything for the community. They just take money out of it."

Robert Markus, a manufacturer in Socksberg, put it this way, "Local businesses are tied to the community and more loyal. Managers of corporate businesses move in and out and don't get involved."

Another manufacturer in Socksberg, Craig Gerdes, expressed a common sentiment about nonlocal businesses: "Corporate businesses do not give to the community.

They aren't allowed to. But they get tax abatements, which I never got, and they don't have to give anything back."

Voicing a similar theme was Nancy Sing, a Caizan retail store owner. She stated, "Local companies are much more likely to get involved than those recruited to come here from out of state. I get discouraged with them."

Walter Klazowski, service business owner in Gatlin City, provides a dramatic illustration of the difference between local and nonlocal businesses.

When the utility here was locally owned, they had what they called their 'trinket fund.' They budgeted $50,000 a year for that fund. It was used for miscellaneous contributions. This was just spare change to them. They also made major donations to the community for big projects. Now, since the utility was purchased by another utility out of state, we're lucky if they donate $5,000 a year in total.

Likewise, interviewees frequently brought to my attention the stark contrast between the community support provided by banks before and after purchase by an outside entity. Bryant Gear in Caizan estimated that the locally owned bank donates an average of $100,000 a year to the community, whereas the nonlocally owned bank gives about $5,000.

Reid Schmidt, the director of a charitable organization in Pikeville, lamented the loss of locally owned businesses, but to be fair, he also provided an example of how the change from local ownership to nonlocal ownership increased the community support provided by one company. He attributed the counterintuitive change to the values of the top management and the culture of the acquiring company. "It all comes down to the values of the people at the top of the business."

In spite of his positive example, Schmidt was particularly troubled by the increasing incidence of CEOs of local branches of consolidated businesses retaining their domicile in another part of the country. Their families remain in the primary domicile while the CEO commutes during the week to the Pikeville operation. When this happens, Schmidt added, the CEO doesn't have kids in the local school, his or her spouse is not in town to attend art gallery shows or sit on the boards of charitable organizations, and the CEO is not available for weekend golf outings at the country club. This means he or she is not as accessible to local elites who would encourage community involvement, and the shared-fate rationale has less resonance. Consequently, the transient CEO group is particularly resistant to social sanctions and shared-fate arguments that normally are effective inducements to community support.

Wilford Krivit, a Pikeville executive, wanted to balance the negative picture most hold of the impact of consolidation on community involvement. He asserted,

Consolidation affects community support both ways. Branches have less resources and power. They have to refer decisions to headquarters and the managers are always looking over their shoulders. But at the same time, the headquarter firms are able to do more for their community. Some communities lose, some gain.

Al Matsumoto was more guarded about the subject:

Consolidation is a serious issue. There's not one answer. It's about corporate attitudes. This is a company that's owned by another company located elsewhere and it operates globally. We have a very strong commitment to the Pikeville community. It's all about people and where people with the company grew up, where they want to place their emphasis, what are their values. There are a lot of large and small companies that are local and they don't give anything because they're taking it all for themselves and their families. The trend is more consolidation. We as business people have to be cognizant as we acquire businesses to the fact that you can't survive if the community you're in doesn't do well.

Research on the impact of variations in ownership on BSP has taken two different paths. One is concerned about the effect of different ownership configurations, such as managerial control vs. owner control and ownership by institutions such as pension funds and mutual funds. The other concentrates on ownership location. First, the ownership configurations. Research conclusions on this subject are mixed. Lisa Atkinson and Joseph Galaskiewicz (1988) found that more concentrated stock ownership is associated with lower charitable contributions. They reasoned that the more control a small number of owners or a single owner have over the distribution of business revenue, the less of it will be donated to charity. Put differently, when managers control the business, more revenue will be donated to charity—sort of a management perk. Anne Buchholz, Allen Amason, and Matthew Rutherford (1999) cite managerial discretion as an important intermediary predictor of charitable donations in midsize companies. However, Peter Navarro (1988) discovered that managerial control was not related to charitable contributions.

The findings about the impact of institutional ownership are a little less ambiguous. Samuel Graves and Sandra Waddock (1994) discovered that the greater the number of institutional owners of a stock, the higher the BSP of the firm as measured by the KLD scale. Richard Johnson and Daniel Greening (1999) examined the effects of mutual fund and pension fund ownership of stock separately. When disaggregated from each other, mutual fund ownership has a neutral effect on BSP, but pension fund ownership is positively associated with it. Considering the rise in institutional ownership of company stock, this is an important matter, although not directly relevant for our study of BSP among small businesses and communities. I will return to the possible differential BSP of managers vs. owners when I examine the impact of the personal features of business operators on BSP. For now, let us turn to the second research path, the matter of local ownership.

When Wendy Atchison's committee solicited input and support from local wealthy families for the Gatlin City theater, their primary target was the group of families who made their fortunes in local businesses. This is the group that David Kamen (1985) called "family capitalists" and Joseph Galaskiewicz credited with the exceptional corporate citizenship evident in the Twin Cities. As noted in chapter 3, the resonance of the shared-fate rationale to this group of business owners/managers should set them apart from businesses without local ties. In addition to Galaskiewicz's two studies of the Twin Cities' grant's economy (1985; 1997), research support for this thesis is provided by McElroy and Siegfried. In 1986 they published the results of their interviews with 229 corporate giving officers and CEOs of large companies headquartered in fourteen large cities. Not surprisingly, they discovered that these companies were more likely to donate to causes in their headquarter's city. When the companies did provide support for other locations, the amount given was smaller than what they gave to causes in the headquarter city.

The lack of support by corporations for communities other than their headquarter's city was common knowledge among my interviewees. But some community leaders were not completely convinced that corporate policy is immutable. That seemed to be the message from Bryant Gear, an insurance business owner in Caizan, when he remarked, "They say, 'Well the home office won't allow contributions,' and we all walk away and accept that. Whereas, I couldn't get away with that excuse." Lamont Blanchard, a minister from Gatlin City, implied that local managers may have more discretion than they want to use. He commented, "Local managers of large corporations are not willing to make the case that local causes should be supported."

Let's look at the empirical data from the Iowa study for more information with which to assess the impact of ownership location on business social performance. In the telephone interviews, ownership location was determined with the following question.

Which of the following best describes the status of this business? Is it . . .

An independent, single establishment firm (meaning this is the only location of this business.)	(68.2%)
Owned by another company.	(5.8%)
Locally owned, but franchised to offer brand name products or services.	(6.6%)
The owner of one or more branch establishments besides the one at this location.	(18.6%)

A franchiser which sells the right to use its   (0.8%)
concept to one or more franchisees.

Don't know and refused.   (1.3%—coded as missing for the
                                                       analysis)

Businesses, whose operators answered the question with response categories 1, 3, 4, or 5, were coded as locally owned. Businesses with response category 2 were coded as nonlocal. An unexpectedly high percentage of sample businesses are locally owned in all sizes of communities (range 90 percent to 96 percent). My concern, when I saw the distribution, was that the low percentage of nonlocal businesses might have been caused by a disproportionately lower cooperation rate among them. However, even if all noncooperating businesses were nonlocal, it would only swell their ranks by 10 percent to 15 percent, still below what we would anticipate in the "new global economy." Considering that physicians, beauty shops, and auto repair shops were the businesses least willing to participate, it is certain that at least some of the refusals were local businesses. With the random selection procedure we used, accompanied by the relatively small deviations in SIC and size of the businesses sampled compared to the population of businesses in the selected communities and counties, I have confidence that the low percentage of nonlocal businesses is reflective of businesses in Iowa. Regardless of the relatively low numbers, nonlocal businesses may be in key positions with regard to community betterment efforts. Thus, if they are in the FIRE sector, or are the largest local businesses, their posture toward community development would have an impact out of proportion to their numbers.

Although the level of local ownership is high in all communities, there is a significant difference between the three community sizes (chi sq. likelihood ratio = 17.64, p = .00). Therefore, the comparison between ownership location and community support and involvement will be made for each community size separately. Figures 4.4 and 4.5 illustrate the average levels of community support and involvement reported by local and nonlocal businesses in the Iowa sample.

Several facts are immediately apparent. Regarding both support and involvement, small-town businesses report higher levels than urban and metro businesses, urban and metro businesses vary little from each other in community support and involvement, and local businesses provide more support and involvement than nonlocal businesses in small towns and metro areas. In urban communities, the operators of local and nonlocal businesses have similar levels of involvement, but local businesses still report higher levels of support than nonlocals. Every piece of evidence we explore on this issue, whether prior research, in-depth interviews, theoretical explanations, or the data from the Iowa telephone interviews, tells the same

Figure 4.4
Support by Ownership Location for Different Sizes of Communities

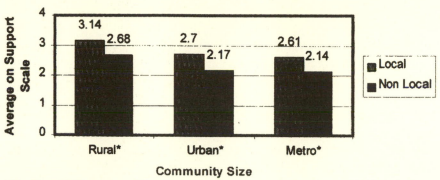

* Significant Difference p < .05

Figure 4.5
Involvement by Ownership Location for Different Sizes of Communities

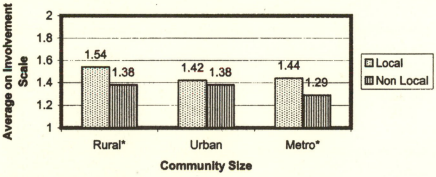

* Significant Difference p < .05

story. Local businesses report higher levels of contribution to local social betterment than nonlocal businesses.

There is another dimension to ownership location that the interviewees brought to my attention. Nancy Sing, a Caizan retail business owner, observed that when a business is purchased by an outside corporate entity, the first thing that happens is that the majority of the white-collar and management jobs are eliminated. These are the people, in her opinion, whom the community relies upon for leadership and volunteering. Furthermore, according to Vince Barker, a nonprofit director in Manasis, the new corporate entity is more profit oriented than the enterprise formerly was. It pares the number of all employees to the absolute minimum and requires more overtime and shift work. Consequently, the employees who remain, regardless of collar color, have less time for community involvement and are not encouraged by corporate management to get involved. Using an often heard refrain, Sing declared, "The consolidated companies are lean and mean when it comes to the community."

Kerry Ferro, the head of a charitable organization in Gatlin City, effectively summarizes the influence of local ownership on business social performance with this comment: "Homegrown businesses predominate here. That probably accounts for the large amount of community support businesses provide. There's a climate here of cooperation."

MANAGERIAL DISCRETION

The predominance of homegrown businesses alone is not enough, however, to account for differences in BSP. In Iowa at least, homegrown businesses predominate everywhere. Yet communities vary significantly, even within the population-size categories, in the amount of BSP reported by resident businesses; and homegrown businesses differ from each other in BSP. More than local ownership is obviously involved. As we already know, business size and industry sector are important considerations. Another firm-level factor remains to be evaluated—the values and the background of the owner/manager. In the BSP model presented in chapter 2, managerial values were given primacy in understanding how firms articulate and actualize their social performance. Given that framework, we would expect managerial values to play a critical role in determining a business's social performance.

As cited in chapter 2, there are a few empirical studies supporting this position. In 1975, when Parket and Eilbert found a positive relationship between profit and BSP among a sample of Fortune 500 companies, they hypothesized that the association between the two was caused by both resulting from good management. They did not test for the relationship, however, nor define what they meant by "good management," other than contend that it resulted in high profits and high BSP. Michael Useem and Stephen I. Kutner (1986) in a study of sixty-two major Massachusetts companies with at least 1000 employees, concluded that the chief executive officer is the single most important influence in setting company giving policies and in selecting recipients of company largesse. Likewise, Judith Thompson and her colleagues, in their 1993 examination of BSP in small businesses, concluded that the owner/manager preference is an important determinant of whether or not a firm donates to charity, how much is given, and in the selection of recipients.

Top management values and discretion were not integrated into the Corporate Social Performance (CSP) conceptual framework until Swanson's 1995 model. Also in 1995, Thomas Jones recognized the significance of the management factor in his reformulated "instrumental stakeholder theory" of CSP. He proposed that top management, as the primary contractor of different stakeholders for the organization, plays a critical role in determining the social performance of the corporation. Their ethics and values permeate the organization, influencing the ethical disposition of employees through self-selection, rules, culture, incentives, and so on.

Reflecting the paucity of interest in, and research-based knowledge of, the subject, Lynn Sharp Paine, addressing the Corporate Crime in America Symposium sponsored by the U.S. Sentencing Commission in 1995, said,

We also need better research not on compliance programs per se, but on the management practices that are used in companies that are good corporate citizens. What this type of research will show, I believe, is that concern for law is reflected in all the core management systems that drive the organization, from its leadership, its supervision, its hiring, its communication, training, education, oversight, control. (1995, p. 434)

Since Paine's call and Swanson's and Jones's theoretical integration of managerial discretion and internal organizational processes into the CSP framework, three studies exploring the role of management values on BSP were published in 1999. Gary Weaver, Linda Klebe Trevino, and Philip Cochran had two of them. They studied a sample of Fortune 500 companies to understand variations in corporate ethics programs. By their own account, their studies provide the first empirical evidence demonstrating that top management's commitment to ethics is associated with both the scope and control orientation of ethics program implementation. External pressure might be the impetus for the ethics program, namely the U.S. Sentencing Commission guidelines; however, their research established that management's values determine the effectiveness of organizational structures and processes adopted to implement the ethics program.

Ann Buchholtz, Allen Amason, and Matthew Rutherford (1999) studied the role of firm resources, managerial discretion, and managerial values on philanthropy in forty-three midsized public companies (defined as having less than $1 billion in sales). They collected information from several of each company's top managers, including the CEO. Managerial values were measured with a forced choice scale asking respondents to weight the relative importance of six different organizational goals; long-term profitability, firm growth, innovation and new product development, stock price appreciation, and service to the community. They used the average ranking of the "service to the community" goal for each company's management team as the indicator of management values regarding BSP.

Their analysis demonstrated that managerial discretion and values were intermediary variables between resource slack and dollars donated to philanthropy. The rather complicated relationship looks like this: Resource slack was a necessary condition for philanthropy. Next, the greater the power of the managers relative to owners (managerial discretion), the more of the resource slack that was given to charity. Finally, management values partially influenced the amount of resource slack donated. Although management values were positively associated with the amount given to charity, they were less influential than expected. Their limited role was attributed to the prevalence of social investing attitudes (Stendardi 1992), wherein managers view philanthropy as a strategic investment to increase profit. In other words, management sometimes committed organizational resources to social betterment because that action conformed with their values about the importance of service to the community. Other times, they contributed to social betterment, even when their values placed service to the community as a low priority because, apparently, they believed it was a way to generate more profit for the business.

Among the questions asked in the Iowa telephone interviews were several that can be used to measure the values and personal characteristics of the owner/manager. For this analysis, I employed a different statistical technique than those utilized previously. Since it would be instructive to examine the relationship of numerous individual characteristics simultaneously on BSP and determine the discrete association of each factor while controlling for the others, I used multiple regression analysis. I have developed three equations estimating community support (one for each community size) and three equations estimating community involvement. Two variables already considered—local ownership and business size—were added in the second stage to each of the six original equations. The advantage of adding local ownership and size was that the relative influence of each of these firm-level factors upon community support and involvement net of the others can be assessed.

In my opinion, the nature of the SIC variable prohibits using it in a regression analysis without the loss of a great deal of information about the association of industry with BSP. It would be necessary to reduce it to two values (probably, FIRE and all other), and although collapsing it thus may not do great disservice to its association with involvement, it would aggregate wholesalers with retail firms who differ significantly with regard to community support. Therefore, I chose not to include industry in the final analysis of the relationship of firm level factors to BSP.

To measure management values I used a set of questions originally developed by Lyman Porter, Richard Steers, Richard Mowday, and Paul Boulian (1974) to measure workers' commitment to their employer. The reliability and validity of the Porter, Steers, Mowday, and Boulian scale has been frequently verified by other researchers. In 1990 Dan Muhwezi modified the commitment scale to measure the commitment of business operators to communities. I changed the Muhwezi scale slightly for this study. The questions that compose the scale and the percentage of respondents who agree or strongly agree with each statement follow. For this analysis, the responses to the questions were summed for each respondent and divided by four to create a single commitment variable.[3]

Please indicate whether you strongly disagree, disagree, neither agree nor disagree, agree, or strongly agree with the following statements about (town).

1. This business does not have much to gain by remaining in (town). (reverse coded for the scale) (Percent who disagree or strongly disagree = 83.1%)
2. Whenever possible, I purchase business supplies locally even when they cost more. (Percent who agree or strongly agree = 77.4%)
3. If given a chance, I would brag about (town) as a good place to locate a business. (Percent who agree or strongly agree = 77.4%)
4. As a business owner/manager, I am willing to expend resources to help the community. (Percentage who agree or strongly agree = 86.4%)

When we contacted businesses for inclusion in the study, we indicated our desire to interview the owner who had primary responsibility for management decisions. If the owner was absent at the time of the call, we arranged an appointment for another time. If the owner(s) was not involved in the business operation, we interviewed the manager with primary decision-making responsibility. Thus, all of our respondents, as closely as we can determine, had primary managerial discretion for the business. Nevertheless, there may be significant differences between owners and managers with regard to community support and involvement. Therefore, the variable that indicates ownership will be included in the regression analysis. It is coded: owner = 1; manager = 0.

Because community involvement looms so large in this analysis, two additional variables were introduced. Prior research has established the importance of education and length of residence in the community as important predictors of involvement.[4] By adding them, I could factor out the influence they might have and get a clearer estimation of the discrete contribution of operator values and business related elements. Education was measured with a nine-category ordinal variable, ranging from 1 = less than 9th grade to 9 = graduate or professional degree.

In the initial multiple regression analyses, the number of years the owner/manager resided in the community was *not* significant, but whether the owner/manager lived in the community or elsewhere *was* significant. Consequently, in the analyses presented here, the variable of whether the respondent lived in the community has been substituted for years of residence. The new "live in" variable was coded as 1 when the business operator lived in the community, 0 when s/he did not.

The means, standard deviations, and bivariate correlations for all the variables included in the multiple regression analyses are displayed in Appendix D. Table 4.3 contains the equations developed to estimate the amount of community support reported by business operators for the three

Table 4.3
Manager/Owner Characteristics and Community Support (Ordinary Least Squares Regression)

	RURAL		URBAN		METRO	
	Eq. 1 (N=885)	Eq. 2 (N=662)	Eq. 1 (N=243)	Eq. 2 (N=163)	Eq. 1 (N=368)	Eq. 2 (N=264)
	Betas		Betas		Betas	
Commitment	.38*	.35*	.43*	.42*	.30*	.30*
Education	.13*	.13*	-.00	.01	.12*	.04
Owner/Manager (owner =1; manager =0)	.04	.07*	.10	.11	.09	.21*
Live in Town (yes =1; no =0)	.17*	.20*	.11*	.16*	.10*	.10
Local Ownership (yes =1; no =0)		.02		.12		.10
Gross Sales (log)		.13*		.34*		.23*
Total Employees (log)		.14*		-.12		-.02
F	59.98*	36.89*	15.62*	10.78*	15.90*	10.98*
R sq	.21	.28	.21	.33	.15	.23

*Significant at p < .05

community size categories. Equation 1 estimates support with only the variables measuring the individual characteristics of the owner/manager. I have displayed the standardized Beta coefficients instead of the unstandardized regression coefficients because Betas allow us to compare the amount of variation in the dependent variable explained by the independent variables relative to each other.

Each Equation 1 for the three community sizes demonstrates the importance of the operator's commitment to the community in explaining the support his or her business provides the community. It explains more than twice as much of the difference in support as the variable with the next closest Beta. The factor in second place differs, depending on the community size. In small towns, where the operator lives is the second most important factor. The Beta for living in the community is almost equally matched by status as owner or manager in bigger places and education in metro communities. In both metro communities and small towns, operators with more education are significantly more likely to report providing support. But in small cities, when other variables are controlled, the education of the operator is not significant in predicting business support for the community. The difference in support reported by owners vs. managers is not significant in rural communities.

Commitment is less dominant in the equations predicting involvement (Table 4.4), although it still has the largest Beta of all variables. Living in town is almost as important as commitment in rural communities and second in importance in urban communities. Where the operator lives is not significantly related to involvement, when other variables are controlled, in metro communities; and the distinction between owners and managers

Table 4.4
Manager/Owner Characteristics and Community Involvement (Ordinary Least Squares Regression)

	RURAL		URBAN		METRO	
	Eq. 1 (N=957)	Eq. 2 (N=703)	Eq. 1 (N=254)	Eq. 2 (N=166)	Eq. 1 (N=386)	Eq. 2 (N=271)
	Betas		Betas		Betas	
Commitment	.32*	.27*	.31*	.36*	.25*	.23*
Education	.10*	.06	.16*	.15*	.19*	.09
Owner/Manager (owner =1; manager =0)	.03	.01	.05	-.03	.18*	.19*
Live in Town (yes =1; no =0)	.27*	.29*	.20*	.21*	.08	.08
Local Ownership (yes =1; no =0)		.05		.09		.11
Gross Sales (log)		.12*		.20		.21*
Total Employees (log)		.09*		-.18*		-.12
F	60.80*	30.12*	14.17*	7.92*	18.84	8.52*
R sq	.20	.23	.18	.26	.16	.18

*Significant at $p < .05$

is significant only for businesses in metro communities. In fact, among personal characteristics in metro communities, commitment, education, and owner vs. manager are about equally important in explaining the difference in involvement among business operators.

Consistent with findings from prior research, education is significantly related to involvement in all sizes of communities. In small towns and small cities, where the primary decision maker lives is more important in predicting his or her involvement in the community than whether the decision maker is the owner or the manager. For businesses in metro areas, the opposite is true. Where they live doesn't matter, but owners are more likely to get involved than managers.

Reid Schmidt, director of a charitable organization, was the interviewee who was most alarmed by the negative ramifications of nonresidence on the community involvement of owners/managers. He was referring to the phenomenon as it is manifested by CEOs of consolidated businesses operating in metropolitan Pikeville. Apparently, this group is still numerically so small that it has not affected the statistics regarding community involvement among metro businesses. However, the significance of the location of residence among business operators in other sizes of towns buttresses Schmidt's concern and is an ominous sign of what the future may hold for locations where commuting owners/managers are becoming commonplace.

The F score for all equations is significant, but the R squares are not large, although common for social science research. They range between .15 and .21, meaning between 15 percent and 21 percent of the difference in support and involvement among businesses is explained by the owner/manager variables contained in the equations. When I introduced the three business variables—ownership location, gross sales, and number of employees—the R squares increase, but not by much. Notice the decline in the size of the sample for all Equation 2s from the sample size for Equation 1s. The drop off is caused by a number of business operators refusing to answer the gross sales question.

With ownership location and business size variables in the equations predicting involvement, operators' education is no longer significant in rural and metro communities. Otherwise, there is remarkably little change in Betas between the two equations for the three community-size categories, in spite of the decline in the N. Since the phenomenon being considered is operators' personal involvement, it is not surprising that individual characteristics account for more of the variation between businesses than business characteristics do. However, a peek ahead to the support equations shows the resilience of individual characteristics, even when predicting support for the community.

Note the negative Beta for number of employees in the two city categories in Table 4.4. Although the Beta in metro Equation 2 is not significant, it appears that owners and managers of businesses with more employees are less likely to be involved in the community than are the operators of businesses with fewer employees. At the same time, gross sales is a significant factor and positively related in all sizes of communities. In small towns, operators of bigger businesses as measured by both number of employees and gross sales are more involved.

As indicated above, an examination of Equations 1 and 2 for support (Table 4.3), shows that individual characteristics remain significant in predicting support even after business characteristics are controlled. In fact, commitment continues to have the largest Beta. The significance of the Beta for gross sales demonstrates its importance in predicting business support, but it does not diminish the role of the personal characteristics of the owner/manager. Two important changes do occur, however. When business size and local ownership are controlled in the second metro equation, education is no longer significant as a predictor of support, and the relationship between owner vs. manager and support is enhanced. This suggests that in metro companies of equal size and ownership location, those managed by the owner will provide more community support than those managed by a manager and the education of the top decision maker is irrelevant to support.

The negative Betas for number of employees in the equations for involvement and support in urban and metro communities sheds doubt on the argument posed earlier that businesses with greater labor intensities are more likely to have higher BSP. The logic that concern for the welfare of employees, or concern about attracting and retaining employees, motivates businesses to work for community betterment appears to apply only in rural communities and in isolated cases elsewhere. Perhaps Craig

Gerdes, the manufacturer in Socksberg, was correct when he said, "Businesses don't have to worry so much about their image in a big city." This is also consistent with Kamen's (1985) contention that in large cities the visibility of individual corporations is less, negatively affecting their BSP. Giant corporations probably still have to worry about their image in big cities as it is hard for them to be invisible anywhere. In this sample, the largest business regardless of location had six hundred employees. A qualitative change may occur in the impact of number of employees on community support after a firm reaches 10,000 employees, or 100,000 employees. There is no ambiguity, however, when it comes to the critical nature of gross sales to involvement and support in all locations.

A rather surprising observation from Tables 4.3 and 4.4 is the lack of significance of local ownership in any of the equations. Based on this analysis, however, I am not ready to discount the findings of prior research and the experience of my interviewees. One explanation for the lack of significance of local ownership when other variables are controlled could be the measure of community support used in this study. The support score of the consolidated utility that did away with the $50,000 trinket fund could be the same as the support score for the utility before consolidation. My measure of support would not capture this important distinction. On the other hand, the correlation between local ownership and support before other variables are controlled is significant and negative for all community sizes as expected. (See Figure 4.4 and Appendix D for these statistics.) Therefore, in spite of the weakness of the measure of support used here, the perceived negative relationship between nonlocal ownership and community support may be explained by other factors common to both nonlocal ownership and nonsupport of the community. One possibility is suggested by the positive association between local ownership and management by owner shown in the correlation matrices in Appendix D. In rural communities, owners have less commitment to the community than do managers, and in metro communities, owners are more likely to report higher levels of involvement and support than managers.

Another possibility is posed by the lack of significance of commitment values with local ownership. The fact that these two variables are not related in this study prompts us to wonder if the lack of support and involvement from nonlocal businesses observed by community leaders results from the fact that nonlocal businesses are run by managers instead of owners who report less commitment to the community. Operator commitment may be the key factor, not ownership location per se. Remembering Reid Schmidt's (director of a charitable organization in Pikeville) example of the parent company that mandated its newly purchased local company to provide more community support than it did previously is a good antidote to the tendency to tar and feather all nonlocal companies together.

As a way to pull together the information reviewed here, I again quote John Crowell, "If there's an asshole at the head of the company, then the company is basically an asshole company." I didn't measure for that particular management quality, but the evidence provided in this section supports the underlying premise of Crowell's statement. The values and the background of top management are important determinants of the social performance of the business. In the Iowa study, they are more important than gross sales and local ownership in predicting how much support and personal involvement businesses report providing to communities.

CONCLUSION

Reflecting upon the evidence presented in this chapter, which businesses are most likely to help implement a community betterment project? First of all, size does matter. Keith Davis and Robert L. Blomstrom (1971) claimed in their formulation of the Iron Law of Responsibility that more is expected from businesses that have more. Here we learn that businesses with more do, indeed, give more. Specifically, businesses with greater resource slack, greater net income, or greater gross sales (depending upon which of the three measures is available) are more likely to provide financial, technical, in-kind, and volunteer support for charitable and community causes.

But size is relative, as the Iowa study shows, and as McElroy and Siegfried discovered in their 1986 research. Both studies demonstrate that size relative to the other businesses in the community is the critical consideration for BSP. Businesses that, by governmental standards, are considered small businesses may be among the biggest businesses in a particular community and the major benefactors for community projects. To an outside observer, business size may be difficult to determine since resource slack is key, not number of employees. In fact, in big towns, community leadership and support are more likely to be provided by prosperous businesses with relatively few employees. This is not true in rural communities where bigger businesses, by all measures, are more likely to contribute to community betterment.

The financial, insurance, and real estate businesses are high on the list of those most likely to help. After the FIRE businesses, retail and agriculture businesses would be likely candidates. Don't ignore the wholesalers, doctor's offices, and nursing homes, but recognize that they will require more effort to recruit than the other business sectors. All else being equal (i.e., size and industry), the next consideration should be to identify business owners or top managers who live in the community, especially for nonmetropolitan areas. In metropolitan areas, business owners are likely to be more receptive to solicitation for help than managers.

The more education the business operator has, the more likely he or she will accept an invitation to get personally involved in a community project. However, in firms that are equally prosperous, the education of the owner doesn't matter much except in small cities. A great deal of evidence indicates that locally owned firms will be more likely to help than nonlocal firms. But the findings from the Iowa study show that, once gross sales and the values and background of the top decision maker are controlled, the effect of ownership location on community support and involvement is not important. Maybe, to paraphrase Caizan insurance business owner Bryant Gear, we walk away and accept too quickly a refusal from a nonlocal business. Perhaps we anticipate refusals and don't utilize the same tactics and arguments we employ to sway local businesses to get involved.

This brings us to what, in the final analyses of the Iowa data, was the most important predictor of a business's social performance—the values of the owner/manager. As the Gatlin City theater group knew, some business owners are more committed to the community than others. They have a reputation for generosity when it comes to community betterment projects. From Joseph Galaskiewicz's research of the Twin Cities (the so called Emerald City), other research that shows the impact of tithing clubs and business networks (Useem & Kutner 1986), analyses I have conducted of the Iowa data (1998), and the accounts of business and community leaders, it's obvious that some communities are fortunate to have higher commitment among their business owner/managers than others. It is also obvious that high community commitment does not happen by accident. In the next chapter, I will examine the culture of communities and its relationship to business social performance.

NOTES

1. I used principal factor extraction to create a factor scale of these four questions. Cronbach's Alpha = .60, and 46 percent of the variance was explained with the items in the factor scale. The correlation of the factor scale with the summative scale is .99. Because the summative scale is more intuitively meaningful, I decided to use that instead of the factor scale in this analysis.

2. I used principal factor extraction to create a factor scale of these four questions. Cronbach's Alpha = .77, and 59 percent of the variance was explained with the items in the factor scale. The correlation of the factor scale with the summative scale is .99. Because the summative scale is more intuitively meaningful, I decided to use that instead of the factor scale in this analysis.

3. I used principal factor extraction to create a factor scale of these four questions. Cronbach's Alpha = .58, and 45 percent of the variance was explained with the items in the factor scale. The correlation of the factor scale with the summative scale is .99. Because the summative scale is more intuitively meaningful, I decided to use that instead of the factor scale in this analysis.

4. The following sources establish the importance of education to community involvement: Parkum and Parkum, 1980; Vedlitz and Veblen, 1980; Schoenberg,

1980; Oliver, 1984; Hodgkinson and Weitzman, 1986; Auslander and Litwin, 1988; Hayghe, 1991; Smith, 1994; Verba, Schlozman and Brady, 1995). Length of residence in the community is another factor associated with community participation. See Onibokun and Curry, 1976; Steggert, 1975; Parkum and Parkum, 1980; Verba, Schlozman and Brady, 1995.

CHAPTER 5

We Have a Little Talk with Them

Ellen Heston, Pikeville attorney, asked me the $64,000 community development question. "What gives some communities the spunk to fight? My hometown is a little town that's like the little engine that could. [This is a reference to the children's story about the little red engine that succeeded in climbing a hill that bigger engines failed to climb after repeating the chant 'I think I can, I think I can.'] What makes my hometown so different from Pikeville?" Anyone who has worked with communities of whatever size or lived in different communities has probably pondered this question. Why do some communities, in spite of their location or resource disadvantages, fare better than other communities with equal or greater advantages? Faring better is translated as a higher quality of life for residents. Social capital may be a partial explanation for the differences between communities in their ability to work together for the common good.

Social capital theorists maintain that communities with high social capital will find it easier to recruit volunteers, secure donations, and implement effective programs because participation is commonplace and expected. These communities have evolved mechanisms to communicate their shared expectations to new residents, to monitor participation, and to reward and sanction appropriately. The social capital dynamics that foster community involvement by residents, whether used positively or negatively, should also impact business operators. The "commitment to community" variable, so important in the analyses presented in the last chapter, may be shaped and reinforced through community social capital.

The ramifications of social capital, however, are not always positive. The same monitoring and sanctioning systems that encourage people to work together for community betterment can, if carried too far, devolve into invasions of privacy and group repudiation of members' personal freedom and individuality. High social capital among subgroups within a community can lead to the exclusion and even the demonization of outsiders. It can result in what has become known as balkanization of a community, creating multiple internally cohesive, tight-knit factions that splinter the community into feuding subgroups.

In the last chapter, I concentrated on firm-level characteristics—the education, commitment, place of residence of the top manager, business size, local ownership—and the part they play in business social performance (BSP). Now I turn to factors external to the firm—community culture and other businesses—to assess how they affect BSP. The place to start is with an elaboration of social capital as a conceptual framework. We will learn from the interviewees how they were recruited and taught the local expectations regarding community involvement and how they now attempt to acquaint new businesspeople with the local customs. Lastly, I will bring in findings from the Iowa telephone interviews.

WHAT IS SOCIAL CAPITAL?

Cornelia and Jan Flora, a highly respected pair of community development experts, have constructed an answer to "the" community development question (Flora 1995). Their "community capitals" framework addresses the question by first examining the resources communities possess that can be marshaled for development. The resources are categorized into four forms of capital; environmental, human, financial, and social. Environmental capital is soil fertility, water quality, air quality, geographical location with regard to transportation grids and metro areas, recreational and visual amenities, climate, and so on. Human capital includes all the skills, ingenuity, health, vitality, and leadership acumen that individuals bring to any enterprise. Money, but also assets like stock equities, roads, buildings, computers, machines, and sewer systems, are financial capital.

The glue that pulls it all together, according to the Floras, is social capital. It is the resource that facilitates the utilization of the other resources for development. Their definition of social capital includes Robert Putnam's definition of the concept in his famous 1993 book *Making Democracy Work* (i.e., networks of relationships, trust, and norms of reciprocity available for efforts to promote the public good). To his definition, they add shared symbols and collective identity. Alejandro Portes and Julia Sensenbrenner (1993) call these two aspects of social capital, "values introjection" and "bounded solidarity." They claim that through shared values (symbols) and collective identity (bounded solidarity), people base part of their self-identity and worldview on their membership in the group, network, or community. It helps explain why someone would contribute money to a cause anonymously or give up his or her life for a group or a cause when there is no hope of reciprocity. As Portes and Sensenbrenner point out, a wealthy Cuban American is likely to help an unemployed Cuban American whom he has never met, realizing that he will probably never get anything in return for the largess. Helping out in this way is part of the group-constructed code and the collective identity and values of the Cuban American community. It is what good Cuban Americans do. Generosity to one another is part of the self-identity of many in the Cuban American community. Also, members of any self-defined group, like Cuban Americans, Mormons, and residents of Socksberg, share with other members of their community common experiences, needs, threats, beliefs, and values. They feel a kinship with each other as a result of their membership in the same group even if they do not personally know each other. All together, networks, trust, norms of reciprocity, shared values, and collective identity promote collective action for mutual gain.

The Floras use the term "capital" in their community development resource framework because it connotes several features of the resources that are significant for development purposes. Here "development" means improvement in areas of life important to the residents of the community, not necessarily economic growth or more jobs. First, except for the Scrooges among us who get pleasure from counting money, capital as it is commonly referred to, has no inherent value. Its worth is a social construction and is derived from its ability to purchase or create goods and services humans value—fulfilling subsistence needs and other human desires. Indeed, it must be used to realize its value. Money buried in a coffee can in the backyard will decrease in value, as will machine tools and human minds and bodies that aren't used. Relationships require periodic renewal, or they atrophy. To realize the value of environmental features for development, they must be used. Fertile soil, moderate climate, or great views become resources for development only when used.

Each of the community capitals can enhance the value of the others and, to a certain extent, can be substituted for each other. The same community outcome may be achieved with different combinations of the capitals depending upon local strengths. Thus, communities with low social capital and high financial capital can hire people to do the work of volunteers. A generous benefactor in Albia, Iowa, made possible a community beautification recipe that started with a larger portion of financial capital than social capital. There is a limit to substitutability, however. Albia's money could have languished had the residents not worked together to decide how to use the resource and leveraged the money with additional funds and volunteer hours. I know of communities that were unable to use funds donated to them because they couldn't agree on its use or couldn't generate the required matching funds. Nevertheless, the principle of substitutability gives us a hint as to the answer to the Heston question.

The instrumental character of capital applied to human beings, environmental features, and relationships has justifiably aroused criticism. Human beings, relationships, and mountain views have inherent value regardless of their utility in creating something else. Some also find the term offensive because it reinforces the dominance in modern life of the economy over other domains of life like family, religion, civic life, and personal development. These criticisms are valid. Even so, at least in community development circles, the flaws of the term are outweighed by the almost immediate insight it provides into the dynamics of development.

Towns and neighborhoods like Heston's hometown that seem to have few advantages but somehow manage to sustain themselves and even prosper are probably maximizing the resource that is all but invisible to the untrained eye—social capital. Heston knew the answer. She followed her question by adding, "It's obviously a mix of people and values. How hard are you willing to work, leadership, what's important to people." I take the liberty of embellishing her comment by adding to it that the tradition of valuing the community and working together successfully for the community at least partially explains why some communities look like the little engine that could. Moreover, social capital can limit the dampening effect of free riders on community development. To explain this function of social capital, I will examine the free-rider dilemma in more depth.

PREVENTING THE TRAGEDY OF THE COMMONS

If we assume that community betterment is a public good as I did in the Enlightened Self Interest Model (Figure 3.1), then those who work to improve their community must confront the problem of free riders. As observed previously, ways have been created to partially privatize the gain so that contributors to public goods are recognized, and, hopefully, rewarded. This is problematic, however, for all of the behind-the-scenes work in visioning, organizing, persisting, calling in favors from friends and acquaintances, and volunteering personal time that are absolutely critical in community betterment. There are rooms in the Gatlin City theater named after major financial donors to recognize their contribution. What form of recognition is there for the people who are truly responsible for the theater renovation, Wendy Aitchison and her dedicated committee? Did they put in all those uncounted hours and put up with all the hurdles and disappointments along the way to get their names in the local newspaper and a handshake from the mayor during the opening night ceremony? No doubt the recognition is appreciated. Nonetheless, it surely is not a sufficient or even a major inducement for all behind-the-scenes work that goes into making communities better places to live.

Everyone in the area can enjoy equally the Gatlin City theater restoration. Why would a relatively small group of theater supporters and donors be willing to bear the costs of restoring the theater when they know others will enjoy the fruits of this effort without contributing anything? The rational thing to do (according to neo-classical economics theory) is to refrain from providing public goods and enjoy the benefit of others' irrationality. An overview of the neo-classical economics perspective toward free riders is contained in the parable of "the tragedy of the commons."

Garrett Hardin's (1968) short essay called "The Tragedy of the Commons" has had a profound impact on modern thinking about free riders and public goods. This is a story about the public lands, called commons, available in medieval English towns for townspeople and peasants to graze their livestock. The timber, wildlife, water, and other natural features of the commons were also shared by all communally. Hardin argued that, since maintaining and upgrading the common land benefited all equally, the gain to individuals from their contribution to the commons was less than the gain they realized from work on their privately owned land or other property or from leisure pursuits. As a result, no one took the initiative and responsibility for the upkeep of the common land. Similarly, everyone was motivated to maximize this "free" resource by grazing as many livestock as possible for as long as possible. These "inherent" characteristics of public goods in general, Hardin claimed, led to overgrazing, overharvesting, and little maintenance, eventuating in the collapse of the British commons. The "tragedy" is that because individuals are prone to pursue their personal gain by being free riders, they imperil the general welfare in public goods situations.

Hardin proposed that the solution to the tragedy was "mutual coercion, mutually agreed upon." However, this part of his story has been frequently overlooked. Instead, the moral that most people take away from the story is that public goods are not sustainable. Either they must be controlled by an autocrat or privatized. When public goods are privatized, proponents claim, someone takes responsibility for the long-term sustainability of the good and has the authority of ownership to enforce sustainable practices. We all gain as a result, in this reasoning.

However, Hardin's account of the English commons' tragedy is taken out of its historical context. In a review of the historical handling of common goods, David Feeny and his colleagues (1990) point out that common land in England was viably sustained for hundreds of years with neither overgrazing nor over use of water, wildlife, or timber. The peasants weren't stupid. They could see that they would all suffer if overharvesting occurred and no maintenance was carried out. Thus, they established standards for grazing, harvesting, and work rotation schedules for upkeep. People who contributed to the maintenance and improvement of the commons were accorded recognition and respect. That was what good upstanding peasants did. Each peasant had a quota for how many of his or her livestock could be grazed and for how long, and, each was expected to help out with work projects. Certain pieces of the commons would be periodically set aside, upon which grazing was forbidden to allow the pasture to regenerate. The herders monitored each other and were given formal sanctioning power through the auspices of law and local magistrates. Of course, we can assume they also used informal sanctioning mechanisms that can be quite effective in small, close-knit communities like medieval towns.

Tragedies of overgrazing started occurring when the aristocracy discovered that they could make more money by sheep herding than by the traditional feudal farming practices. However, to raise sheep profitably, they required more land. Peasants were displaced from their traditional feudal lands to towns, releasing more land for sheep herding and providing needed labor for the burgeoning industrial revolution. The enclosure laws were passed privatizing much of the commons, so that what land remained was woefully inadequate for the needs of the increasing numbers of landless peasants. Also at this time, laws were changed and magistrates became less sympathetic to peasants' pleas for support in enforcing their traditional standards for commons upkeep and grazing quotas. It is little wonder that the commons became a tragedy. However, is the tragedy a lesson in the inherent unsustainability of public goods or a lesson in the use and abuse of class power?

Supporting the later interpretation are the findings in Eleanor Ostrom's 1990 book on common pool resources. Common pool resources include common pastures, irrigation systems, and terraced farm lands owned by communities in various parts of the world. Her research demonstrates that clearly defined communities of place can maintain public goods for extensive periods of time, in some instances for a millennium, without the tragedy that befell Hardin's commons. Key elements in the sustained provision of these public goods are a stable community with an ethos that values the resource, and those who improve and maintain it, and effective mechanisms to monitor and control its use.

We are now positioned to apply the morals of Feeny's commons and Ostrom's research on common pool resources to business social performance and community betterment. The values underlying business social performance were elaborated in chapter 3. Briefly, they are social contract obligations, moral responsibility, and enlightened self interest rationales. My focus here is to elaborate how the values are communicated to newcomers and reinforced among longtime residents, and discuss what techniques of surveillance and reward and punishment discourage free riders.

IN THE BEGINNING ARE RELATIONSHIPS

Whatever the prevailing culture about community involvement and business support for community, it is communicated to people through other people. The message can be transmitted through words or action, or both. The more affection and respect the receiver has for the sender, the more effective the message. This implies, of course, that the receiver knows the sender. So, the first step is building relationships. Socksberg banker Nick Grafton provided an example of how relationships are established and then lead to community involvement among business operators:

John Piquo started smoozing with the new business people. Their company had just built a plant on the outskirts of a neighboring town. Took them out to lunch, had them over for dinner, invited them to play golf, that kind of thing. It paid off for us as a business. We got their accounts, but also it brought them into the community down here. They were glad to serve on committees. Some of them are only here for a year or two. Their spouses didn't come with them. They were kind of looking for things to do. They're a smart, diverse group, and we're excited to have them participate.

Probably the majority of relationship building is informal and takes place in a hundred variations of Grafton's example. Being informal does not mean such activity is necessarily haphazard or unplanned, however. A CEO in Pikeville, Bill Mannes, provided a typical example of deliberate informal efforts toward relationship building. He said,

Communications and relationships are the whole bag. It's as simple and as complex as that. We develop friendships with new public officials and new CEOs. We socialize together. We have retreats. We get together for parties, drinks. We make sure they're involved.

Wilford Krivit, another Pikeville chief executive, underscored the fact that relationship building is not left to chance in Pikeville when he reported,

You've got to have meaningful reasons for the top leadership to get together. There's got to be formal ways, but also informal ways. They've got to get up against each other and talk. Over the years, just two of us have had lunch with various people in the community just for the sake of developing a relationship and opening a dialogue. Got to have prolific, free, and open discussion.

The process of developing relationships has its formal side also. In all five of the case-study communities, some institution in town is charged with the responsibility of welcoming new business people to town and engaging them in the community. In Caizan it is the community development corporation. Lance Butterfield, a realtor in Socksberg, reported that new businesses get a "little birthday kiss" when they open and, subsequently, on their anniversary. This involves a visit from some of the Community Development Corporation (CDC) business members who present the new owner or manager with a gift. Butterfield left the nature of the gift unspecified. However, whatever the gift, the visiting business operators inquire into the new business's needs, convey their concern about the business's welfare, provide information about local services, invite the business owner to join the CDC and the Chamber, and establish a personal link with the business operator. Members of the Chamber perform the same function, without the "kiss" part, in Manasis, Gatlin City, Pikeville, and Socksberg.

Communities may also create regular opportunities for the CEOs of the largest local businesses to meet and socialize. One small-town development director created a CEO committee that meets once a month for breakfast. Ostensibly, the purpose of the group is to give the director advice about development goals and techniques. Another hardly concealed purpose is to involve this group in the community and develop linkages between them. In Pikeville, the major corporate CEO group started meeting regularly after they all worked together on a major downtown attraction. They realized the potential benefit in maintaining the ties that had been established. Now, being invited to join the Pikeville CEO group is a coveted signal that a CEO has entered the ranks of the city's elite.

Service organizations like the Jaycees, Rotary Club, and Kiwanis also actively recruit new business people as members. One of their selling points is that joining the club is a way to network and build relationships with other local businesspeople. As Jill Slaughter from Manasis commented, "There's no better place [than service clubs and chamber membership] to get your business contacts, develop a network. It's a way to meet people and get help with problems." A critical feature of local service clubs is that each tends to focus on a slightly different aspect of community betterment. This offers a variety of local causes and approaches to those causes that should appeal to a broad range of interests.

The larger the community, the more complicated and hierarchical the system for assimilating new business operators into the community seems to be. At the top are the CEOs. In Pikeville, this group is further divided with the CEOs of the major companies singled out for special attention. Directors of nonprofit organizations attempt to recruit them for their boards. Other CEOs invite them to join the most prestigious country club. Public officials and Chamber representatives try to develop a relationship with the individual.

After the CEO group, I was told that the next level in the hierarchy of involvement is the Rotary Club, where the second tier of business executives meet and smooze. None of the CEOs of major corporations whom I interviewed belonged to the service clubs. Following the Rotary Club in no particular order are the other service clubs.

As indicated previously, the system for building ties between owners and top managers and the community may be thwarted when business executives commute every weekend to their home in the mountains or on the coast. Also potentially threatening, according to Pikeville charitable organization director Reid Schmidt, is the practice of CEOs living in the suburbs and/or acquiring a second home in another location. It seems logical that having a home in two locations would split the loyalty of local capitalists between their "summer home" community and their "winter home" community. Even though the analysis of the Iowa data contained in the last chapter did not find that top manager's place of residence was a significant detractor from business support in metro areas, it was significantly related to support in smaller communities.

THE SHARED VALUE OF COMMUNITY BETTERMENT COMES NEXT

You should now have a picture of the importance that interviewees accord to relationships in building businesses' support for communities and the variety of formal and informal techniques that are utilized to build these linkages. Networking between business people is nothing new however, and it is not necessarily a tool for community betterment. For that to occur, the behavior modeled and the messages sent within the network must convey the value that the community is important and the expectation that businesses should contribute to the public good. Bryant Gear explained how the business operators in Caizan go about transmitting the value of community support:

We encourage by example mostly. When new businesses see what we do in Caizan, they usually get involved too. We also talk up specific projects and try to convince them of the value of that project.

The significance of modeling is echoed in findings from McElroy and Siegfried's 1986 study of 229 large companies. This group of businesses tended to increase their contributions when other local firms set an example of generosity.

Modeling is rather passive and does not necessarily require the presence of relationships. It may seem obvious, but it bears emphasizing, that most people get involved in public affairs because someone they know invited them to join (Oliver 1984). Relationships are the first element in creating social capital and preventing free riders because they facilitate and personalize invitations to participate. Over and over again, interviewees told me a version of, "I got involved because somebody I know invited me to participate." Sometimes it was their boss. More often it was a friend or acquaintance. About one of four interviewees indicated that they got involved because it was expected in the families in which they grew up. Even among this group, however, the specific civic club or project that was the beneficiary of their civic-mindedness depended upon someone in that group inviting them. It works like this according to Bill Mannes, Pikeville business leader: "We make an effort to go to new business owners and CEOs and engage them in community activities. Get them on the boards of community institutions, the Chamber, arts, etc., and get them interested in local issues."

Harriet Ernst, who owns a retail store in Socksberg, illustrated another role that relationships play in promulgating the value of community betterment. She decided that Socksberg needed a youth sports complex. She talked to her friends and acquaintances one-to-one, convinced them of the need for the complex, and convinced them to work to provide it. Once on board, they each agreed to contact ten other businesspeople and solicit their support. From this base of support, a fundraising drive was launched and eventually the sports complex was built.

The mechanism of growing a "tree" of support for a project by utilizing one-to-one relationships was mentioned by several interviewees when they described community betterment projects in which they had participated. The core group of supporters is akin to the trunk of the tree whose influence extends out through their individual relationships to branches, i.e., to others who do the same with their relationships. This continues until the leaves are reached and a whole tree of support has been created. Roger de la Renta, retail manager in Manasis, put a slightly different twist on the process when he reported, "It works like this: you get the core people involved and then they go out and drag in the others you need."

Al Matsumoto, a Pikeville financial institution chief executive, was more blunt about how personal relationships facilitate community support:

If a CEO I know comes to me about a project he's endorsing, and that I agree with, and asks me for money to support it, if I can, I probably will support it. I know at some juncture I'm going to want to go to that person's company and ask him/her for support.

The norm of reciprocity implicit in the social capital framework couldn't be illustrated better. Matsumoto added, however, that his willingness to help people he knows with their projects, only goes so far. Support that involves a large commitment of money, time, or personal reputation would be scrutinized more closely, and other factors would become more important determiners of his decision to assist with the project. As a result, any substantial community improvement project requires people in the network to solicit the support of others who are not in the network. Of course, this depends on the size of the town. In a small town or small city, the network might include all the critical players.

According to Lance Butterfield, Socksberg realtor, there is another way that relationships help get people involved or overcome the resistance of a key individual. "People always have friends. If you can't convince them head on, you go to their friends and get them to talk to them," he said. Butterfield made the comment that is the title for this chapter when I asked him how he would encourage a new business person to get involved in the community. He laughed as he responded, "We have to train new business people. We sit them down and have a little talk with them." I don't think he meant to be taken literally. Most of us would be put off by this kind of treatment. Instead, I believe he was stating his opinion about the strength and clarity of the community support message that established business people in Caizan send to new business operators. The content of the message, according to responses to the question, "How would you convince another business person to provide support to the community?" was always a version of the enlightened self-interest rationale. Usually, the shared-fate and the public relations versions were combined in the message.

IN ORDER TO DISCOURAGE FREE RIDERS

The strength of belief in the shared-fate and public relations values of business community support is apparent in the reaction of businesspeople to their counterparts who don't support the community. The following comments provide us with a sense of what nonsupportive businesses face from other businesses. First Robert Markus, a manufacturer, described how business people react to a nonsupportive business in Socksberg:

There's a lot of groaning and moaning. There's never any outright . . . I don't think anyone would say anything to their face. There's one business in town that whenever there's a big event, they won't throw any money in or pay for advertising because they know everybody's coming to town anyway. They're not well liked.

Businesses that don't help out aren't looked upon very well. Sometimes, businesses will refrain from using their services for a period of time. They have to learn the unwritten rules. (Corey Zander, accountant in Manasis)

All businesses should be involved. I get kind of upset when they don't help out. We blackball businesses that don't get involved. Ninety percent do. (Doug Avala, Socksberg insurance owner)

If a business came in to town that didn't support the community, they wouldn't last very long here. (Craig Gerdes, Socksberg manufacturer)

Later Gerdes elaborated the finer nuances of acceptable community support in Socksberg:

The town was renovating a park and adding a band shell. Four or five business guys worked on this for years. In the last year, another business owner who hadn't been involved at all up until this point, threw in a bunch of money under the condition that the band shell be named after him . . . and he got it! Well . . . you don't do things to have things named after you. You do it for pride in your community or you just want to. When you have an ulterior motive, you want to be remembered for what you gave, you're thinking wrong. To most people in Socksberg, that's very unpopular. On the other hand, there are circumstances where it's okay for a donation to be immortalized by having your name on something. If it's a ton of money.

In metropolitan Pikeville, community and business leaders expressed frustration about nonsupportive businesses but seemed to have fewer tools at their disposal for dealing them. This may be due to the larger size of the big businesses in Pikeville and their greater power relative to the collective of other local businesses. That is, a very large business and its management may be accorded special privileges, whether the company is viewed as a good corporate citizen or not. This possibility highlights the fact that the effectiveness of negative sanctions in shaping behavior is related to how dependent the nonconforming business is upon the "enforcers." If the enforcers have no legal or economic hold over the business and no personal ties to the top management, their negative sanctions are not likely to have much impact. Being disliked by other local businesspeople may not matter much to the CEO of a giant transnational company who is under pressure to show 12 percent profit from the local operation and who plans to move back to headquarters as soon as possible—assuming she can meet corporate's profits goals.

Before we jump to any general conclusions about the inability of community businesses to sanction big businesses, we need to consider the role of positive sanctions (rewards) in shaping the behavior of business operators. For, as any animal trainer or psychologist will attest, rewarding desired behavior is more effective in changing behavior than is punishing undesired behavior. I will elaborate the full range of rewards for community support in the next chapter. For now, I will consider only those that are an integral part of the relationship network of business operators in a community.

Melvin Timm, a CEO and influential business leader in Pikeville, recalled for me the inception of an exclusive "club" whose members are the CEOs of Pikeville's biggest businesses. What brought them together at the time was their shared desire to see a civic center built downtown. Once the project was successfully completed, they recognized the value in sustaining their relationship. They created the Betterment Group, to which each contributed enough money annually to hire staff and run an office and contribute somewhere around a million dollars a year to betterment projects. The group was expanded in the years that followed to include other CEOs who were willing to contribute the required dues (on a sliding scale based on a formula that included business size).

There was no shortage of CEOs willing to contribute the required money. Timm attributed the popularity of the Betterment Group to its exclusivity and the prestige of membership. Membership represented inclusion among an elite group—the opportunity to regularly rub shoulders with the movers and shakers of Pikeville and the state. Timm and his colleagues were advised by leaders of a similar group in Cleveland to restrict membership to the CEOs of the largest companies. In defying this advice, they ran the risk of diluting the exclusivity of the group somewhat, but in the process they created a powerful incentive for CEOs of smaller companies to contribute funds for community betterment; in some cases, it was their first contribution.

Several studies offer insight into the rewards to businesses when their top management is part of a network of other businesses, influential or otherwise. In a fascinating historical study of Dutch accounting firms from 1880 to 1990, Johannes Pennings, Kyungmook Lee, and Arjen van Witteloostuijn (1998) found that the more ties firm professionals had to outside entities (i.e., the larger the firm's network), the greater the probability of firm survival. A study of New York diamond traders published by Mark Granovetter in 1985 established the importance of embedded social relations in economic transactions. The fact that the traders knew each other, trusted each other, and had a shared code of expected behavior, facilitated the diamond trade in a much more economically efficient manner than could occur without the relationships between the traders.

Brian Uzzi conducted two studies analyzing the impact of networks on business performance. In 1996 he examined the network among businesses in the clothing industry in New York City and in 1999, the association between access to capital at reasonable rates for businesses and their acquaintanceship ties with bankers. In both studies, he found that firms with more relationship ties fared better than those less well-connected. Clothing industry businesses with more ties had a higher probability of survival, and businesses with relationships with bankers were more likely to secure needed capital at reasonable rates. The upshot of these research studies is that relationships with other businesses are good for business.

Likewise according to Mark Granovetter's 1973 research and Ron Burt's research in 1992, networking can pay off for individuals, as well, when they engage in job searches and in efforts to be promoted within a firm. Developing relationships with other businesspeople may promote the thinly disguised community booster agenda of the established business leaders, but it clearly can also promote the self-interest of the new businesses and the self-interest of the new owner or manager's career. Hence, being included in the inner circle of influential business leaders in a community, and obtaining their respect, can offer tangible personal and business rewards. If the cost is being engaged in the community, it may seem a small price to pay.

Inclusion in the inner sanctum of powerful business leaders is not a viable reward in small towns where all or almost all businesses are relatively small. Nor is it a feasible option for the vast majority of the tens of thousands of small businesses in metropolitan areas. However, networking with other businesspeople in service clubs and the local Chamber of Commerce still provides many of the benefits identified in the research just mentioned. Businesspeople in small towns need capital, business leads, advice for dealing with problems, and inclusion in lucrative business ventures that can result from relationships with other businesspeople. In addition to the rewards inherent in networking, small towns seem to possess very effective techniques for monitoring and sanctioning (positively and negatively) business social performance. [Examples of community sanctions of businesses are provided elsewhere in this book, especially in the next chapter.] Whatever mechanisms are employed, research shows that businesses in small towns hold ethical values in higher regard than small businesses in metro areas (Smith and Oakley 1994), and small businesses rate doing business in a small town as having a large positive effect on their business ethics (Brown and King 1982). Therefore, it is safe to assume that small-town business leaders possess tools that are at least as effective in promoting common values and doling out sanctions as those employed in metropolitan areas.

Is the net effect of proselytizing the value of community support, sanctioning recalcitrant businesses, and rewarding good corporate citizens sufficient to eliminate free riders? Certainly not. We have heard repeatedly from interviewees about nonsupportive businesses, and we know from national and Iowa statistics that all businesses are not good corporate citizens. A more critical question, however, is, do the practices just mentioned lessen the dampening effect of free riders on businesses' contributing to community betterment? Let's look first at the findings from prior research and then at the Iowa data to address the question.

Galaskiewicz in his 1997 restudy of the Twin Cities grants economy relayed stories about instances of sudden increases in community support that occurred after new CEOs in town served a year or two on local boards. He credited assimilation into the local business network for the aboutface in the giving patterns of new CEOs, but he noted that local civic and voluntary associations were partially responsible for the continued viability of the networks. A similar pattern of business contributions conforming to prevailing standards established by other businesses was found by McElroy and Siegfried (1986). They compared the United Way contributions of the large firms in their sample with giving from other local businesses. If a businessperson were so inclined, United Way contributions offer a great opportunity for free-riding. To the contrary, they discovered that "executives responded favorably to the increased expectations spawned by escalating contributions of other firms rather than make an effort to enjoy the benefits of others' corporate contributions without the expense of their own donations" (1986, p. 407). In other words, business executives were likely to give more, not less, when other businesses were generous in contributing.

Michael Useem submitted the McElroy and Siegfried data to additional analyses in 1991 and concluded that as intercorporate influence increases, companies allocate more of their budget to the arts. Contributions to educational, human, and health causes were less likely to be influenced by others' level of giving. Also, businesses located in cities where businesses favor giving to culture, give a higher proportion of their budget to culture. Useem and Kutner (1986) reported similar findings among their sample of large corporations operating in Massachusetts. Slightly more than 50 percent of these firms reported that they were modestly or strongly influenced to give to a particular cause if another major corporation had already given. The larger the other corporation, the more influence they wielded on corporate giving amounts.

Peter Navarro (1988) sampled 249 of the largest companies in the United States to determine the factors associated with corporate giving. He concluded that, among other influential variables, operating in a metropolitan area with a corporate tithing club increased the proportion of gross sales contributed to charity. Corporate tithing clubs are associations of businesses in a particular location who pledge to contribute an agreed-upon percentage of their before-tax profit, or gross sales, to charitable causes.

The research evidence is consistent and convincing. Large corporations positively influence each other to contribute to the provision of public goods. No wonder Jeff McCaffrey, a Manasis minister, called Hans Becherer's (Deere's CEO at the time) support of a community betterment project the "kiss of life" for the project. He knew that, since Deere is the largest private sector employer and arguably the most prestigious firm in the local area, Becherer's active support would strongly influence other businesses to follow suit and provide support.

The Iowa data allow us to explore the influence of external factors, i.e., community and other businesses, on business social performance among a large cross section of small businesses. To review, the elements shown in the last chapter to be associated with business support for the community were: size of business; the operator's place of residence, education, and commitment to the community; and whether the top decision maker was the owner or manager. All these factors are internal to the business, or firm-level variables. From among this group, commitment to the community had the largest correlation with business support and involvement in the community when all other variables were controlled. Building on that framework, the most logical way for external elements to impact business social performance is through the operator's commitment to community. I will start then by examining elements that might be associated with the owner/manager's commitment to the community.

Five questions asked in the telephone interviews can be used to measure business operators' perceptions of the prevailing community values toward working for the public good. They were drawn from Thomas Glynn's 1981 overview of indicators of community phenomena.

	Average Score		
	Rural	Urban	Metro
If you do not look out for yourself, no one selse in (town) will. 1 = Strongly disagree to 5 = Strongly agree (reverse coded)	3.42	3.37	3.46

When something needs to get done in (town), the whole community usually gets behind it. 1 = Strongly disagree to 5 = Strongly agree	3.42	3.51	3.16
Community clubs and organizations are interested in what is best for all residents. 1 = Strongly disagree to 5 = Strongly agree	3.65	3.65	3.40
Please rate the friendliness of (town) on a scale of one to seven with 1 being very un-friendly and 7 being very friendly.	5.35	5.34	5.31
How would you rate (town) on trust using a scale of 1 to 7 with 1 being very trusting and 7 not trusting? (reverse coded)	4.95	4.73	4.53

These questions were combined in a factor-scaling procedure to create a single variable called collective action.[1] Figure 5.1 is a graph that depicts the relationship between operators' commitment to the community and their perception of the level of local collective action for different sizes of communities.[2] It is clear from the graph that in all sizes of communities, as perceived level of collective action increases, business operators' commitment to the community increases. The correlation between the two for the whole sample is statistically significant ($r = .471$, $p = .00$), and the correlations are significant for the three community sizes also (rural $r = .52$, urban $r = .48$, metro $r = .36$).

As a way to measure business operators' receptivity to the influence of other businesses, I used two questions included in a series of items that asked about operators' assessment of the importance of various strategies for business success. The exact wording was:

Figure 5.1
Commitment and Perception of Collective Action for Different Community Sizes

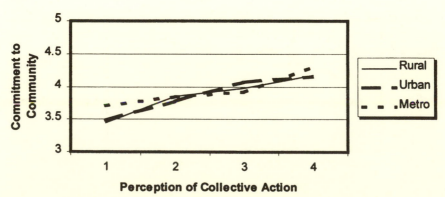

The next section of questions deals with the different things businesses do to succeed. Please rate the following business strategies by their importance to the success of your present business on a scale of 1 to 5 with 1 being not important and 5 being extremely important. How would you rate . . .

	Average Score		
	Rural	Urban	Metro
Cooperating with other local businesses	3.94	3.73	3.62
Networking with businesses outside the community for mutual gain	3.45	3.26	3.24

Each operator's responses to the questions were summed and divided by two to create a networking variable. The relationship between commitment to community and networking is displayed in Figure 5.2. Again, in all sizes of communities, the more important networking is evaluated to be to business success by the owner/manager, the greater his or her reported commitment to the community. This relationship is also statistically significant (r = .231, p = .000).

Up to this point, the findings suggest that business operators' commitment to the community is likely to conform to what they perceive to be the local values regarding collective action and to be associated with operators' networking values. But will the association persist after the effect of all the other important factors is controlled? To answer that question, I use regression analysis to calculate a standardized coefficient (Beta) for each independent variable net of the others. The result will be an equation predicting commitment similar to those generated in the last chapter to assess how firm and top management characteristics related to business social performance.

Figure 5.2
Commitment by Networking Importance for Different Community Sizes

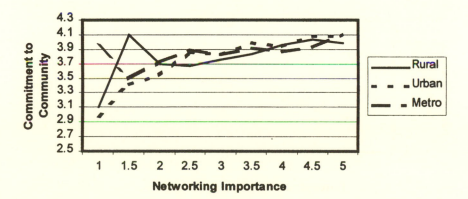

Table 5.1 contains the equations predicting the level of community commitment for business operators in the three community sizes. Regardless of community size, both collective action and networking are significantly related to commitment. Moreover, collective action has the largest Beta; networking is second. These results support the contention that business operators' commitment to the community is influenced by the prevailing values of collective action, and that those who believe that networking is important to their success tend to have higher commitment. These two factors are more important in predicting commitment than the operator's education or place of residence, the size of the firm, and its ownership location.

Let's take this one step further and determine if there is any direct association between values of collective action and networking with community support. To do that, I calculated another set of regression equations with support and involvement as the dependent variables. Table 5.2 contains the equations predicting business support for the community for the three community sizes. The Betas for commitment remain relatively unaffected, with values of collective action and networking included, and continue to be the largest coefficients. Networking is significant for rural and metro businesses, while collective action is important for businesses in urban communities. Gross sales continues to be an important predictor of sup-

Table 5.1
Commitment to Community, Perceptions of Community Collective Action, and the Importance of Networking by Community Size Categories (Ordinary Least Squares Regression)

	Commitment to Community = Dependent Variable Betas		
	Rural	Urban	Metro
Owner (1 = yes, 0 = no)	-.02	.06	.01
Education	.06*	.10	.11
Live in Town (1 = yes, 0 = no)	.05	.14*	.12*
Local Ownership (1 = yes, 0 = no)	.02	.01	.06
Gross Sales (log)	.16*	.18*	.11
Collective Action	.47*	.42*	.34*
Networking	.19*	.33*	.14*
F Score	49.69*	12.72*	8.08*
R Squared	.35	.38	.19

$^*p < .05$

Table 5.2

Collective Action and Networking Variables as Predictors of Business Support for Community Controlling for Operator/Business Characteristics (Ordinary Least Squares Regression)

	Betas		
	Rural	Urban	Metro
Commitment	.30*	.29*	.30*
Owner (yes = 1, no = 0)	.09	.15	.24*
Education	.16*	.03	.06
Live in Town (yes = 1, no = 0)	.16*	.18*	.08
Local Ownership (yes = 1, no = 0)	.02	.13	.08
Gross Sales (log)	.21*	.29*	.23*
Collective Action	.02	.17*	-.03
Networking	.21*	.08	.21*
F	33.42*	9.57*	11.09*
R Sq	.30	.35	.27

* Significant at p < .05

port, as does living in town for rural and urban businesses. It appears that networking for rural and metro businesses and collective action in urban areas are related to business support in ways independent of their influence on commitment. Thus, even with commitment controlled, they are associated with the support businesses provide communities.

The role of networking and collective action values follows the same pattern in predicting business involvement in community (See Table 5.3). In the metro equation, networking almost reaches significance with the probability associated with the Beta at .06. Again, both are apparently associated with involvement independently, that is, over and above the role they play in influencing commitment. In fact, commitment is no longer significantly associated with involvement for urban businesses when collective action is in the equation.

To summarize, business operators in rural and metropolitan communities who believe that networking is important to their success are more likely to be committed to the community, support the community, and be involved in leadership roles in the community. Operators in urban communities that are perceived to possess high levels of collective action are more likely to be committed to the community, support the community, and be involved in the community. When it comes to predicting support, networking or community collective action (depending on community size), factors

Table 5.3
Collective Action and Networking Variables as Predictors of Business Operators' Involvement in Community Controlling for Operator/Business Characteristics (Ordinary Least Squares Regression)

	Betas		
	Rural	**Urban**	**Metro**
Commitment	.24*	.16 n.s.	.24*
Owner (yes = 1, no = 0)	.01	.04	.19*
Education	.09*	.16*	.10
Live in Town (yes = 1, no = 0)	.25*	.21*	.07
Local Ownership (yes = 1, no = 0)	.06	.09	.09
Gross Sales (log)	.18*	.13	.14*
Collective Action	-.01	.30*	.00
Networking	.14*	.06	.11
F Score	24.87*	7.41*	6.56*
R Square	.24	.29	.18

* Significant at $p < .05$
n.s. This Beta was .158 rounded up to .16 $p = .08$

external to the firm, are exceeded in importance only by the operator's commitment and firm size.

Drawing upon the findings from the Iowa data, prior research, and insight provided from the accounts of business and community leaders, it is clear that business operators are affected by the social milieu around them. If their business is located in a community that they perceive has high collective action and one where other businesses support the community, they are more likely to provide support. Of course, other personal, business, and community factors are at play as well. Human beings are complicated. So long as people have free will, different life experiences, and different world views, we will never be able to totally predict their behavior. The best we can achieve is to reduce the error in predicting what they will do.

Community culture and the prevailing values of other businesses are important considerations in local business social performance. Building relationships between business owners/managers and transmitting the expectation that businesses in a given community contribute to community betterment through modeling, one-on-one persuasion, and personal invitations can make a difference in the operator's commitment to the community. Included in this package of relationships and values transmission are informal negative and positive sanctions to discourage free riders. Relationships, collective identity, shared values, and trust are the components of Neal and Jan Flora's definition of social capital.

This chapter started with the Heston question about why some communities with few apparent resources are able to survive and prosper. Using the Flora's framework, I suggested that community development involved a recipe composed of varying portions of four different community capitals: financial, human, environmental, and social. Social capital is the invisible glue that facilitates the development of the other resources for community improvement and can be partially substituted for other resources. I proposed that social capital is a critical aspect in controlling free riders and sustaining public goods. One outcome of community social capital is working together for the public good. It was a small conceptual step to the application of the social capital framework to the cultivation of business social performance in communities. Evidence presented above showed that business operators are influenced by community culture and prevailing values about collective action.

NOTES

1. Principal components extraction method was used. The percent variance explained by the collective action factor variable is 43.46 and Cronbach's alpha is .65.

2. The collective action variable created from factor scaling was collapsed into quartiles and coded from 1 to 4 for depiction in the graph in Figure 5.1.

CHAPTER 6

Soul Food or Penance: The Rewards and Punishments of Community Service

"We have given and given for years. The award, the public recognition, and acknowledgment are big deals to us."

"You put yourself on a dart board and let people launch darts at you when you get involved in the community."

"It gives you a great sense of satisfaction seeing the community better off."

"Most people don't appreciate how involved the business sector is and how much money they put into projects to make them work."

These comments describe what businesspeople (or anyone else for that matter) can expect to receive in return for their community service—recognition, animosity, lack of appreciation, satisfaction, and frustration. Clearly, the rewards and punishments of business social performance (BSP) are complex and ambiguous. We need to distinguish at the outset between those consequences of business social performance that impact the success of the business and the consequences to the personal well-being of the owner/manager. That the scholarship devoted to this subject has ignored the latter is no doubt partially due to its almost unanimous focus on giant corporations. Notable exceptions aside, the majority of studies of the consequences of BSP utilize indirect sources of information, such as annual reports, IRS data, Fortune 500's environmental and community service ranking, and the Kinder, Lydenberg and Domini social investing index. The motivation and reaction of owner/managers to their businesses' charitable contributions or community involvement are not available from these sources. Moreover, it is difficult to get survey responses from, or personal interviews with, the CEOs of the megacompanies that are the center of attention in the discipline in order to learn about their motivations and reactions.

One solution to this problem has been to infer personal motivation, costs and rewards based upon whether the top decision maker is the owner or manager and the compensation of top management as a percent of income (See Navarro 1988; Fry, Keim, and Meiners 1982; and Atkinson and Galaskiewicz 1988). It is presumed that owners will be more concerned with the success of the business than managers and, therefore, less willing to give business resources to social causes. Managers, on the other hand, will be more generous since it is a way for them to increase their prestige in the local community and demonstrate their power over business resources. Regardless of the conclusions of this line of research, inferring the decision maker's motivation and the personal consequences of BSP from the association between ownership patterns and BSP is perilous.

Overall, the literature has ignored the human side of the BSP equation. The result is a myopic focus on the economic effects of BSP to companies without regard for the motivations, costs, and rewards to the top decision makers. This is unfortunate because managerial values are an important influence on businesses' support for the community, and, of course, on operators' personal involvement in the community (See analyses of the Iowa data shown in chapter 4; Buchholtz et al. 1999; Weaver et al. 1999; Burlingham and Kaufmann 1995; Useem 1991; McElroy and Siegfried 1986; Useem and Kutner 1986). From other research studies and further analyses of the Iowa data in chapter 5, we discovered that the way community culture and business networks impact BSP is through relationships with and influence upon the top decision maker. The lack of research-based knowledge about the personal costs and rewards to owners/managers of BSP distorts our understanding of the subject and, more critically, handicaps efforts to encourage BSP. My research is able to partially address that shortcoming. The first goal of this chapter, therefore, is to summarize from the in-depth interviews what business leaders reported to be the rewards and punishments of community support and involvement to themselves personally. Then I turn to an examination of the relationship of BSP to business success, the central tenet of the enlightened self-interest rationale.

Keep in mind one caveat about information derived from this set of interviews. Most of the interviewees were selected because they had knowledge of the business-community interface—which meant, in most cases, that they were businesspeople with a history of community support. Even though some were selected at random, the sample was biased toward business operators who had had a positive experience with community involvement and support. Therefore, their accounts may be a fair depiction of the experience of committed, involved businesspeople but should not be generalized to all business owners and managers nor to those who at one point got involved in community service but quit for one reason or another. Still, understanding the experience of this group can be very illuminating and may provide insight into the personal motivations of the managers and owners of companies that are good business citizens.

IT'S THE WAY I FEED MY SOUL

It is hard not to be impressed with John Crowell. He is a striking, personable CEO of a successful manufacturing plant who described his community support in terms of zen philosophy. "Supporting the community is the way I feed my soul. It's my survival and my path to wholeness and perfection," he declared. Other business operators may have been less philosophical and poetic, but they were, nevertheless, equally profound when I asked them about the rewards and costs of their support for the community. The place to begin is with rewards. All but one of the interviewees let me know that the rewards outweighed the costs and that they would be as supportive again if they were to start over. The dissenter stated that he would do it over again because it was the right thing to do, but believed the downside was stronger than the rewards.

Psychological rewards were the number one personal payback for community support identified by business leaders. At the top of the list of psychological rewards was recognition. Roger de la Renta, the retail manager from Manasis, articulated the common sentiment with this comment:

We give college scholarships and sometimes we get thank you notes. We think that's pretty impressive. It's gratifying. Makes you feel good personally. Last year we were nominated by the community for a citizenship award. It was an honor. We have given and given for years. The award, the public recognition, and acknowledgment are big deals to us.

De la Renta's response shows his positive reaction to both official forms of recognition such as awards and unofficial forms like thank you notes. Forms of recognition for good corporate citizenship are numerous, from plaques and building names to awards, banquets, pins, parties, pictures and articles in the local newspapers, and personal thank yous. "We say thank you a lot," said Jim Thomas, Socksberg's mayor.

A close second in terms of psychological rewards was having an impact on the future of the community. Al Matsumoto, a Pikeville business leader, put it this way, "It gives you a great sense of satisfaction seeing the community better off. You go to bed at night knowing you've made a difference." Business leaders from small towns and cities whom I interviewed thought the advantage of their smaller-sized communities was that the effort of one individual could have an impact on the community. However, Matsumoto and other Pikeville business leaders felt the same way about the effect they have had on metro Pikeville's future. Of course, non-Iowans probably think that even the metro areas in Iowa are small towns compared to "real cities" like Chicago and New York. Stereotypes of Iowa aside, the issue is how size of place affects feelings of empowerment and efficacy among residents. Conclusions from current research debunk the old notion that people who live in bigger places feel more powerless and hold less affection for their community than those in towns with smaller populations. Similarly, evidence from my interviews suggests that the appeal of being able to impact the community's future as a motivation for BSP cuts across business leaders in all communities regardless of size.

Personal satisfaction and sense of accomplishment were identified almost as often as was the chance to make a difference. Socksberg manufacturer Robert Markus summed up this view:

It's hard to measure the payoff in dollars and cents. It's more about community pride. It gives you a sense of pride and satisfaction to see flowers in the parks and see kids playing in the parks.

I like working with youth. How much reward I'll get back, I don't know but you see the expressions on their faces and that's enough. (Keith Runciman, realtor in Caizan)

Although satisfaction and sense of accomplishment are similar to the ability to make a difference, because interviewees distinguished between them, I gave them separate mention. A community service director, Reid Schmidt, provided this assessment of the significance of the psychological rewards of community service to business leaders:

I'm often humbled by the Pikeville business leaders. They have a very strong passion for community service, even the social service piece. You have to realize that for some of them, it's their last big call professionally. It's their chance to be a part of issues of broader scope than the matters that have been the focus of their life until this point. These are men who haven't been involved in broad human issues before, and they find them to be important and rewarding. They get real hooked on it.

Adding veracity to Schmidt's perspective is a comment from Melvin Timm, one of those Pikeville business leaders to whom Schmidt referred. According to Timm,

I get a lot of stimulation out of this. This is my home. I like it here. This has been a lot of fun.

Moving to consideration of other rewards, De la Renta mentioned the pleasure that can accompany socializing and human interaction as a positive aspect of community service. Wilfred Krivit, Pikeville business executive, echoed that theme when he said, "Aside from the tremendous amount of satisfaction you get from the work itself, you build a huge number of acquaintanceships and some friends." As noted in the last chapter, building acquaintanceships and friendships can assist one's career and one's business. Banker Jerome Rossides admitted without hesitation that one benefit he has realized from his community work is career advancement. Business owners among my interviewees mentioned this feature often, but I classified their reactions as a business advantage and will cover them later in the chapter.

Another by-product of the social interactions that are an integral part of community service is personal growth and development. Bill Mannes encourages the staff of his Pikeville business to get involved in the community. He believes its good leadership training for them. As for himself, Mannes quipped,

It's improved my speaking skills, taught me to appreciate diverse perspectives, introduced me to people from all situations and walks of life, kept me from getting mentally lazy, and put my face out in front of people.

Completing the list of personal rewards was the advantage that community betterment can bring to business operators' families. By working for improvements in the local quality of life like school, parks, safety, economic, and cultural upgrades, they believed they were indirectly helping members of their own families.

AND NOW FOR YOUR PENANCE

I was astonished to learn the extent and severity of the costs of community support reported by this group of businesspeople who, overall, describe their experience as positive. I can only wonder about the experiences of those who discontinued supporting the community because the costs were too high. Earl Fowler, a Gatlin City business leader, explained.

You put yourself on a dart board and let people launch darts at you when you get involved in the community. There isn't a business around that hasn't been slapped down. Some of them just don't want to admit it.

Some business operators did disagree with Fowler, however, reporting that they had not experienced any negative consequences for their support for the community. Again, businesspeople from the non-metro areas expected that their negative experiences were part of life in small towns and cities and that their counterparts in the big cities would escape the worst of it. In part, reports from metro interviewees supported this hunch. However, there were costs involved in community service in the metro area too, and some of them were severe.

Fowler's comment hints at the most often cited disincentive to community support. It is the negative side of recognition. People know or can easily learn who you are and some of them vehemently disagree with you and criticize you. Matsumoto was the leader of a task force implementing a major community improvement project in Pikeville. His task force made some unpopular decisions, and, as their leader, he was the one who drew the public's ire. The newspaper took a stand against the task force and criticized Matsumoto. It was a painful experience for him. Reporting a similar experience was Michael Palmer, who owns a business in Caizan and has served on the school board and city council. He has had his share of scrapes with public controversy, probably more from his time on the school board than on the city council. He advised, "You can't be a local leader without making some people mad at you. You might as well accept that going in." Rossides, a Pikeville banker, had to seek another job over conflicts of interest that arose from his community work. He maintained that his community service has helped his career in the long run, yet it had to be a devastating experience at the time.

Several owners of retail businesses told me frankly that they refused to get involved in anything that had the slightest chance of being controversial. Elizabeth Rebello, who owns a Gatlin City restaurant, asserted "I stay as apolitical as possible without being apathetic." That stance doesn't always save them, though. Sometimes, neutrality on an issue is construed by protagonists as support for the opposing side. It's a no win situation.

Being a lightening rod for negative public comments is one thing. However, the lack of civility turned into something more serious for three interviewees. One received a death threat and the other two, threats of personal injury. Joe Black, business owner and mayor of Gatlin City, discounted the seriousness of the death threat that he received from an angry citizen. He said, "It was only one person, and I figured it was just a bluff." Maybe so, but I suspect that many in his situation would have reevaluated their commitment to public service in light of this potentially severe consequence.

De la Renta described what happened to him:

We provided funds to bring a speaker to town. Well, somebody called me and read me up one side and down the other about the speaker's position. He proceeded to tell me I'd better be careful. I was shaking. You think you're doing the right thing and look what you get.

Crowell, who received a letter threatening him with personal injury, was clearly disturbed and hurt by it. One community was embroiled in a particularly acrimonious debate over a zoning and building request. The businesspeople who served on the zoning board, those who sold supplies to the facility after the decision to build it was approved, or who contracted to build the facility "were crucified" according to minister Lamont Blanchard.

Nancy Sing, a retail business owner in Caizan, sums up the feelings of many of those who no longer are involved in community support:

People don't want to be on the city council or school board any more because they'll just chop your throat. It didn't use to be that people would attack you so. Now they get agitated about the littlest things. Retired people do a lot of complaining. They've got lots of money and lots of time.

No one wants the kind of recognition just described, but some business people felt their community work wasn't even acknowledged—especially by the public. "In Pikeville," Bill Mannes reported, "I don't think the man on the street realizes that these kind of efforts do go on. Most people don't appreciate how involved the business sector is and how much money they put into projects to make them work." Businesses in small towns, where people are supposed to know everything about each other, don't seem to fare any better when it comes to public appreciation. As Robert Markus from Socksberg pointed out, "A lot of the time, community work is really thankless because people just expect that the park will be there, and the park equipment and softball diamonds will be there. They expect the government to build it and maintain it, I guess." Socksberg retail businessowner Harriet Ernst expressed the same feeling when she reported,

I haven't had anybody come up and thank me. I spent two years studying the school reorganization issue, hundreds of hours working on it. I recruited others, I kicked in money for advertising and planning. No one thanked me, except the superintendent.

The second most frequently reported drawback to community support was the time commitment and burnout. This was one negative consequence of community support unanimously cited by the metro business leaders. In their accounts, community work constitutes time taken from family and recreation, and to their critics, it is time taken from the business. I heard secondhand about a CEO who was active in the community and was subsequently fired. His replacement refused to get involved, claiming that the reason his predecessor was fired was because the home office believed he was too active in the community and not tending to the business as he should be. Whether the account is true or not, as stories like this get told and retold, they may make other CEOs of public companies with nonlocal boards wary of supporting the community.

The other dimension of the time factor is burnout. The Gatlin City manufacturer, John Crowell, vividly described the situation:

There are ten or twelve people who are involved in everything. Pretty soon you see these husks walking around. They've nothing left. I go through burnout cycles every three or four years. Say yes to everything for a while. Then get off everything and say no for a year or so. Right now I'm on twelve nonprofit and three for-profit boards, plus Rotary, and discussion groups that meet on a weekly basis. I'm not quite to the husk point, but getting close.

Business operators in small towns, small cities, and metro areas alike expressed concern about time pressures. In small towns, however, the concern appeared to be verging on alarm. Mitch Eisenstadt from Socksberg summed it up: "There's too few people, too much work." As business owners retire without finding a buyer to keep the business going, as local retail stores are replaced by Walmarts and branch convenience stores, as people commute to work in distant communities, and as more and more shopping dollars are spent in large retail centers, there are fewer people in small towns available for community service. Our focus here is the personal negative consequences of business social performance and not the state of businesses in small towns. It should be clear, though, that the two are related.

In the same way that community support provided personal satisfaction to some business operators, it could also be a source of frustration for them. According to Pikeville community leaders, business operators are decisive and accustomed to quick action. They become frustrated with the necessity of consensus building, dealing with political disagreements, and the slowness of public bureaucracies that are necessary features of community betterment efforts. The case seems logical. However, only one Pikeville businessperson mentioned frustration as a negative consequence, and he didn't elaborate. None of the interviewees from the smaller towns identified frustration with the process of community betterment as a drawback of community service.

Let me close this section with a comment from Denise Bassett, an architect in Gatlin City, who summarized the consequences of her community support with these words:

I lost some business because of my support for the bond issue, and it was personally stressful. But it wasn't that bad. In the long run the plusses outweigh the negatives. I wouldn't have missed it for the world.

HIDDEN DONATIONS AND BOYCOTTS

The consequences of business support for the community to the personal well-being of the owner or managers are not unique. That is, the same menu of costs and rewards undoubtedly applies to anyone involved in community affairs, or who supports a social cause or community project, regardless of career or organizational affiliation. Since business owners and managers represent their businesses and often contribute business resources to public betterment, the well-being of another entity, albeit a so-cially constructed one, is involved as well. In this section, I will focus on the central proposition of the enlightened self-interest rationales—that good business citizenship will be rewarded with greater business success.

As indicated in chapter 3, even though a great deal of research energy has been devoted to this topic, the findings are inconclusive. To support that claim, I cited articles by Peter Arlow and Martin Gannon (1982), Steven Wartick and Philip Cochran (1985), and Jennifer Griffin and John Mahon (1997) who have all reviewed the research evidence and found that results were incomparable across studies, or poorly designed, or contradictory. We must look elsewhere for insight into the impact of BSP on business success. In the main, my select group of business interviewees believed that their in-volvement and support for the community was good for their business. Nevertheless, several cited instances of loss of business or suspected loss of business resulting from their community work.

Ellen Heston, an attorney in Pikeville, made a comment that is appar-ently often repeated among her friends in the legal profession: "I don't do a lot of pro bono work on purpose, but I end up with a lot of it." To amplify what she meant and show how the comment applies to community social responsibility, Heston gave me an example of a recent divorce case in which she represented an indigent, illiterate mother of two young children whose husband had deserted her. The woman pleaded with Heston to take her case promising to pay $5 a month for the rest of her life if necessary to pay the legal fee. Heston could have referred her to legal aid but knew that the woman, was desperately in need of public assistance and child support from her husband and couldn't wait for help from the overworked public attorneys. She took the case as an act of kindness. However, providing legal assistance to indigent citizens is also a service to the community. It repre-sents time and money "donated" by her business to the community, for which there is little hope of enhanced business success as a result, or even of acknowledgment by the community. If the legal fee is paid, and Heston fully believes it will be, she will still not be reimbursed for the risk of default involved, for the extension of credit, or any interest to cover inflation. Any MBA would tell her that this is an unsound business practice.

As a pharmacist in Socksberg, Greg Opinski has often donated to the community in a similar way. He told me about customers with prescrip-tions to be filled who don't have insurance and can't afford the cost of pre-scription. What can he do? There is a sick child, or a friend, or infirm elderly person whose well-being is dependent upon getting the medicine. He fills the prescription and offers credit, or a deep discount. These are acts of kind-ness, but they are also business contributions to the common good, to the community. They, too, go unrecognized and unacknowledged. As business owners, Heston and Opiniski have the discretion to provide these contributions. At the same time, as small business owners, they do not have a corporate policy to legitimize turning someone down.

Heston's and Opinski's charitable acts are not the kind of community service with which most of us are familiar. More commonly, we think of donations, organizing, networking, soliciting, planning, and general volunteering. These, too, can result in loss of business revenue through angry residents and lost customers. Bryant Gear in Caizan lost a $5,000 account because a customer didn't like the development corporation, and Gear had just been elected its president. Five interviewees reported that they had lost business due to their support of various projects. Especially problematic were school reorganization issues, building and zoning decisions, and bond issues—the same areas that caused personal stress for the owner/manager. Michael Palmer, whose comments about the personal liabilities of community involvement were included above, also noted, "We lost a lot of business over our role in the school consolidation issue. It took a long time to recover."

Reverend McCaffrey described a community betterment project he led in Manasis. He, other religious leaders, public officials, and a number of business leaders organized to build a new mental health facility in town. People living in and around the part of town where the facility was to be built were vehemently opposed to the project. They picketed his church and the businesses involved, garnered a lot of publicity from television and local newspaper coverage, and organized a boycott of the businesses. McCaffrey didn't know if business revenue was actually impacted by the publicity and boycotts, but it definitely discouraged businesses from supporting other community projects that have even a hint of controversy.

One Socksberg business donated a substantial amount of money to build a tech center at the local high school and was boycotted for the donation. It was unpopular with those who believed that upgrading that particular high school, instead of others, would lay the groundwork for closing the other schools in the future if declining enrollment necessitated school closures. Generally, it is difficult to know exactly how much revenue is lost through boycotts and threats "to take my business elsewhere." Some business owners were sanguine about their losses as indicated by this comment from Doug Avala: "I lost business when I supported the school closing, but I figure, that's life." Keith Runciman expressed a similar reaction:

I got slapped for helping with the building project, but you've got to do what you think is right. Anyhow, no matter what you do, someone will get mad at you.

IN THE LONG RUN, IT'S GOOD FOR BUSINESS

Paul Komendras moved to Caizan years ago as a young attorney eager to establish a law practice. Soon after settling in, he was asked to spearhead the drive for a tax referendum for school construction. It was a heated and controversial campaign. He remembered worrying about what the drive would do for his business but figured he didn't have much to lose, since he didn't really have a business yet and had little else to do with his time. He said,

I got to know a lot of people in town as a result of working on the project. That helped build my business. Also, after the drive was over, and we won, the leader of the opposition moved all of his legal business to me. Thought I did a good job.

The advantages of the networking associated with community service have been noted previously and were mentioned by several interviewees in construction, service and retail businesses as advantageous to their businesses. Owners and managers of retail firms also believed that the positive public image associated with community support increased their clientele and the loyalty of their customers. This was one basis for the public relations variant of the enlightened self-interest model developed in chapter 3. Elizabeth Rebello, restaurant owner, reported that, every year, she provides a banquet dinner to the Gatlin City High School athletes. As a result of her generosity, she maintained, students, their families, and their friends frequent the restaurant more often. She is convinced that her business is positively affected by her donation to the athletic teams, plus other contributions she makes to the community.

To submit Rebello's proposition as one basis for the public relations variant of the enlightened self-interest model to an empirical test, I turn to the Iowa telephone data. Business success was measured with a question asking respondents to rate the success of their business (on a scale from 1 to 5 where 1 = very unsuccessful and 5 = very successful) using their own definition of success.[1] Even in the rural communities where I expected to find a somewhat pessimistic picture of business success, operators' assessments were generally quite positive. Since there was no significant difference in the distribution of businesses by industry nor in success ratings in the three community-size categories, all businesses are grouped together for this analysis. The average rating of success was 4.06 with 77.4 percent indicating that their business was either a 4 or a 5 on the scale.

In order to check the veracity of this subjective measure of business success, I compared the success evaluation of business operators to their plans for the future. I figured that operators planning to expand their business would rate their business as significantly more successful than those planning to get smaller. The average success rating for businesses planning to expand was 4.1 compared to 4.0 for those intending to stay the same and 3.7 for those planning to get smaller—a statistically significant difference. Also, I calculated the correlation between the operator's evaluation of success and the change in number of employees in the last five years. My reasoning was that successful businesses would be more likely to add employees or at least stay the same than would unsuccessful businesses, who would be more likely to have declined in employment. Hence, if the subjective measure of success is valid, there should be a positive association between change in employment and the success rating. Indeed, there is. The correlation is .06, small but statistically significant. Together, these tests help to establish the validity of the success question as an indicator of business success.

Returning to Rebello's thesis that retail businesses have more to gain than other businesses by supporting the community, refer to Figures 6.1 and 6.2. I divided the sample by industry classification and, for each industry, compared community support to business success. In order to display the relationship in a bar chart, I divided the support scale into four categories ranging from low to high support. Each category represents approximately 25 percent of respondents.[2] Since neither success nor Standard Industrial Classification (SIC) code varies significantly by community-size category, the comparison of SIC, success, and support will be conducted for the sample as a whole. Figure 6.1 shows that, with the exception of agricultural businesses, firms that provide more support to the community in every industry are more successful, but that the differences reach statistical significance only for wholesale, retail, and service businesses. The zero order correlation coefficents between success and the uncollapsed support variable for each SIC category reveal similar findings. The associations between the variables for retail ($r = .24$, $p < .01$), services ($r = .16$, $p < .01$), and wholesale ($r = .29$, $p < .01$) businesses are significant, and the coefficients are not significant for the other SICs except manufacturing ($r = .29$, $p < .05$). I'll return

Figure 6.1
Business Success by Community Support by Standard Industrial Classification Code

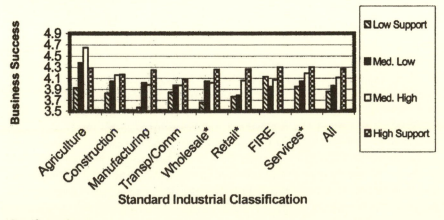

*Significant Anovas

to consideration of the support—success relationship for manufacturing enterprises below.

Rebello's thesis is supported. Retail businesses, along with service and wholesale companies, that support the community are more successful than those that do not. However, this test does not tell us which comes first, success or support. It could be that successful firms have more resources and thus are more likely to support the community, rather than community support causing greater success. Prior evidence provided in this book can be used to support both positions. In chapter 4, I demonstrated that gross sales was a strong predictor of community support. Gross sales is not the same as business success. A business can have high gross sales and even higher debts to equal a net loss—unsuccessful, by almost everyone's definition. But, it does suggest that slack resources are necessary for contributions to community causes. Presumably, successful businesses will likewise have greater slack resources at their disposal to contribute to the community. On the other hand, prior research has shown that businesses that are dependent upon sales to households, like retail and some service businesses, are more likely to see a direct payback to their business from philanthropic contributions.

In order to test for causation, we must have data from the same or comparable samples from two different time periods. If companies that support the community at time A have increased success in time B compared to time A, then we will know that support precedes success and can notch up the probability that support causes success. For now, we must be content with ambiguity about the direction of causation in this matter. Rebello's advice to retail business owners is to play it safe and assume that those who do not support the community will suffer the consequences in fewer customers and lower sales.

For the analysis shown in Figure 6.2, the involvement scale was divided into four categories as was done with the support scale.[3] We see an entirely different kind of relationship between community involvement and business success than the support—success relationship shown in Figure 6.1. In three industries—manufacturing, transportation, and FIRE—the businesses that have the highest perceived success are in the low-medium involvement category. In three of the five industries with significant differences, the operators who are most involved are not in the most successful businesses. It is difficult to discern a pattern between involvement and success. Since all relationships shown in Figure 6.2 except for wholesale businesses are nonlinear, it is not surprising that none of the correlation coefficients for success and the uncollapsed involvement variable by SIC are significant. There appears to be less predictability about the role community involvement plays in business success when examined by industry type.

Figure 6.2
Business Success by Community Involvement by Standard Industrial
Classification Code

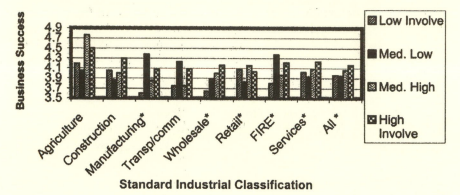

*Significant Anovas

Another tenet of the public relations variant of the enlightened self-interest rationale is that community support and involvement will increase employee retention and attraction, which, in turn, will enhance business success. This tenet was derived from numerous comments from interviewees reported elsewhere, especially in chapter 3, and prior research (e.g. Turban and Greening 1997; McElroy and Siegfried 1985). To provide an empirical test of the relationship between BSP and employee turnover, I divided the sample into the three community sizes again and used the same two BSP indices, each collapsed into four categories from high to low as before.

Figure 6.3 illustrates the relationship between employee turnover and community support by community size. Statistical tests of significance (analysis of variance) revealed that community support is not related to the amount of employee turnover experienced by businesses.[4] Nevertheless, the businesses that reported providing the highest support have the lowest turnover, except in rural communities where their turnover is second lowest. Urban and metro businesses in the medium-high category of support have the second lowest turnover. These findings are consistent with what we would expect of good business citizens, i.e., they are good places to work as well as sources of support and leadership for the community. Further, it tends to substantiate the belief that good business citizens are more successful at retaining their employees. What confounds this notion is the failure of the differences to reach statistical significance and the relatively low turnover displayed by nonsupportive rural businesses.

Once again, there is no apparent pattern to the information displayed in the bar chart of community involvement and a measure of business success/employee turnover (Figure 6.4). The differences illustrated in the

Figure 6.3
Turnover Rate by Community Support by Community Size Categories

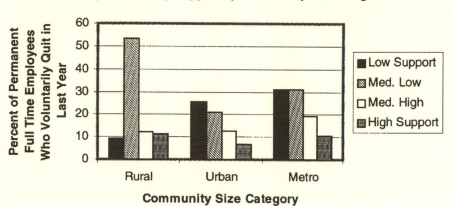

Figure 6.4
Turnover Rate by Community Involvement by Community Size Categories

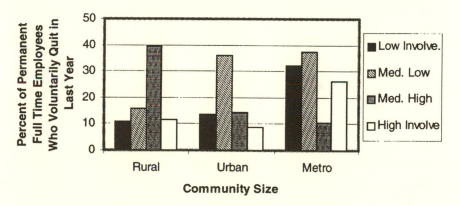

chart are not statistically significant in any of the community sizes. In rural and urban communities, business operators that report the greatest involvement in the community have the lowest or almost the lowest turnover rate. However, that is not true for metro businesses. Also, the least involved businesses do not have the highest turnover rates in any community category. Involvement clearly does not affect business success or turnover in a simple, direct fashion.

The interviewees who most frequently mentioned the importance of company profile for employee retention and attraction were the manufacturers. A comparison of turnover rate by community support and involvement for manufacturers fails to reach the level of statistical significance for involvement but is significant for support ($r = -.33$, $p < .01$). The correlation coefficient between success and support was also significant for manufacturers. Both pieces of evidence, taken together, substantiate the conclusion that for manufacturers, supporting the community is associated with business success, although involvement in the community has no impact on it.

There are a number of possible explanations for the lack of statistical significance for the support/turnover relationship in the sample as a whole. The one-year time frame for turnover may be too short. The historically low unemployment level in Iowa during the research period may have affected the relationship. Perhaps, attraction of employees, which was not measured, is more critically affected by BSP than is retention. Finally, perhaps, the kind of support and involvement measured in the telephone interviews does not capture the BSP factors that affect employment issues.

Let us turn now to an examination of community support and involvement as they affect business success for the sample as a whole. The best way to investigate the association between business success with community support and involvement is to remove the category distinctions and calculate correlations using Pearson's r. When that is done, the correlation of business success with community support is significant for all three community sizes: $r = .23$ ($p < .05$) for rural businesses, .16 ($p < .05$) for urban businesses, and .16 ($p < .05$) for metro businesses. Involvement is significantly associated with success for rural businesses only, $r = .15$ ($p < .05$). Both Iowa businesses that report providing more support for the community and rural businesses that are more involved in the community perceive that they are more successful than businesses reporting lower BSP levels.

An important consideration is the impact of business size on this relationship. Perhaps, bigger businesses, which we already know contribute more to the community, are also more successful. If so, then the relationship between success and BSP is not real and results instead from the association of both with size of business. To determine the likelihood of this possibility, I recalculated the correlations, controlling first for gross sales (log) and then for total number of employees (log). The relationships do not change appreciably with number of employees and gross sales controlled, except that for metro businesses, when gross sales is controlled, the correlation for support and success is no longer significant.

ALL TOGETHER: THE CONSEQUENCES OF BUSINESS SUPPORT FOR COMMUNITY

We can conclude from these analyses that businesses that provide more community support perceive themselves to have greater business success. This applies, regardless of their size, except for metro businesses for which the relationship of support and success is not significant for businesses of equivalent gross sales. Employment size has no affect on the relationship. We saw in Figure 6.1 that the relationship between support and success is positive in all industries, but statistically significant for retail, service, and wholesale businesses. Employee turnover is perceptibly lower for businesses providing the most community support, but not sufficiently so to meet the test for statistical significance, except for manufacturers for whom the association is significant. Community involvement does not appear to be directly related to perceived success, except for rural businesses, nor is it related to employee turnover. This evidence substantiates the public relations variant of the enlightened self-interest rationale—doing good is good for business. At the very least, the findings suggest that businesses that support their community do not experience less success than other businesses.

Over and above the ramifications of BSP to business success are their effect on the owner/manager personally. A number of psychological rewards of community service were identified by interviewees, including recognition, a sense of accomplishment, a chance to make a difference in the community's future, the opportunity for social interaction and networking, personal growth and development, and the satisfaction of improving the quality of life for one's family. On the negative side, if reports from interviewees apply more broadly, serving in a local office is fraught with hazards and costs. This is especially the case for school board positions, but planning and zoning boards and city councils can also draw considerable citizen rancor. Community service can entail stressful, frustrating, and threatening personal experiences for the business owner/manager. Other personal costs include lack of acknowledgment, burnout, less time available for recreation and family, negative career consequences, and frustration. Overall, however, business operators believed their community service was a positive personal experience. Even so, a path to popularity it is not.

The presentation in this chapter of the rewards of business social performance may leave us wondering why all businesses aren't good corporate citizens. It seems to make such good business sense to support the community. This impression is too simplistic, however, and ignores the instances when business interests and community interests do not coincide. Consider the example of the Sara Lee plant closure in New Hampton, Iowa. Losing six hundred jobs, and the property taxes paid by Sara Lee, will be devastating to the community of New Hampton. However, Sara Lee must think the move will be good for its business. Here we have a clear conflict of interest between community and business. How can Sara Lee justify the damage the loss of the company will bring to New Hampton?

Sara Lee might argue that New Hampton is not the relevant community in their rendition of the shared fate between business and community. They might point to the positive impact the move will have on the community receiving Sara Lee's New Hampton operations. And they could cite the argument, based in part on a misreading of Schumpeter's economic theory of creative destruction, that the United States as a whole will gain if the move makes Sara Lee a stronger and more efficient company. If the plant closure results in greater quality or lower costs for their baked goods, they might emphasize the benefit to the consumers throughout the United States. Sara Lee could contend that the relevant community is the nation as a whole, not the community of New Hampton. Put differently, their justification might be that New Hampton has to suffer a little pain for the greater good of us all. Further, they might argue that New Hampton will be better off in the long run without so much of its economic welfare tied to one company. New Hampton now has a great opportunity to strengthen their local economy, or more glibly, a chance to turn their lemons into lemonade.

Clearly, determining whether businesses and communities have a shared fate requires that we agree on what's good for the community, good for business, the relevant time frame, and the relevant community (the world, nation state, states, regions, incorporated municipalities or neighborhoods). There are basic assumptions of economic theory and values about economic vs. human activity that must be confronted and resolved.

Sara Lee's plant closing in New Hampton serves to illustrate that the statement, "What's good for the community is good for business," fails to capture many of the nuances of contemporary community/business tensions and challenges. The issues raised in the example result from events occurring outside the community, some of which are captured by the term "globalization." In the next chapter, I examine the challenges posed by globalization to BSP and present the strategies utilized in some communities to enhance the shared-fate rationale, address the challenges of globalization, and nurture community friendly businesses.

NOTES

1. The exact wording is "Please rate the success of your business by your own definition of success on a scale of 1 to 5 with 1 being very unsuccessful and 5 being very successful."

2. Low support = 1–2.24, low med. = 2.25–2.99, high med. = 3.0–3.74, high = 3.75–5.

3. Low involvement = 1.0–1.24, low med. = 1.25–1.49, high med. = 1.5–1.74, high = 1.75–2.0.

4. Correlations between the uncollapsed support and involvement variables with the turnover rate are also not significant.

CHAPTER 7

Molding the Conscience of Capitalism

In this chapter I take the point of view of community leaders and ask "What can be done to encourage good business citizenship?" To effectively address this matter, however, it is necessary to first return to one of the arguments against business social performance (BSP) presented in chapter 3. Edward Stendardi (1992), Clark Smith (1994a & b), S. Prakesh Sethi (1996), and others contend that conditions are so different in today's new global economy that even profitable firms are under pressure to be more profit driven and less socially responsible. Following this line of reasoning, businesses can only justify contributions to social betterment that produce short-term, measurable economic benefits. In the new global economy, they contend, philanthropy must be defended as a business opportunity.

The "new global economy" argument against BSP is so insidious and compelling that it must be examined in depth before the lessons derived from the research presented in this book can be taken seriously. Realizing that such an examination would require a lengthy side trip from the topic of BSP, I postponed it until now. I begin with an explanation of the key factors usually associated with economic globalization. After establishing a base of common meanings, I will present a critique of this position and discuss the consequences of belief in economic globalization. I argue that acceptance of the inevitability of economic globalization tends to invalidate the evidence of prior experience and research about BSP to communities. I will end the chapter, and the book, with a review of the advice provided in the literature and given by Iowa business and community leaders about nurturing businesses that share a common fate with their communities and encouraging businesses to be good citizens.

THE NEW GLOBAL ECONOMY

Cultural and economic globalization are often incorrectly conflated with each other causing confusion and misspecification. George Ritzer (1993) coined the term "McDonaldization" to express succinctly the main features of cultural globalization. McDonaldization describes a situation where no matter where one travels in the world, he or she can find a Coke, eat at McDonalds or Pizza Hut, watch *Seinfeld* on TV, listen to Madonna on the radio, and tune into world events presented in English by a CNN reporter. Thus, the first element of cultural globalization, according to Ritzer, is the worldwide penetration of Western culture—cuisine, dress, entertainment, and even the English language. In Ritzer's framework, a sinister consequence of the entry of Western popular cultural forms into a country or region is the elimination of competing indigenous forms. Eventually, there is less total global diversity in cultural forms and a corresponding loss of local control and identity.

Actually, it is simplistic to refer to this process as the dominance of Western culture in the world. Several "Western" nations feel as threatened by McDonaldization as the traditional Islamic countries do. For example, the French government decries the increasing encroachment of the English language in France and strongly denounces the growing prevalence of American popular culture in France. Similarly, regional and ethnic variations in language, food, beverages, music, etc. within the United States have been muted considerably since the 1950s, although a recent revival of local micro breweries and demonstrations of ethnic heritage are evidence that local cultural diversity remains important to people.

Cultural globalization, therefore, refers to the hegemony of primarily American corporate cultural products (e.g., Coke, Bud, McDonald's, Disney entertainment parks, TimeWarner movies, TV, books) over other regional and national cultural forms. Obviously, cultural globalization, dominated as it is by corporate entities, is related to economic globalization. Nonetheless, because there are important differences as well, I distinguish between them and focus on the latter.

Scholars who have defined what is usually meant by economic globalization (see Hirst and Thompson 1999; Gordon 1988; McMichael 1996; Gertler 1997) identify the following as its unique characteristics: At the top of the list in terms of importance is the greater mobility of capital in today's economy as compared to former times. Huge sums of capital can be invested and disinvested in currency or innovative financial instruments (hedge funds, derivatives, mutual funds) in the time it takes an electronic message to travel from computer to computer. Since capital is so fluid and can move so easily, locations are pressured to create a good business climate to encourage and retain capital investment. This equates to political stability, few regulations, low labor costs, low taxes, minimal social safety net for workers, the provision of infrastructure, and economic incentives. Further, the return on capital resulting from investment in financial transactions (e.g., currency trading, equity options, commodities trading, hedge funds) sets the benchmark by which other investments (in productive and extractive enterprises) are judged—frequently placing the latter at a disadvantage in attracting investment.

A second distinguishing feature of economic globalization is the emergence of transnational corporations (TNCs) possessing qualitatively different mechanisms of coordination and control than those used by national and international corporations of previous times. Electronic communications, but also innovative management systems, allow TNCs to manage far-flung economic enterprises efficiently, in a way not available before. In the name of economic rationality, the TNCs have no allegiance to a mother country. It is true that they possess power and financial resources that surpass what most nation-states can marshal, but that is nothing new. Economic entities such as the Hudson Bay Company, the Rothschild banking enterprise of 19th century Europe, and railroad trusts like that of the Vanderbilts in 19th century United States commanded vast economic empires, more powerful than most nations of their day. Therefore, it would be a mistake to consider the great power of some businesses in the current economy a defining feature.

Facilitating the hypermobility of capital and the enhanced mechanisms of organizational coordination are the revolution in information technology and the ideological conversion of policy makers to an economic principle called "comparative advantage." Computers, the Internet, fax technology, and satellite communication systems make it possible to move capital quickly and decentralize production processes worldwide while maintaining control and coordinating efficiencies from corporate headquarters. However, the technological ability to move capital quickly or decentralize production processes around the world does not mean that it is financially feasible or politically expedient to do so. For that to occur, there has to be an agreed-upon, secure currency exchange system, laws and regulations that advantage capital over other economic resources and financial investments over production investments, political entities that guarantee contract compliance, and political stability. The motivation to create this political and social infrastructure for the global economy is prompted by belief in the economic theory of comparative advantage.

The English economist David Ricardo is usually cited as an early exponent of the set of propositions known as the principle of comparative advantage. He posited that investment capital should and will flow to the products or resources that provide the greatest return. The nature of the most lucrative investments will vary by nation and region. Therefore, it is in the best interests of people in a particular geographic area to focus on those economic activities that net the greatest return to capital, export the surplus production of those items, and import everything else. Put differently, nations should concentrate their resources on the production of those items that represent their economic "comparative advantage" over other nations and regions. By producing more than is needed to accommodate the local market, economies of scale will be realized, making production even more efficient—and profitable. The necessities and desires of life that are no longer produced locally, because resources are devoted to the production of the export commodity, can be imported from places where their production is most economically advantageous. Ricardo envisioned that, through regional economic specialization, products and resources would be made available to world customers in the most economically efficient manner possible, returns to capital would be maximized, and all would enjoy a higher standard of living as a result.

According to the principle of comparative advantage, the Japanese would be better served if they concentrated their resources on the production of high tech, value-added items like cell phones and machine tools instead of rice farming. (Although prior to World War II they were rather forcibly advised to concentrate on rice farming and leave industrial products to the "industrialized" nations.) Certain places in Indonesia and Louisiana are better suited economically for rice cultivation since land is cheaper in those locations and large tracts of it can be placed under cultivation. This allows Louisiana rice farmers to use machinery instead of the relatively expensive labor present in both the U.S. and Japan. Since Indonesian labor costs are cheaper than Japanese labor costs, even labor-intensive cultivation on small tracts of land is more economically efficient in Indonesia than cultivation in Japan. Therefore, to realize the greatest economic advantage and the greatest good for all, the Japanese should import their rice from Louisiana and export cell phones and machine tools in exchange.

Proponents of the principle of comparative advantage claim that the Japanese government is irrational in stubbornly protecting national rice cultivation and inconsiderate of Japanese consumers who could possibly buy Louisiana rice cheaper than Japanese rice and then have money left over to improve their quality of life by upgrading their cell phones. The theory of comparative advantage is the philosophical justification that legitimizes World Bank and the International Monetary Fund pressure on nations to specialize in coffee production for export instead of yams and cassava for local consumption or cell phone production instead of rice cultivation, to create a business-friendly climate, and to open home markets to international competition.

Philip McMichael (1996) argues that public policy conversion to the principles of comparative advantage is a fairly recent phenomenon. The economic policies based on the principle of comparative advantage contrast sharply with what he calls the development project that characterized economic policy for the thirty years immediately following World War

Two. At that time, the United States and its allies used economic policy to forestall the hyperinflation and economic devastation that occurred in Europe after World War I—a situation implicated as a cause of World War II—and to curb the spread of Communism in the Third World. The strategy entailed establishing the World Bank and the International Monetary Fund and furnishing grants and loans to nations to build their human, social, financial, and physical infrastructure for economic development. It was believed that national development, constructing schools, hospitals, roads, dams, a banking system, among other things, would eventually improve the quality of people's lives, promote political stability, and discourage the spread of Communism. According to McMichael, the economic stagnation and inflation of the 1970s led to replacement of the development project with the globalization project. This new policy orientation admonishes nations to specialize economically and make themselves attractive in the global market as the path to an improved standard of life for their citizens.

Associated with economic globalization and the theory of comparative advantage is the specialization of workers and communities worldwide. Special skills are required of workers who are able to compete effectively in the new global economy. According to Robert Reich in his book *The Work of Nations* (1992), the most skilled workers are the symbolic analysts, those workers able to effectively create and manipulate symbols—numbers, computer programs, financial instruments, and words. These workers will be richly rewarded in the global economy. Correspondingly, workers without these skills will not provide the labor value most desired by companies and will face lower wages and heightened job insecurity. In this schema, if the workers in the low-paying jobs had just gone to college, majored in something useful like engineering or accounting, made the right contacts, and kept their skills current, they wouldn't be in the deplorable position they're in now. Their unfortunate lot is of their own making—and not due to national policies that discourage public investment in human capital or to companies moving operations to low-wage countries and rural areas, busting unions, and establishing increasingly "winner take all" wage structures.

In a similar vein, Rosabeth Moss Kanter (1995) calls the fortunate members of the new labor force "cosmopolitans." She describes them as being rich in the three Cs: concepts, competence, and contacts. The term "cosmopolitans" was chosen to emphasize the critical importance of regular interaction between the new global elite workers in a specific urban geographic location. For Kanter, there are three kinds of places specializing in elite economic activities: the Silicon Valleys, where thinkers create new ideas with money-making potential; places like Cleveland and Spartanburg, North Carolina, with the technical know-how and infrastructure to make things from ideas; and trading and financial centers like New York and Miami.

Saskia Sassen (1991, 1998) takes a more global view of this phenomenon in her books about "global cities." Accordingly, the centers of economic activity in the new global economy are located in only a handful of truly international cities: London, New York, Tokyo, Hong Kong, and Paris, among them. These locations contain the skilled people, the diverse, stimulating culture, and the social, financial, and political infrastructure that create the synergy for new ideas and the mix of expertise necessary for turning ideas into economic actualities. She contends that global cities attract and support people with complementary specialties who then become the engines of economic value and efficiencies. Below the global cities, in Sassen's framework, are cities that act as centers of regional economic activity like Kansas City, Nagasaki, and Liverpool. The rest of the world is hinterland, either supplying raw materials and cheap labor or providing repositories for the externalities of global city economic activity like land fills and prisons.

Economic globalization, therefore, refers to an economy with extreme fluidity and mobility of capital, controlled by huge transnational companies with few ties or allegiance to any nation, spawned by a revolution in information technology and management systems, and supported by an international social and political infrastructure that is legitimated by the economic principle of comparative advantage. This theory postulates that the standard of living of all will benefit with regional and national economic specialization. Parallel phenomena are the evolution of an elite class of symbolic analysts, whose expertise, interactions, and creativity drives the new economy, and the emergence of locational centers of economic activity, specializing either by scope of economic activity (Sassen's global and regional cities) or type of economic activity (Kanter's idea, craft, or trade centers).

One end-product of economic globalization is heightened economic interdependence between far-distant locations. Another, potentially more frightening, outcome is the economic dependence of locations (nations and communities) on corporations that possess no allegiance to place. In the paradigm of the new global economy, businesses are the transcendent institution, independent of the welfare of any particular community. Hence, the shared-fate rationale of BSP is largely irrelevant. Further, the balance of power between communities and businesses is so one-sided in favor of businesses that the social contract stipulating the social responsibility of businesses is unenforceable. At the same time, the quality of life and survival of communities is increasingly dependent upon the booms and busts of the tightly linked global economy. In following the principle of comparative advantage, communities have staked their welfare on the success or failure of a small number of industries like coffee production, furniture manufacturing, or computer software. In a sense, they are gambling on the continued economic viability of one or a few specialties.

Since locations import what they don't specialize in, they have an additional dependence on the economic and political vicissitudes of other parts of the world. To illustrate, if Japan specializes in high tech products and services and leaves rice cultivation to Louisiana and Indonesia, not only is its economy and quality of life affected by the world market for high technology products, but it is also subject to the political, economic, and environmental circumstances in the locations growing rice. Suppose the rice crop in Louisiana is wiped out by floods one year. The Japanese will have no choice but to pay the inflated price the Indonesian rice brokers can then demand. Of course, the Japanese could substitute wheat and corn products for rice, or different kinds of rice for their preferred variety. Nevertheless, the choice between an inflated price for a dietary staple or selecting a less palatable substitute would be forced upon them, and, in either case, they remain vulnerable to the vagaries of distant places and powerful TNC brokers.

THE MYTH OF THE NEW GLOBAL ECONOMY

The general acceptance of the reality of economic globalization among scholars, especially American scholars, is bewildering. There is no shortage of criticisms of the consequences of economic globalization and the policies that support economic globalization, but almost universal acceptance of its existence. This leads to the general impression that globalization is a scientific fact, like the force of gravity. However, a few scholars, mostly Europeans, offer a powerful critique of the claim that today's global economy is qualitatively different from previous economies. British scholars Paul Hirst and Grahame Thompson (1999) use historical data to examine the key propositions of the new global economy. They assert that the globalization argument, as espoused by extreme globalists like Riech (1992) and Ohmae (1990), is based on a fuzzy conceptualization of what globalization means, inappropriately generalizes from the financial sector to all sectors of the economy, and depends on information that extends no further back in history than World War II.

To ascertain whether the capital invested in productive enterprises has been as mobile as financial investments, Hirst and Thompson (1999) and another scholar David Gordon (1988), each independently analyze international trade patterns dating back to the middle 1850s. They also investigate the nature of, and changes in, foreign direct investment (investment made by businesses) in production over this extended period of time. With this broader historical perspective, both sets of scholars conclude that international trade was more open prior to 1914 than at any time since then, as measured by the ratio of international trade and capital flows to gross domestic product. Gordon concludes that the increase in the percent of production occurring in less developed countries (LDCs) since 1980 has simply allowed them to recoup the losses in production that they suffered from 1948 to 1966.

Hirst and Thompson (1999) add that most international trade is between the developed (G7) nations of Europe, North America, and Japan, and most foreign direct investment is within those countries. The majority of the foreign direct investment outside the G7 countries consists of investment in a few LDCs—the so-called newly industrialized countries like South Korea and Taiwan, and investment in countries possessing huge local markets. Examples of the latter situation would be foreign direct investment in India, China, and Brazil, aimed at producing for local consumption not for international trade. Such LDCs as Uganda, Afghanistan, and Peru remain on the periphery of world trade and investment, a situation unchanged in the putative new global economy.

If Hirst and Thompson and Gordon are correct, how can we account for the decline in employment in the manufacturing sector in the United States? If U.S. firms are not transferring production processes to cheap-labor third-world countries, why the precipitous decline in manufacturing employment since the 1950s? These authors admit that some manufacturing jobs have been exported, but they claim that the majority of the decline results from increases in manufacturing productivity in the United States and changes in consumption patterns. Some support for their position is furnished by Arthur Alderson in his analysis of deindustrialization in the developed countries of the world (1999). He reports that the decline in manufacturing jobs is associated with the outflow of direct investment. However, using a technique known as "counterfactual history," he adds that "a significant reduction in the percentage of the labor force in manufacturing in the advanced industrial societies was practically unavoidable, as all the OECD countries had reached maturity by the close of the 1960s. Owing to this economic success, deindustrialization in the post-1970 period would have been considerable even if the performance of manufacturing had been stronger or the upswings in direct investment and southern imports had not occurred." (p. 718)

Another defining feature of economic globalization is the evolution of new footloose transnational corporations possessing superior management mechanisms of control and coordination. According to the economic globalization paradigm, TNCs are truly global citizens that do not identify with any nation. Hirst and Thompson (1999) use data from the annual reports of the world's largest corporations to ascertain whether they are truly devoid of economic bias toward their mother country. The researchers note the difficulties of cross-cultural comparisons as companies report the same activities differently within the same country, and legal reporting procedures can vary considerably from country to country. Nevertheless, analyses of the location of assets, sales, and profit generation leads them to conclude, "Multinational corporations still rely on their home base as the centre for their economic activities, despite all the speculation about globalization. From these results we should be reasonably confident that, in the aggregate, international companies are still predominantly multinational corporations (with a clear home base to their operations) and not TNCs (which represent footloose stateless companies. . . .)" (p. 84). It is true that there is a trend toward decentralizing operations, but Gordon points out that the trend started in the 1930s and has not qualitatively changed in the last twenty years. In other words, although these companies operate in international markets, they remain oriented toward their mother country in terms of sales, assets, and as the locus of innovation and leadership.

Meric Gertler (1997), a Canadian researcher, provides additional evidence that companies are oriented toward their mother countries even in their international operations. His research also directly challenges the claim that investments in production (manufacturing) are as mobile as transactions in financial investments. Gertler studied the advanced machinery technology industry in Ontario. He discovered that this industry relies on socially constructed definitions of technology, labor relations, and regulations, such that economic transactions within the same culture are more efficient regardless of the physical distance between consumer and producer. For example, a German manufacturing firm operating in Ontario will find it more economically expedient to use machine tools made by German companies and supported by German technical consultants than to purchase Canadian or American ones, even though the latter are in closer proximity. This effect, Gertler concludes, is mitigated somewhat, but still exists, for large multisite and multinational consumers who possess sufficient in-organization expertise and resources to address problems associated with the installation, customizing, and maintenance of production technology. Additionally, Gertler points to a couple of the newest, most popular innovations in production management—the just-in-time system of inventory control and customized manufacturing. In as much as both innovations require close spatial clustering of producers and suppliers, they demonstrate that at least a few contemporary management innovations discourage decentralizing production operations.

Jefferson Cowie in *Capital Moves: RCA's Seventy-Year Quest for Cheap Labor* (1999) makes a different case against the proposition that TNCs are uniquely different than the multinational companies of prior days. In an excellent historical examination of RCA, Cowie confirms that at least one large company moved operations repeatedly in its history to escape gradual increases in labor costs and labor organizations. RCA's first plant was in Camden, New Jersey, where thousands of largely female immigrant laborers were employed at low wages. In the 1940s, due to the escalation of labor costs in Camden, RCA opened a plant in Bloomington, Indiana. The area had a high level of unemployment and offered rural women with a "good work ethic" as workers. By the 1960s the situation in Bloomington had changed. Workers were no longer desperate for any job and organized to secure better pay and benefits. This was RCA's cue to move its assembly operations to Memphis where they could hire African Americans at lower wages. Although the Memphis move was never completely implemented, Bloomington workers and the community were forewarned of the fragility of RCA's commitment to them. RCA's last move (thus far) has been to Ciudad Juarez in Mexico in search of docile, low-cost labor. The Memphis and Bloomington facilities are now closed.

Summing up his research, Cowie declares, "Understanding capital migration to Mexico in the context of a lengthy history of plant locations and relocations clearly challenges the view that the globalization of capital signals a radical departure from previous systems of labor control" (p. 179). Furthermore, RCA historically demanded concessions and infrastructure from local taxpayers at each location as a condition of moving operations there. Cowie quotes E.E. Shumaker, president of the RCA-Victor Company, in a 1929 speech to the Camden Chamber of Commerce: "The industry I represent can only grow if we can build cheaper here than elsewhere. That means taxes must be low. It means we must have a Delaware River port and transportation advantages" (p. 16). Perhaps companies are not so different after all in the new global economy.

In light of their own and other's analyses of the key features of economic globalization, Hirst and Thompson (1999) announce that "Globalization as conceived by most extreme analysts is a myth." They and other critics of the fact of economic globalization do not deny that international trade has increased since 1950 and that some corporate entities are inordinately powerful. Nor do they dispute that nation-states feel constrained by global economic actors in formulating national strategy. Their argument is that the situation is nothing new. However, they continue, belief in economic globalization paralyzes national radical economic reform and cripples the labor movement in the United States. Under the new global economy rubric, less-developed countries are forced to abandon investment in social and human infrastructure in lieu of finding their comparative economic advantage in the world market. The belief legitimates the power of megacorporations over place-based entities, whether nations or communities, and justifies denying noneconomic claims on business resources, such as legal, ethical, and discretionary social responsibilities.

IMPLICATIONS FOR BUSINESS RESPONSIBILITY TO COMMUNITIES

Hirst and Thompson (1999) and Gordon (1988) argue that the danger in accepting the extreme version of economic globalization is that the belief itself bestows more power on multinational corporations than their economic position warrants. Important though that outcome is, I suggest that there are two less-obvious results pertinent to business social performance and community welfare. For one, if we are convinced that the current economy is qualitatively different from preceding ones, then we must assume that the experiential and research knowledge gathered in the old economy probably does not apply in this new situation. Doubts about the knowledge base of past practices and government policies may preclude using them, or doubts may be sufficient to make formerly successful practices ineffective.

As a case in point, past procedures for involving CEOs in Pikeville haven't worked very well for the CEO who jets to his "real home" every weekend. Certainly, modern technology makes his long commute possible. Possibly, the company board appointed him CEO because they wanted someone who would focus narrowly on internal business operations and not "waste" time and energy on external community relations. But is the failure to connect the commuting CEO to the community the result of the new global economy? Should community leaders scrap the community-building strategies that rely on building relationships and promoting a sense of shared fate between business leaders and the community? Are these "old fashioned" techniques outdated in the new lean and mean global economy? The evidence from the literature and that presented in this book suggests that the answers to these questions are "unknown," "no," and "no." However, the new global economy paradigm causes people to have less confidence in these "old practices," leaving them feeling powerless to influence business social performance. Globalization has become the catchall explanation for failures to elicit community commitment from business operators, causing premature closure of analysis of the situation and only a cursory consideration of alternative explanations.

Suppose economic globalization is overstated. How would that change our impression of the events attributed to globalization? The uninvolved Pikeville CEO might simply be the kind of person who would not get involved in affairs of the community under any circumstances. The Sara Lee plant closing in New Hampton, Iowa, would be just another example of poor citizenship by global capitalists, like RCA's century-long search for cheap docile labor and a friendly business climate, rather than an illustration of the new global economy. The devastation to New Hampton would be the same with either explanation, but recognizing that it is a familiar situation suggests that there might also be tried and proven solutions or alternatives.

Suppose the reason for the consolidation of banks and utility companies evident today is the altered regulatory climate rather than the new global economy. Changed regulations may have resulted from fears or beliefs about globalization, or the inordinate power of the financial industry in the political affairs of the United States or any number of related factors. Still the causal link between the consolidation of the financial and utility industries and new global economy is indirect at best. Again, posing a different explanation for the phenomena places it within a familiar context and suggests that there may be effective historical remedies available for the problems associated with consolidation. Believing that the cause is economic globalization too often translates to mean that previous knowledge does not apply to the new situation. Hence, the paralysis predicted by Hirst and Thompson (1999).

A second manifestation of the belief in economic globalization pertinent to our investigation of BSP is that it rivets our attention on transnational corporations even more than when we saw them as "mere" multinational corporations. As I demonstrated in the first chapter, the overwhelming majority of economic actors are small businesses. In the new global economy, if considered at all, they are viewed as totally dependent upon the economic engine of large companies. Bennett Harrison (1994) attempts to disabuse us of the notion that small businesses are consequential players in the new economy. He maintains that they are dependent upon large businesses who are their customers, their source of natural resources, or their suppliers. Big businesses are preferenced in the political and regulatory arenas over small businesses. Although there is the common wisdom that small businesses are more innovative and flexible than big businesses, Harrison claims that they simply don't have the resources or personnel to develop ideas into products or respond quickly to market changes. The rise in small business employment experienced in the last twenty years, he argues, is due to the practice of big businesses outsourcing noncore functions to lower-wage small businesses. It is not an indication of their superior performance in the new global economy. The obsession with TNCs leads policy makers and communities to ignore, or consider irrelevant in the new global economy, the research base that highlights the important role small businesses can play in improving the quality of life in communities.

If we look outside the new global economy paradigm where TNCs dominate, we find another view of the role of small businesses in the contemporary economy. Michael Piore and Charles Sable brought the small business districts of Northern Italy to world attention in their 1984 book *The Second Industrial Divide: Possibilities for Prosperity*. These small firms are loosely organized in networks that contain a diverse range of skills and contacts related to garment manufacturing. They pool their resources and are able to effectively compete against large businesses in this cutthroat industry. Other small business districts in Germany, Denmark, Japan, Taiwan, and Italy are described in books by Grabher (1993), Forsgren et al. (1995), and Perry (1999). According to these scholars, small businesses can work together to form a strong viable economic entity that is not solely an appendage of big businesses. Indeed, the international Organization for Economic Co-Operation and Development encourages countries to utilize the "cluster approach" (their term for networking) as the keystone strategy for economic development and to spur industrial innovation and success (1999).

Closer to home, a network of small businesses has evolved in the Ohio Appalachian Region nurtured by a development organization called ACEnet (Appalachian Center for Economic Networks). Director June Holley commented in a 1997 article by David Riggle, "We've found that creating healthy, locally owned small businesses can be a great thing for communities, especially if the businesses are willing to train and hire people who are unemployed and use local resources wisely" (p. 28). ACEnet builds networks of firms within a community that support each other and share resources, staff, equipment, and ideas. It provides assistance with business plans, tax issues, marketing, and technology, and coordinates a revolving microloan fund. By 1997, forty businesses were selling products in ACEnet's kitchen incubator store, twenty were using the processing facility, and one hundred businesses had utilized the center's advisory services and library.

Another community developer, Walter de Silva in Alberta, Canada, helped establish a different kind of business network. Starting with the town of Lloydminster, De Silva and others built a supply and service replacement network throughout the northeast portion of Alberta.[1] Information from businesses operating in the area is gathered to ascertain the products and services they sell, what resources, supplies and services they use, the source and cost of those inputs, and what waste material results from their operations. Local suppliers are then linked to local customers. When no local supplier exists and the demand is sufficient, other local businesses are encouraged to offer the product/service, or it is viewed as a business opportunity for a local business start-up. Reverse market shows where high-volume buyers get together with suppliers to exchange information are another mechanism to link local buyers and sellers. Staff look for ways that business waste products can generate economic advantage, such as establishing business chains where the waste products from one business becomes the input for another business. The business network is coordinated by staff, whose salaries are paid by the network businesses and who are assisted by members of a local high school computer clubs.

De Silva and his colleagues apparently do not believe in the principle of comparative advantage. The import replacement program in Alberta partially decouples local businesses from the vagaries of economic actors in distant parts of the world. Policy makers in Alberta encourage import substitution as a community-building strategy, because when a business purchases its supplies and services locally, it helps to enrich other local businesses that hire local employees, pay local taxes, and contribute to the community. These additional employees send their kids to the local school and purchase groceries at the local store. The local grocery store and the school district have more employees and money available to purchase local supplies and services. In this way, dollars recirculate in the local economy, contributing additional value to the community. Also, the process generates economic diversity as people with various skills and backgrounds are able to find job opportunities in the local area. Within the first year of the Lloydminster import replacement program, over $600,000 of contracts were negotiated among twenty-two businesses (Buchanan and Murray 1995). The local economic gain in that year from the retained and recirculated dollars was estimated at $1.5 million.

The enthusiasm for small business networks is partially based on prior research that concludes that local economies built on many small businesses, instead of one or two large companies, are more robust and less subject to boom-and-bust economic cycles. They are associated with greater civic involvement and greater income equality among residents. An early study by C. Wright Mills and Melvin Ulmer (1946) spurred by Congress's interest in the consequences of industry concentration found that the level of well being was higher in small business cities than those dominated by one or two large businesses. Providing a contemporary test of the Mills and Ulmer findings, Charles Tolbert, Thomas Lyson, and Michael Irwin (1998) examined census data from 3000 U.S. counties. They concluded that counties with greater numbers of small manufacturing companies, retail firms, and family farms had enhanced general socioeconomic welfare as compared to those with large manufacturers, fewer retail firms, and fewer family farms.

Gary Green (1994), however, cautions us that the benefits to communities from small businesses may be less than expected. Based on findings from his study of more than 1700 small businesses in rural Georgia counties, he supports Harrison's conclusions that small businesses as a whole are less innovative than medium and large companies and that they are not much different from medium-sized firms in the amount of goods and services they purchase from other local businesses. Moreover, they are less likely to offer health care and retirement benefits to employees than larger businesses—a component of community welfare that should not be underestimated. Even so, Green advises communities to encourage small-business formation and to work to mitigate these potential drawbacks by providing the businesses with assistance in business planning, implementing new technology, and networking together so that they can offer more lucrative employee benefits.

By diverting attention from small businesses, the new global economy paradigm disempowers communities as they attempt to improve their wellbeing and encourage good business citizenship. Utilizing advice that focuses on the economic advantage of big businesses, many communities (and states) employ a quixotic development strategy aimed at luring large businesses to town. Unfortunately, even the winners in industrial recruitment strategies may end up losers. Such is the outcome for Bloomington, Indiana, and New Hampton, Iowa. Both were successful in the game of industrial recruitment when they managed to land the RCA plant and Sara

Lee plant, respectively. As they have also discovered, the favor of relocating, large businesses may be fickle and fleeting.

MOLDING THE CONSCIENCE OF CAPITALISTS

If we overcome the crippling malaise caused by belief in economic globalization and look at the evidence presented in the literature and the research presented in this book, we find three general approaches to increasing business social performance in communities. The first approach involves designing public policies that favor the businesses that are most amenable to the social-contract and shared-fate rationales and, therefore, more likely to be loyal community citizens. Included here are techniques designed to support good business citizenship and generate a diverse local economy of small businesses. My elaboration is not intended to be exhaustive but, instead, to be indicative of the wide array of possibilities for action available to promote BSP. For each of the three general approaches, I list here the specific techniques and provide a more detailed description of the techniques following the overview.

Public policies and programs to create and nurture good business citizens:

1. State economic development policies that favor good business citizens
2. Stipulations in state corporate charters about expectations for BSP
3. Business retention and expansion programs
4. Access to capital at reasonable rates for small businesses
   - State economic development funds
   - Local banks and other lenders
   - Revolving loan funds
   - Community foundations
5. Import replacement programs
   - Supplier chains
   - Energy conservation programs
   - Local food systems
6. Local entrepreneurship
   - Infrastructure
   - Youth programs

The next approach pertains to creating a social environment in which business operators will be likely to provide support for the community. This requires building relationships, a sense of shared identity, and norms of collective action and reciprocity within the community or, in other words, generating community social capital.

To increase social capital:

1. Leadership programs
2. Inclusive and community-oriented business and service clubs
3. A reputation for success
4. Youth community involvement
5. Study circles

The last approach contains those strategies intended to motivate the business owner or manager as an individual to get involved and support the community.

Inducements for the top decision maker:

1. Business success
   - Networking with other businesses
   - Consumer sanctions
   - Employee morale, attraction, and retention
2. Personal psychological rewards
3. Gain for family and friends
4. The principles of effective volunteer recruitment and retention

POLICIES AND PROGRAMS TO CREATE AND NURTURE GOOD BUSINESS CITIZENS

When I asked James Black, mayor of Gatlin City what advice he'd give other communities that wanted to create a mutually supportive business-community relationship, he responded by referring to state economic development policies. He said,

I think the disengagement of some businesses is the result of failure on the state's part. We spend money on economic development in the wrong place. We chase industry and new businesses. We could put that money into existing local businesses. Our emphasis on businesses ought to be to support businesses that will provide good jobs for our children and support the community.

Black alerts us to the fact that state policies play an important role in determining the kind of businesses that populate local communities. State governments have at their disposal corporate chartering, business incentive, business assistance, and business regulation mechanisms that influence local economic activity. They set the overall philosophy and context of economic and development policies that determine what local governments can do.

State policies can favor businesses with a record of good citizenship. In a prior section, I discussed at length the control that state governments possess over corporations in their chartering capacity. In that regard, they have ultimate power to grant "life" to corporations or to "kill" them for irresponsibility. Until modern times, one condition for receiving and retaining a corporate charter was service to the public good in ways over and above economic responsibilities. States could reassert their control over corporations by reintroducing the expectation of business social performance into corporate chartering regulations.

Obviously, this would require concerted efforts among states, prompted by a groundswell of public support, to facilitate their reassertion of control over corporations. Opponents of this approach would no doubt argue that tampering with corporate charter regulations is tantamount to threatening civilization as we know it. Given the current political climate, a more achievable, albeit still very ambitious, goal might be to require corporations, as part of their charter obligations, to conduct and submit regular audits of their social performance.

Short of using their ultimate weapon, states can take less controversial steps to enhance BSP. Through their economic development functions, they can help communities determine the kinds of businesses and development strategies that match local needs, and they can encourage them to invest their public resources accordingly. I have worked with local community leaders who express anger at state officials who will not reveal the identity of a business (at the business's request) that is considering locating in their community. Community leaders complain that when they learn the name of the company at the last minute, they often must come up with an incentive package with neither time for community input nor for adequate analysis of the background of the company and the costs and benefits of the venture to the community. Not only does this handicap communities in their negotiations with relocating businesses, but it also discourages them from charting and executing a development program tailored for their own needs and values. State governments also influence the economy of local communities in that they provide development expertise and training to local leaders. Hence, if their experts encourage industrial recruitment over retention and expansion programs, if they emphasize programs based on the principle of comparative advantage and denigrate local business networks, then communities will likely lean their policies in the favored directions.

Shifting now from state to community strategies to foster good business citizenship, Gatlin City minister Lamont Blanchard informed me that the best approach to improving business social performance is for communities to "concentrate resources on supporting local business that will have loyalty to the community." The findings from the Iowa telephone data challenge us to move beyond quick conclusions about the BSP of local vs. non local businesses to consideration of factors more directly linked to BSP such as the values of top management, the prosperity of the business, where the owner lives, and whether the top decision maker is the owner or a manager. The key, therefore, is to design programs and invest public resources in businesses that will be or are good citizens. The test should be behavior based on belief in the statement "What's good for the community is good for business." If their record indicates that a business does not believe in the statement, then it probably is not worthy of public support.

What are some initiatives that communities can implement to nurture and support businesses that currently are or are inclined to be good citizens? George Morse from the University of Minnesota Extension and Tom Ilvento from University of Delaware Extension have each worked to develop nationally recognized "business retention and expansion" (BR&E) programs. Through BR&E programs, community leaders learn how to connect with local business operators and develop the support system to facilitate their success. Additionally, BR&E is a format for dialogue between business operators and other community residents. It can help establish common ground and the recognition of the mutuality of interests between businesses and community.

A necessary ingredient for healthy local capitalism is access to capital at reasonable rates. With consolidation in the banking industry, most communities have lost local banks and face the possibility of leaner and meaner lenders. Community leaders in both Caizan and Gatlin City were so convinced of the importance of a local bank to community welfare that when local banks were lost through consolidation, they successfully encouraged the start up of new locally owned banks in their communities. Within the last three years, two new locally owned banks have started doing business in Gatlin City, and one has opened in the smaller Caizan.

The town of Aurura, Nebraska, illustrates another way to provide capital to designated businesses and for other quality of life projects like recreation facilities, college scholarships, and adult education. Aurura has its own community foundation established with money from local benefactors who choose to invest in or bequeath to Aurura community improvement. The foundation furnishes some funds for new business ventures and business expansions as well as for small-business assistance initiatives. Some communities and development organizations, such as ACEnet, support small business ventures by initiating and coordinating revolving loan funds. Micro-loan revolving funds have received acclaim in international development circles for their success in aiding economically disadvantaged people become business owners.

Import substitution programs, like that developed by DeSilva in Alberta, are another effective tool to nurture local capitalism. I include in this category energy conservation programs and food systems programs. An example of a successful community wide energy conservation program is Sioux Center, Iowa's (a town of about 5,000 people), program coordinated by Ron Horstman. Sioux Center has its own locally owned public utility.

They have cut the price of energy to consumers three times since 1980 through their conservation programs. As a result, it now costs less to run a business in town since the energy required for facilities and processing is lower. Home ownership is cheaper because utilities cost less. The money saved on utilities can be spent on a more expensive home, or in local retail stores. All, residents and businesses alike, enjoy the additional public revenue available for betterment projects or tax reductions realized from the lower cost of heating, cooling, and providing electricity for public buildings and schools. Furthermore, the conservation program provides business for local entrepreneurs engaged in energy conservation such as energy auditors and insulation contractors.

Local food systems programs tie local food producers to local consumers through farmers' markets, community-supported agriculture programs, and "buy local" food initiatives in schools, hospitals, and restaurants. The small farmers who benefit financially from direct marketing to local consumers are more likely to support the community than large corporate agriculture operations, use local suppliers and service providers, and comprise a larger population base for local schools, retailers, and churches.

Another approach to developing a strong base of local capitalism is to provide the infrastructure for local entrepreneurs. The relationship of entrepreneurship to business social performance is based on the assumption that local residents with presumably some commitment to their community will maintain that commitment once they become business owners. It follows then that efforts to encourage local start ups and aid in their success should increase the ranks of business owners with a commitment to the community.

The key to the success of ACEnet's entrepreneurs is the business assistance, cost sharing, idea generating, and personal support aspects of the network. Experienced businesspeople and staff help new operators generate business plans, assist with marketing strategies, provide tax advice, and so on. Business and community leaders in Atlantic, Iowa, sponsor entrepreneurship classes taught by a business consultant from a neighboring community college. The instructor provides consultation to students beyond the class and establishes a support group of class members who continue to meet and share ideas after the class is completed.

A promising avenue for encouraging entrepreneurship is to work with local youth to motivate them to consider entrepreneurial careers. Junior Achievement has traditionally sponsored school programs with this goal in mind. A recent initiative in Iowa, funded by The Papajohn Center for Entrepreneurship, involves junior high students in a summer residential camp, the objective of which is to encourage the skills and values of entrepreneurship early in people's lives.

Pikeville business leader Al Matsumoto captured the theme of this approach to increasing business social performance when he said, "There is no good way to prevent consolidation and where the CEO chooses to live. Emphasis needs to be placed on supporting new start-up businesses and small businesses that are still locally owned."

THE SOCIAL CAPITAL CONTEXT

Social capital consists of relationships, trust, norms of reciprocity, shared values, and collective identity. The Floras contend that it is the glue that pulls together other community resources and encourages community members to work together for the common good. Social capital, when accompanied by effective monitoring and sanctioning mechanisms, can discourage free riders and, in that way, stimulate people to work for public goods such as community betterment. Like other members of the community, business owners and managers are influenced by the social context that encourages or discourages working together.

As I indicated in chapter 5, social capital is not an automatic recipe for collective efforts for the public good. Without shared values and a sense of common identity, social capital can lead to solidarity within multiple small groups who constantly feud with each other. Even when all the components of social capital are in place, it can facilitate stagnation and stymie personal freedom. Social capital is a tool whose effective utilization for community betterment depends upon the context in which it is developed and used.

Previously in the book, I summarized the techniques employed by Iowa business and community leaders to build relationships between business and community leaders, to create and transmit shared values about community support, and to sanction nonsupportive businesses. The significance of community culture to BSP was affirmed in the analyses of the Iowa data. Although there were differences by size of community, overall business operators who describe their communities as possessing high levels of collective action (i.e., willingness to work together for the common good) express greater commitment to the community and in turn provide more support for the community. Similarly, those business operators most likely to be receptive to the values and norms of the resident business population (i.e., they identified networking and cooperative relationships with other businesses as important strategies for business success) reported higher commitment to the community.

Strategies to increase BSP derived from this knowledge base consist of techniques to build relationships, generate shared values and norms of reciprocity, and discourage free riders. Residents of Caizan and Gatlin City credited community-sponsored leadership classes with helping people get to know each other, learn about their community, develop leadership skills, and establish a pattern of working together. The leadership programs that are most effective in establishing relationships of the kind that can be utilized for community betterment are multisession formats spanning several months that recruit a diverse range of citizens. There are numerous organizations available to assist communities with leadership training. Consultants from universities, colleges, and community colleges; university extension programs; and state economic development departments are but a few of the available resources.

Interviewees also emphasized the importance of business and service clubs as catalysts for relationship building and values transmission. Several interviewees noted the critical role the Chamber of Commerce plays in relationship building and setting the tone for the business-community interaction. Max Oringer, who is a community leader in Caizan and has lived in several other communities, declared, "Communities where I've seen really strong business support for the community are places with strong Chambers that bring businesses together and develop team spirit among the business people themselves."

It helps to have skilled professional staff running the chamber. As Jill Slaughter, business leader from Manasis, advised,

Invest in a good Chamber head. Don't try to get by with volunteers. The head must be someone who is respected in the community and by business leaders—someone who is gifted. He or she won't be cheap, but it will be well worth the cost.

Effective community business links are facilitated when the Chamber moves away from traditional thinking about membership to be more inclusive of diverse businesses and community residents. Alice Canty, who owns a beauty shop in Socksberg, recounted her experience with the Socksberg Chamber.

Before the new Chamber head, I was never invited to join the Chamber. The reason was they thought beauticians were second class citizens. Now care centers and beauticians and even teachers belong to the Chamber. We all get together once a month for a happy hour 'Business after 5'. It's a big change.

In addition to building relationships, interviewees mentioned the importance of establishing a pattern of successful project completion. According to business leader Lance Butterfield, all the work on a community- supported housing project was worth it, even though only one house has been completed, because, "people will know we can do a project. We've demonstrated a can-do attitude, persistence, and learned how to put together a package like this."

Of like mind is Jeff McCaffrey from Manasis who commented, "Successful community development projects create an expectation of success and that has implications for resources and the ability to get support for future projects. Also, if change is already occurring, then, additional change is less of a problem." The lesson in these comments is to start with small projects likely to be successful and publicize the project, the work that went into the project, and the successful aspects of projects that, from the outside, might look like failures.

What these leaders fail to mention in their comments, but was expressed by other leaders and highlighted in the example of the Gatlin City theater renovation project, is that successful projects are important also because they establish positive relationships between the people who worked on the project, a basis of trust between them, and norms of reciprocity. Earl Fowler business owner in Gatlin City articulated this aspect of community work.

You need to agree to disagree, and you have to support other people's ideas. People in some communities are focused too much on their own agenda, and if they don't get what they want immediately, they try to nix other people in what they want. You have to build comradery and say "I know this really isn't important to you, but it's important to me. If you'll support me on this, I'll support you later on."

Working together on projects helps people know each other well enough so they can negotiate implicit trust-based agreements that are so necessary for community betterment.

The Papajohn Entrepreneurship Camps and the Junior Achievement program are both based on the conviction that it is necessary to start with young people to effectively encourage more entrepreneurial activity. For the same reason, several communities have initiated programs to get children and youth involved in community service. In Manasis, for example, Vince Barker is working with local schools to encourage the integration of community service into the high school curriculum. Keith Runciman volunteers to work with Caizan youth church programs. He always designs the youth program with a large component of community service in it. Another benefit of youth involvement heralded by Runciman has to do with parents of involved youth. He said, "Once I get the youth involved, then they ask their parents to help out. We usually end up with as many parents as young people in our projects."

Another social-capital building mechanism developed in the United States but perfected in Sweden is the study-circle methodology. Generally study circles are small groups of residents who meet in each other's homes over an extended period of time to study an issue, learn a skill, or discuss a general theme. Each meeting usually includes a meal and is facilitated by a group member who has volunteered for special training. Ron Hustedde and his associates from the University of Kentucky brought study circles to Kentucky communities as part of a program on conflict resolution. Other groups, including the National Issue Forum, the Wallace Foundation, Positively Iowa, and numerous faith-based organizations, now use study circles as a way to build social capital among their constituents. The Study Circle Resource Center[2], funded by a nonprofit organization dedicated to advancing deliberative democracy in the United States, offers free assistance and nominally priced materials for communities interested in the study circle method of community building. Although it requires a substantial commitment in resources, it can to be an effective tool in the community-building tool box (see Ron Hustedde's 1996 evaluation of the Kentucky project).

GOING DIRECTLY TO THE TOP

An economic base of prosperous small businesses and family farms and abundant social capital sets the stage for business social performance. The real actors in the drama, however, are the business owners and top managers who sign the donation checks, serve in public office, and personally work to produce various public goods. In the end, it all comes down to their commitment and disposition toward community support.

Community leaders have at their disposal an array of formal and informal inducements to influence top decision makers to be good community citizens. In chapters 5 and 6, I examined in detail the personal and business ramifications of BSP. I presented findings from the Iowa data that demonstrated that business success and community support are positively related. Other business operators, public officials, consumers, family, friends, and the public at large can reward behavior that conforms to their values regarding community support and can punish nonconforming behavior. It works something like this: A network of good business citizens may be more apt to include like-minded business operators in lucrative new ventures; provide them assistance, inside information, and capital at reasonable rates; use their services or products; not undercut them in negotiations; and so on. All of which would equate to a business advantage to good citizens over poor citizens.

Many business operators interviewed for this research, and those interviewed for other research projects, stated their belief that good business citizenship helps them be more profitable by improving their ability to attract and retain employees. I could not support the claim of improved employee retention for supportive Iowa businesses. In metro and urban communities, supportive businesses had lower turnover than nonsupportive businesses, but the differences were not great enough to reach statistical significance. However, my sample consists of small businesses, and for them, size of community might make a difference in how much publicity they receive for their acts of business citizenship. Also, during the data-gathering period, Iowa was experiencing unprecedented low unemployment, and that might have changed normal patterns of employee retention. Therefore, the benefit to business success from high BSP realized through employee morale, attraction, and retention is still a salient argument.

Informed, "cause conscious" consumers can affect the success of businesses and thereby influence the BSP of businesses. Iowa business operators reported numerous instances of consumers' threatening to take their business elsewhere, and even threats of personal harm to operators, over disagreements on community issues. Some disagreements resulted in actual loss of business. At the national level, we are all aware of the power of consumers evidenced in national boycotts or threats of boycotts spurred by consumer anger over businesses' practices on environmental or social matters.

The effectiveness of rewards and sanctions from business networks, employees, and consumers depends upon the knowledge these groups possess regarding a business's citizenship. We heard two different impressions of the notoriety associated with community involvement and support from business leaders. On the one hand, Earl Fowler vividly describes the negative feedback business operators sometimes receive for their community support. He likened community service to putting your face on a dartboard and letting people throw darts at you. But Harriet Ernst, Robert Markus, and Bill Mannes each lamented the lack of knowledge among the general public about the contributions businesses make to the common good. Both perspectives point to the fact that many citizens operate with flawed or inadequate information about the role of business in community betterment.

Public knowledge of the quantity and quality of community support provided by particular businesses influences business citizenship in another way too. The recognition afforded by positive publicity in local newspaper, awards, ceremonies, honors, banquets, and symbolic testaments (such as plaques, pins, and jackets) is a psychological reward to civic-minded business owners and managers and, in a small way, counteracts some of the negative consequences of community service. Recognition was the most frequently mentioned personal reward for community service identified by my interviewees.

As director of a charitable organization in Pikeville, Reid Schmidt faces the formidable task of recruiting volunteers in an age of declining volunteerism and of raising money from businesses that receive an ever escalating number of requests for funds each year. Within his national organization, Reid's office is always among the top five in the amount of funds raised from businesses (on a per capita basis). So I listened very closely to Schmidt's advice about how to get business operators to be supportive of the community.

In Schmidt's schema, you've got to start with a concrete project or theme in mind:

People generally want to be helpful, but they need to know exactly what they're supporting. You've got to have a hook or a theme. Then, you've got to make it fun. It's kind of like high school homecoming. You and your core people must be creative. Come up with celebrations, contests, anything that makes it memorable and enjoyable. And like homecoming, the enthusiasm of a few good folks pulls the others along. Leadership is important. The appeal will be much more successful if it relates to something meaningful to them personally and you can demonstrate the tie.

In my interviews, business leaders stressed the high value they assign to being able to accomplish something that will make a difference in the community and/or to the future of their family. "Being able to accomplish something" highlights the significance of a successful project outcome, which in turn underscores the critical importance of a good planning, effective organization, and knowledgeable project execution.

"And another thing," Schmidt added, "you've got to make it as easy as possible for them to help out. Use their time and talents efficiently. Develop a division of labor among volunteers depending on the talents and resources they bring to the project. You don't want to ask a CEO to stuff envelopes. It's a waste of the unique resource they offer, i.e. contacts and clout. Lastly, you find creative and meaningful ways to thank people."

People who volunteer to help with an ill-conceived project that wastes their time and skill and offers little chance of success, will require considerable cajoling to get them involved a second time, if it is possible at all.

THE PUBLIC RESPONSIBILITY FOR BUSINESS SOCIAL RESPONSIBILITY

Through the evidence presented in this book, I have had the opportunity to expose a side of capitalism seldom seen and little know. I've attempted to show that capitalism is not monolithic. The interests of large corporations are frequently incongruent with the interests of small-business owners. Many small-business owners and managers express frustration about the public and economic forces (like business consolidation) that they believe threaten their businesses and their communities. As much as *Newsweek* and the general public, they are concerned about the decline in good business citizenship. The case that communities and businesses are mutually interdependent is more compelling for small-business operators, although it resonates with some big businesses as well.

In spite of the prevailing dismal assessment of civic mindedness and business social performance in the United States, this book contained good news. The majority of capitalists in Iowa express commitment to their community, provide support for their communities, and are personally active in the community. Moreover, communities are not simply the passive recipients of business largesse or abuse. Instead, they can purposefully influence the social performance of businesses operating within their confines. The techniques outlined above provide a taste of the kind of policies and programs that logic and experiential and research evidence suggest can affect BSP.

However, to effectively employ the insights presented in this book and create new innovative approaches to the subject, we must be convinced that good business citizenship is an obligation, not just a discretionary act of individual business owners and managers. Further, we must understand that it can be shaped by public policy at the national, state, and even the local level. For if we see the putative decline in business social performance as intractable, as caused by global forces beyond our control, then we will fail to utilize the remedies at hand, and will be unable to initiate new ones.

Individual, community, and state efforts to direct and reward good business citizenship do matter. To think otherwise is to increase the probability of the outcome we dread. Minneapolis, the so-called Emerald City,[3] has a tradition of strong business support for the community. Such a tradition is a double advantage to communities that possess it in that the institutions and values that encourage BSP are already in place. Equally important though, community leaders approach new challenges to BSP with a can-do attitude born of prior successes.

The chances of conscientious capitalism improve in accordance with the public expectation that businesses have ethical and discretionary social responsibilities and the willingness of public officials to design policies that actualize those expectations. The conscience of capitalism depends on all of us, not just business owners and managers. We must all be convinced that "Good corporate citizenship is not optional."

NOTES

1. The information on DeSilva's import replacement program comes from his appearance as a guest speaker at the "Quality Jobs for Quality Communities" conference at Iowa State University Feb. 1999. At that time he also conducted a seminar for faculty and graduate students. An earlier published account of Alberta's import substitution program can be found in Gary Buchanan and Eloise Murray's 1995 article in *Small Town* magazine.

2. For information on study circles contact The Study Circle Resource Center, P.O. Box 203, Rt. 169, Pomfret, CT 06258.

3. This term was first used by John D. Rockefeller III to refer to Minneapolis in a speech to the Minneapolis Chamber of Commerce, June 30, 1977.

References

Abrams, Richard M. 1979. "Private Enterprise and Public Values: The Modern Corporation." *Society* (Mar.-Apr.): 44–51.

Alderson, Arthur. 1999. "Explaining Deindustrialization: Globalization, Failure or Success?" *American Sociological Review* 64 (5): 701–721.

Apperle, Kenneth, Archie B. Carroll, and John D. Hatfield. 1985. "An Empirical Examination of the Relationship between Corporate Social Responsibility and Profitability." *Academy of Management Journal* 28 (2): 446–463.

Anshen, Melvin. 1970. "Changing the Social Contract: A Role for Business." *Columbia Journal of World Business* (Nov.-Dec.): 6–14.

Aram, John D. 1989. "The Paradox of Interdependent Relations in the Field of Social Issues in Management." *Academy of Management Review* 14(2): 266–283.

Arlow, Peter, and Martin Gannon. 1982. "Social Responsiveness, Corporate Structure and Economic Performance." *Academy of Management Review* 7: 235–241.

Atkinson, Lisa, and Joseph Galaskiewicz. 1988. "Stock Ownership and Company Contributions to Charity." *Administrative Science Quarterly* 33: 82–100.

Auslander, Gail K., and Howard Litwin. 1988. "Sociability and Patterns of Participation: Implications for Social Service Policy." *Journal of Voluntary Action Research* 17(2): 25–37.

Baltzell, E. Bigby. 1979. *Puritan Boston and Quaker Philadelphia: Two Protestant Ethics and the Spirit of Class Authority and Leadership.* New York: Free Press.

Besser, Terry, and Nancy Miller. 2001. "Small Business Community Values and their Relationship to Management Strategies." *The Journal of Socio-Economics* 30(6): 221–241.

Besser, Terry. 1998. "The Significance of Community to Business Social Responsibility." *Rural Sociology* 63(3): 412–431.

Bockelman, Wilfred. 2000. *Culture of Corporate Citizenship: Minnesota's Business Legacy for the Global Future*. Lakeville, Minn.: Galde Press, Inc.

Bowen, Howard R. 1953. *Social Responsibilities of the Businessman*. New York: Harper & Brothers.

Brown, Daniel J., and Jonathan King. 1982. "Small Business Ethics: Influences and Perceptions." *Journal of Small Business Management* (Jan.): 11–18.

Buchanan, Gary, and Eloise Murray. 1995. "Import Replacement: The Lloydminster, Alberta, Experience. *Small Town* (May-June): 10–13.

Buchanan, James M. 1968. *The Demand and Supply of Public Goods*. Chicago: Rand McNally.

Buchholtz, Ann K., Allen C. Amason, and Matthew A. Rutherford. 1999. "Beyond Resources: The Mediating Effect of Top Management Discretion and Values on Corporate Philanthropy." *Business and Society* 38: 167–187.

Burlingame, Dwight F., and David A. Kaufmann. 1995. *Indiana Business Contributions to Community Service*. Center on Philanthropy, Indiana University: Indianapolis, Ind.

Burt, Ronald S. 1983. "Corporate Philanthropy as Cooptive Relations." *Social Forces* 62: 419–426.

Burt, Ronald S. 1992. *Structural Holes: The Social Structure of Competition*. Cambridge, Mass.: Harvard University Press.

Cannon, Tom. 1994. *Corporate Responsibility: A Textbook on Business Ethics, Governance, Environment: Roles and Responsibility*. London: Pitnam Publishers.

Carroll, Archie B. 1979. "A Three-Dimensional Conceptual Model of Corporate Performance." *Academy of Management Review* 4(4): 497–505.

Chrisman, James J., and Richard W. Archer. 1984. "Small Business Social Responsibility: Some Perceptions and Insights." *American Journal of Small Business* IX(2): 46–58.

Chrisman, James J., and Fred L. Fry. 1982. "Public vs Business Expectations: Two Views of Social Responsibility for Small Business." *Journal of Small Business Management* (Jan.): 19–26.

Cochran, Philip L., and Robert A. Wood. 1984. "Corporate Social Responsibility and Financial Performance." *Academy of Management Journal* 27(1): 42–56.

Corson, John J., and George A. Steiner. 1975. *Measuring Business' Social Performance: The Corporate Social Audit*. New York: The Committee for Economic Development.

Cowie, Jefferson. 1999. *Capital Moves: RCA's Seventy-Year Quest for Cheap Labor*. Ithaca, NY: Cornell University Press.

Davis, Keith. 1975. "Five Propositions for Social Responsibility." *Business Horizons* June: 19–24.

Davis, Keith, and Robert L. Blomstrom. 1971. *Business, Society and Environment: Social Power and Social Response*. 2nd ed. New York: McGraw-Hill.

Evan, William E., and R. Edward Freeman. 1988. "A Stakeholder Theory of the Modern Corporation: Kantian Capitalism." In *Ethical Theory and Business*. 3rd ed. Tom L. Beauchamp, and Norman E. Bowie, eds. Englewood Cliffs, N.J.: Prentice Hall Inc.

Feeny, David, Fikret Berkes, Bonnie J. McCay, and James M. Acheson. 1990. "The Tradegy of the Commons: Twenty-Two Years Later." *Human Ecology* 18: 1–19.

Flora, Cornelia Butler. 1995. "Social Capital and Sustainability: Agriculture and Communities in the Great Plains and Corn Belt." *Research in Rural Sociology and Development* 6: 227–246.

Flora, Jan L., Jeff Sharp, Bonnie Newlon, and Cornelia Flora. 1997. "Entrepreneurial Social Infrastructure and Locally Initiated Economic Development in Nonmetropolitan U.S." *The Sociological Quarterly* 38: 623–644.

Folger, H. Russell, and Fred Nutt. 1975. "A Note on Social Responsibility and Stock Valuation." *Academy of Management Journal* 18(1): 155–160.

Fombrun, C., and M. Shanley. 1990. "What's in a Name? Reputation Building and Corporate Strategy." *Academy of Management Journal* 33:233–58.

Forsgren, Mats, Ingemund Hagg, Hakan Hakansson, Jan Johanson, Lars-Gunnar Mattsson. 1995. *Firms in Networks: A New Perspective on Competitive Power*. Stockholm: The Center for Business and Policy Studies.

France, Mike and Andrew Osterland. 1999. "State Farm: What's Happening to the Good Neighbor? *Business Week* (Nov. 8): 138–146.

Frederick, William C. 1986. "Toward CSR3: Why Ethical Analysis is Indispensable and Unavoidable in Corporate Affairs." *California Management Review* 28(2): 126–141.

Frederick, William C. 1994 (1978). "From CSR1 to CSR2: The Maturing of Business and Society Thought." *Business and Society* 33(2): 150–164.

Freeman, R. Edward. 1984. *Strategic Management: A Stakeholder Approach*. Boston: Pitman/Ballinger (Harper Collins).

Friedman, Milton. 1962. *Capitalism and Freedom*. Chicago: University of Chicago Press.

Friedman, Milton. 1971. "Does Business Have a Social Responsibility?" *Bank Administration* (April): 13–14.

Fry, Fred L., and Robert Hock. 1976. "Who Claims Corporate Responsibility? The Biggest and the Worst." *Business and Society Review* 18: 62–65.

Fry, Louis W., Gerald D. Keim, and Roger E. Meiners. 1982. "Corporate Contributions: Altruistic or For-Profit?" *Academy of Management Journal* 25(1): 94–106.

Galaskiewicz, Joseph. 1985. *Social Organization of an Urban Grants Economy: A Study of Business Philanthropy and Nonprofit Organizations 1981*. Orlando, FL: Academic Press.

Galaskiewicz, Joseph. 1997. "An Urban Grants Economy Revisited: Corporate Charitable Contributions in the Twin Cities, 1979–1981, 1987–1989." *Administrative Science Quarterly* 42: 445–471.

Gertler, Meric S. 1997. "Between the Global and the Local: The Spatial Limits to Productive Capital." In *Spaces of Globalization: Reasserting the Power of the Local*. Kevin R. Cox, ed. New York: The Guilford Press.

Glynn, Thomas. 1981. "Psychological Sense of Community: Measurement and Application." *Human Relations* 34(7): 789–818.

Gordon, David M. 1988. "The Global Economy: New Edifice or Crumbling Foundation?" *The New Left Review* 168: 24–65.

Grabher, Gernot, ed. 1993. *The Embedded Firm: On the Socioeconomics of Industrial Networks*. London: Routledge.

Granovetter, Mark S. 1973. "The Strength of Weak Ties." *American Journal of Sociology* 78(6): 1360–1380.

Granovetter, Mark S. 1985. "Economic Action and Social Structure: The Problem of Embeddedness." *American Journal of Sociology* 91(3): 481–510.

Graves, Samuel B. and Sandra A. Waddock. 1994. "Institutional Owners and Corporate Social Performance." *Academy of Management Journal* 37(4): 1034–1046.

Green, Gary P. 1994. "Is Small Beautiful? Small Business Development in Rural Areas." *The Journal of the Community Development Society* 25(2): 155–171.

Griffin, Jennifer, and John Mahon. 1997. "The Corporate Social Performance and Corporate Financial Performance Debate: Twenty-five Years of Incomparable Research." *Business and Society* 36 (Mar.): 5–32.

Grossman, Richard L., and Frank T. Adams. 1996. "Exercising Power over Corporations through State Charters." In *The Case Against the Global Economy: And For a Turn toward the Local*. Jerry Mander and Edward Goldsmith, eds. San Francisco: Sierra Club Books.

Gutman, Herbert. 1976. *Work, Culture, and Society in Industrializing America: Essays in American Working Class and Social History*. New York: Knopf.

Haley, Usha C.V. 1991. "Corporate Contributions as Managerial Masques: Reframing Corporate Contributions as Strategies to Influence Society." *Journal of Management Studies* 28(5): 485–509.

Hardin, Garrett. 1968. "The Tragedy of the Commons." *Science* 162: 1243–1248.

Hardin, Russell. 1982. *Collective Action*. Baltimore: The Johns Hopkins University Press.

Harrison, Bennett. 1994. *Lean and Mean: The Changing Landscape of Corporate Power in the Age of Flexibility*. New York: Basic Books.

Hayghe, Howard V. 1991. "Volunteers in the U.S.: Who Donates the Time?" *Monthly Labor Review* (Feb.): 17–23.

Hirst, Paul, and Grahame Thompson. 1999. *Globalization in Question: The International Economy and the Possibilities of Governance*. 2nd ed. Cambridge, U.K.: Polity Press.

Hodgkinson, Virginia A., and Murray Weitzman. 1990. *Giving and Volunteering in the United States*. Washington, D.C.: Independent Sector

"How Business Students Rate Corporations." 1972. *Business and Society Review* 2: 20–21.

Hustedde, Ronald J. 1996. "An Evaluation of the National Issues Forum Methodology for Stimulating Deliberation in Rural Kentucky." *Journal of the Community Development Society* 27(2): 197–210.

Johnson, Richard A., and Daniel W. Greening. 1999. "The Effects of Corporate Governance and Institutional Ownership Types on Corporate Social Performance." *Academy of Management Journal* 42(5): 564–576.

Jones, Thomas M. 1995. "Instrumental Stakeholder Theory: A Synthesis of Ethics and Economics." *Academy of Management Review* 20: 404–437.

Kamens, David H. 1985. "A Theory of Corporate Civic Giving." *Sociological Perspectives* 28(1): 29–50.

Kanter, Rosabeth Moss. 1995. *World Class: Thriving Locally in the Global Economy*. New York: Simon and Schuster.

Kedia, Banwari L., and Edwin C. Kuntz. 1981. "The Context of Social Performance: An Empirical Study of Texas Banks." In *Research in Corporate Social Performance and Policy*. 3rd ed. Lee E. Preston, ed. Greenwich, Conn.: JAI Press.

Keim, Gerald D. 1978. "Corporate Social Responsibility: An Assessment of the Enlightened Self-Interest Model." *Academy of Management Review* (Jan.): 32–39.

Kinder, P.D., S. D. Lydenberg, and A.L. Domini. 1990. *Social Screens Key to Ratings*. Cambridge, MA: Kinder, Lydenberg, and Domini and Co.

Kuttner, Robert. 1996. *Everything For Sale: The Virtues and Limits of Markets*. Chicago, IL: The University of Chicago Press.

Lerner, Linda D., and Gerald E. Fryxell. 1988. "An Empirical Study of the Predictors of Corporate Social Performance: A Multi-dimensional Analysis." *Journal of Business Ethics* 7: 951–959.

Levitt, Theodore. 1958. "The Dangers of Social Responsibility." *Harvard Business Review* 36(5): 45–49.

Logan, John R., and Harvey L. Molotch. 1987. *Urban Fortunes: The Political Economy of Place*. Los Angeles: University of California Press.

Longenecker, Justin G., Joseph A. McKinney, and Carlos W. Moore. 1989. "Ethics in Small Business." *Journal of Small Business Management* (Jan.): 27–31.

Lynd, Robert, and Helen Lynd. 1937. *Middletown in Transition*. New York: Harcourt Brace Jovanovich.

Makin, C. 1983. "Ranking Corporate Reputations." *Fortune* 107(1):33–44.

Martin. S.A. 1985. *An Essential Grace*. Toronto: McClelland and Stewart.

McAdam, T.W. 1973. "How to Put Corporate Responsibility into Practice." *Business and Society Review/Innovation* 6: 8–16.

McElroy, Katherine Maddox, and John J. Siegfried. 1985. "The Effect of Firm Size on Corporate Philanthropy." *Quarterly Review of Economics and Business* 25(2): 18–26.

McElroy, Katherine Maddox, and John J. Siegfried. 1986. "The Community Influence on Corporate Contributions." *Public Finance Quarterly* 14(4): 394–414.

McMichael, Philip. 1996. "Globalization: Myths and Realities." *Rural Sociology* 61(10): 25–55.

Miller, Nancy, and Terry Besser. 2000. "The Importance of Community Values in Small Business Strategy Formation: Evidence from Rural Iowa." *Journal of Small Business Management* 38(1): 68–85.

Mills, C. Wright, and Melville J. Ulmer. 1946. "Small Business and Social Welfare." *Report of the Smaller War Plants Corporation to the Special Senate Committee to Study Problems of American Small Business*. 79th Congress, 2nd session, Document 135.

Mintzberg, Henry. 1983. "The Case for Corporate Social Responsibility." *The Journal of Business Strategy* 4(2): 3–15.

Moskowitz, Milton. 1972. "Choosing Socially Responsible Stocks." *Business and Society Review* 1: 71–75.

Moskowitz, Milton. 1975. "Profiles in Corporate Responsibility." *Business and Society Review* 13: 29–42.

Muhwezi, Dan R. 1990. *Corporate Contributions: An Empirical Assessment of the Underlying Factors Among Small Business Organizations*. Ph.D. dissertation, Iowa State University.

Navarro, Peter. 1988. "Why Do Corporations Give to Charity?" *Journal of Business* 61(1): 65–93.

Ohmae, Kenichi. 1990. *The Borderless World*. London and New York: Collins.

Oliver, Pamela. 1984. "If You Don't Do It, Nobody Else Will: Active and Token Contributors to Local Collective Action." *American Sociological Review* 49: 601–610.

Onibokun, Adepoju G., and Martha Curry. 1976. "An Ideology of Citizen Participation: The Metropolitan Seattle Transit Case Study." *Public Administration Review* 36: 269–277.

Organisation for Economic Co-Operation and Development. 1999. *Boosting Innovation: The Cluster Approach*. Paris: OECD Proceedings.

Ostrom, Elinor. 1990. *Governing the Commons*. New York: Cambridge University Press.

Parket, I Robert, and Henry Eilbirt. 1975. "Social Responsibility: The Underlying Factors." *Business Horizons* (Aug.): 5–10.

Parkum, Kurt H., and Virginia Cohn Parkum. 1980. "Citizen Participation in Community Planning and Decision Making." In *Participation in Social and Political Activities*. David Horton Smith, Jacqueline Macaulay, and Associates, eds. San Francisco: Josey Bass.

Pennings, Johannes M., Kyungmook Lee, and Arjen van Witteloostuijn. 1998. "Human Capital, Social Capital, and Firm Dissolution." *Academy of Management Journal* 41 (4): 425–440.

Perry, Martin. 1999. *Small Firms and Network Economies*. New York: Routledge.

Piore, Michael J., and Charles F. Sabel. 1984. *The Second Industrial Divide: Possibilities for Prosperity*. New York: Basic Books.

Porter, Lyman, Richard Steers, Richard Mowday, and Paul Boulian. 1974. "Organizational Commitment, Job Satisfaction and Turnover among Psychiatric Technicians." *Journal of Applied Psychology* 59: 603–609.

Portes, Alejandro, and Julia Sensenbrenner. 1993. "Embeddedness and Immigration: Notes on the Social Determinants of Economic Action." *American Journal of Sociology* 98: 1320–1350.

Preston, Lee E., and James E. Post. 1975. *Private Management and Public Policy: The Principle of Public Responsibility*. Englewood Cliffs, N.J.: Prentice Hall, Inc.

Pruzan, Peter, and Simon Zadek. 1997. "Socially Responsible and Accountable Enterprise." *Journal of Human Values* 3(1): 59–79.

Putnam, Robert D. 1993. *Making Democracy Work: Civic Traditions in Modern Italy*. Princeton, N.J.: Princeton University Press.

Reich, Robert B. 1992. *The Work of Nations: Preparing Ourselves for 21st Century Capitalism*. New York: Vintage Books.

Research and Policy Committee, Committee for Economic Development. 1971. *Social Responsibilities of Business Corporations: A Statement on National Policy*. New York: Committee for Economic Development.

Ricardo, David. 1917. *The Principles of Political Economy and Taxation*. New York: E.P. Dutton & Co.

Riggle, David. 1997. "Networking for Small Business Creation." *In Business* (July/August): 28–30.

Ritzer, George. 1993. *The McDonaldization of Society: An Investigation into the Changing Character of Contemporary Social Life*. Newbury Park, CA: Pine Forge Press.

Samuelson, Paul A. 1954. "The Pure Theory of Public Expenditures." *Review of Economics and Statistics* 36: 387–389.

Samuelson, Robert J. 1993. "R.I.P.: The Good Corporation." *Newsweek* 122:41.

Santiago, Frank, and Thomas Beaumont. 1999. "IBP Manager Accused of Delaying Care." *Des Moines Register* (Dec. 14): 10S.

Sassen, Saskia. 1991. *The Global City: New York, London, Tokyo*. Princeton, NJ: Princeton University Press.

Sassen, Saskia. 1998. *Globalization and Its Discontents*. New York: The New Press.

Schoenberg, Sandra Perlman. 1980. "Some Trends in the Community Participation of Women in their Neighborhoods." *Signs* 5: 261–268.

Schumpeter, Joseph. 1939. *Business Cycles: A Theoretical, Historical, and Statistical Analysis of the Capitalist Process*. 1st ed. New York: McGraw-Hill Book Company, Inc.

Sethi, S. Prakash. 1979. "A Conceptual Framework for Environmental Analysis of Social Issues and Evaluation of Business Response Patterns." *Academy of Management Review* 4(1): 63–74.

Sethi, S. Prakash. 1996. "Moving from a Socially Responsible to a Socially Accountable Corporation." In *Is the Good Corporation Dead? Social Responsibility in a Global Economy*. John W. Houck and Oliver F. Williams, eds. Lantham, MD: Rowman & Littlefield Publishers, Inc.

Sinclair, Michelle, and Joseph Galaskiewicz. 1997. "Corporate Nonprofit Partnerships: Varieties and Covariates." *New York Law School Law Review* 61(3&4):1059–1090.

Smith, Craig. 1994a. "From Responsibility to Opportunity." *Fund Raising Management* 25(2): 34–36.

Smith, Craig. 1994b. "The New Corporate Philanthropy." *Harvard Business Review* (May-June): 105–116.

Smith, David H. 1994. "Determinants of Voluntary Association Participation and Volunteering: A Literature Review." *Nonprofit and Voluntary Sector Quarterly* 23(3): 243–263.

Smith, Patricia, and Ellwood F. Oakley III. 1994. "A Study of the Ethical Values of Metro and Non-metro Small Business Owners." *Journal of Small Business Management* 32(4): 17–27.

Steggert, Frank.X. 1975. *Community Action Groups and City Governments: Perspectives from Ten American Cities*. Cambridge, Mass.: Ballinger.

Stendardi Jr., Edward J. 1992. "Corporate Philanthropy: The Redefinition of Enlightened Self-Interest." *The Social Science Journal* 29(1): 21–30.

Swanson, Diane L. 1995. "Addressing a Theoretical Problem by Reorienting the Corporate Social Performance Model." *Academy of Management Review* 20(1): 43–64.

Thompson, Judith Kenner, and Howard L. Smith. 1991. "Social Responsibility and Small Business: Suggestions for Research." *Journal of Small Business Management* 29:39–44

Thompson, Judith K., Howard L. Smith, and Jacqueline N. Hood. 1993. "Charita-
    ble Contributions by Small Businesses." *Journal of Small Business Manage-
    ment* 31(3): 35–51.
Tolbert, Charles M., Thomas A. Lyson, and Michael D. Irwin. 1998. "Local Capital-
    ism, Civic Engagement, and Socioeconomic Well Being." *Social Forces*
    77(2): 401–28.
Turban, Daniel B., and Daniel W. Greening. 1997. "Corporate Social Performance
    and Organizational Attractiveness to Prospective Employees." *Academy
    of Management Journal* 40(3): 658–672.
U.S. Census Bureau. 1992. *Economic Census.* Table 1: Employers and
    Nonemployers. Accessed at www.census.gov.epcd.www/smallbus.
    html#empsize.
U.S. Census Bureau. 1997. *Economic Census.* "The Number of Firms, Establish-
    ments, Employment, Annual Payroll, and Estimated Receipts by Indus-
    trial Division and Enterprise Employment Size for 1996." Accessed at:
    www.census.gov/epcd/ssel_tabs/view/tab3_99b.html#tot.
U.S. Sentencing Commission. 1995. *Corporate Crime in America; Strengthening the
    'Good Citizen' Corporation.* Proceedings of the Second Symposium on
    Crime and Punishment in the United States: Washington, D.C.
U.S. Small Business Administration.1993. *Our 1992 State Profile.* Office of Advo-
    cacy, Washington, D.C.: Small Business Administration.
Useem, Michael. 1988. "Market and Institutional Factors in Corporate Contribu-
    tions." *California Management Review* Winter: 77–88.
Useem, Michael. 1991. "Organizational and Managerial Factors in the Shaping of
    Corporate Social and Political Action." *Research in Corporate Social Perfor-
    mance and Policy* 12: 63–92.
Useem, Michael, and Stephen I. Kutner. 1986. "Corporate Contributions to Cul-
    ture and the Arts: The Organization of Giving and the Influence of the
    Chief Executive Officer and of Other Firms on Company Contributions
    in Massachusetts." In *Nonprofit Enterprise in the Arts: Studies in Mission
    and Constraint.* Paul J. DiMaggio, ed. New York: Oxford University Press.
Uzzi, Brian. 1996. "The Sources and Consequences of Embeddedness for the Eco-
    nomic Performance of Organizations: The Network Effect." *American So-
    ciological Review* 61: 674–698.
Uzzi, Brian. 1999. "Embeddedness in the Making of Financial Capital: How Social
    Relations and Networks Benefit Firms Seeking Financing." *American So-
    ciological Review* 64: 481–505.
Van Auken, Philip M., and R. Duane Ireland. 1982. "Plain Talk about Small Busi-
    ness Responsibility." *Journal of Small Business Management* (Jan.): 1–3.
Varadarajan, P. Rajan, and Anil Menon. 1988. "Cause-Related Marketing: A
    Coalignment of Marketing Strategy and Corporate Philanthropy." *Jour-
    nal of Marketing* 58: 59–60.
Vedlitz, Arnold and Eric P. Veblen. 1980. "Voting and Contacting: Two Forms of
    Political Participation in a Suburban Community." *Urban Affairs Quar-
    terly* 16: 31–48.
Verba, Sidney, Kay Lehman Schlozman, and Henry E. Brady. 1995. *Voice and
    Equality: Civic Voluntarism in American Politics.* Cambridge, Mass: Har-
    vard University Press.

Waddock, Sandra A., and Mary Ellen Boyle. 1995. "The Dynamics of Change in Corporate Community Relations." *California Management Review* 37(4): 125–140.

Wartick, Steven L., and Philip L. Cochran. 1985. "The Evolution of the Corporate Social Performance Model." *Academy of Management Review* 10 (4): 758–769.

Weaver, Gary R., Linda Klebe Trevino, and Philip L. Cochran. 1999. "Corporate Ethics Programs as Control Systems: Influences of Executive Commitment and Environmental Factors." *Academy of Management Journal* 42(1): 41–57.

Weaver, Gary R., Linda Klebe Trevino, and Philip L. Cochran. 1999. "Integrated and Decoupled Corporate Social Performance: Management Commitments, External Pressure, and Corporate Ethics Practices." *Academy of Management Journal* 42(5): 539–552.

Wilson, Erika. 1980. "Social Responsibility of Business: What Are Small Business Perspectives?" *Journal of Small Business Management* (July): 17–24.

Wilson, Ian. 1974. "What One Company Is Doing About Today's Demands on Business." In *Changing Business-Society Interrelationships*. George A. Steiner, ed. Los Angles: Graduate School of Management, UCLA.

Wood, Donna J. 1991. "Corporate Social Performance Revisited." *Academy of Management Review* 16(4): 691–718.

Appendix A: Telephone Interviews

SAMPLING STRATEGY

The research for this book started in 1994 when the Rural Development Initiative was started with funding from the Iowa State University Agriculture and Home Economics Experiment Station. That summer, faculty and staff in the Iowa State University's Department of Sociology surveyed almost 15,000 residents of ninety-nine small Iowa communities to assess aspects of community life in small towns. Details of the residents' evaluation of their community are contained in the publication, *Sigma: A Profile of Iowa's Rural Communities*. All reports mentioned here can be obtained by calling Lori Merritt at Iowa State University Department of Sociology (515–294–8368).

One finding of the survey was that a majority of small-town citizens believed the most serious threat facing their communities was the demise of businesses. Their concern prompted a 1995 study of a random sample of 1,008 business owners and managers in 30 of the original 99 communities. In the summer of 1997, we received additional funds from the Iowa State University Agriculture and Home Economics Experiment Station to complete the picture of Iowa businesses by examining for-profit organizations in Iowa's cities. The purpose of the 1997 phase of the study was twofold: 1) to add a critical piece to our understanding of life in Iowa; and 2) to ascertain in what way urban businesses differ from rural businesses, if at all. The results of these studies were published in reports entitled *The Sigma Business Sector: A Profile of Business in Iowa Small Towns, Doing Business in Iowa's Metropolitan Cities, Doing Business in Iowa's Small Cities,* and *How Size of Town Affects Doing Business in Iowa*.

Rural Business Sample

The sample communities for the rural phase study consisted of 30 communities randomly selected from the ninety-nine communities previously mentioned. (One community had been randomly selected from each of Iowa's ninety-nine counties.) Only towns with 500–10,000 in population were considered.

Telephone interviews with business operators were preceded by a pilot study of all the businesses in one town (with a population in 1990 of approximately 1,000 people), purposively chosen from among the remaining sixty-nine communities. A team of faculty and graduate students went door-to-door and interviewed either the owner or manager of all of the businesses in town.

Subsequent to the pilot study, we refined our survey instrument and purchased a list of all of the businesses located in each sample town from American Business Lists, a private organization in Omaha, Nebraska. The list contained the owner's name, address, telephone number, and other basic business information. American Business Lists assembles business information from the Yellow Pages and business White Pages of telephone directories, annual reports, and federal, state, and municipal government data. They then verify the information by calling each business at least once a year. In addition, we verified the accuracy of the lists by comparing the purchased list of our pilot community to our own field data, and double-checking Yellow Page entries with the lists for communities of less than 2,500 in population, whose business districts are likely to be small and hard to locate in consolidated telephone directories that serve those areas. We were satisfied that the lists were a close approximation of the population of businesses in those towns.

Our definition of a business establishment was that it be a for-profit organization and have a business listing (Yellow or White Pages) in the telephone directory. This allowed us to include businesses that do not pay sales tax, but are important components of the small town business scene, such as attorneys, accountants, hospitals, farm suppliers, nursing homes, physicians, etc. Our experience in the pilot community led us to eliminate businesses that did not have a specific place designated for business only and that did not have a business listing in the telephone directory, even if they had a sales-tax permit. We discovered that these "businesses" in the pilot community were side occupations of people otherwise engaged in the labor market or in other businesses. Examples of these businesses are selling Avon or Stanley products, lawn work, plowing gardens in the spring, contract farm work, welding services, auto repair services, craft making, and catering. The total number of businesses in the sampling frame was 3,440.

From the sampling frame of business names, we randomly selected a stratified sample of business owners and managers. In order to ensure a significant number of businesses from the smaller towns and still stay within budget, we sampled a larger proportion of the businesses in those towns. Table 1 below provides a summary of the sampling goals and the actual average sample size by community size categories. In all the analyses in the book, the data from the rural businesses were weighted to represent all businesses in Iowa towns of 500 to 10,000.

A list of sample communities, population size, their sample size, and cooperation rate follows (Table A1). We oversampled the target sample size by 10 percent, expecting refusals, changes in business status, and so on. In all, 1,008 business owners and managers were interviewed for a cooperation rate of 89 percent.

Table A1
Sample Details

Name Rural Community	1990 Population	Cooperation Rate
Albia	3,870	72%
Allerton	599	66%
Bedford	1,528	67%
Calmar	1,026	71%
Cherokee	6,026	70%
Clarence	936	79%
Denison	6,604	69%
Donnellson	904	74%
Eagle Grove	3,671	75%
Elma	653	83%
Esterville	6,720	80%
Farmington	655	67%
Jefferson	4,292	74%
Le Claire	2,734	78%
Mapleton	1,294	78%
Mediapolis	1,637	74%
Missouri Valley	2,888	75%
Olin	663	78%
Pacific Junction	548	71%
Pleasantville	1,536	65%
Pomeroy	762	75%
Sac City	2,516	76%
Sheffield	1,174	81%
Sibley	2,815	73%
Traer	1,552	80%
Ventura	590	77%
Waukon	4,019	74%
Webster City	7,894	69%
Winfield	1,051	73%
Woodward	1,197	66%

Urban Communities	1990 Population	Cooperative Rate
Bettendorf	31,015	68%
Cedar Falls	34,884	67%
Fort Dodge	24,755	69%
Muscatine	23,096	59%
Newton	15,116	66%
Spencer	11,194	66%

Metropolitan Communities		
Cedar Rapids	113,482	61%
Des Moines	193,422	53%
Iowa City	60,923	56%
Sioux City	83,791	57%

Small City Business Sample

From among the twenty-two towns in Iowa between 10,000 and 50,000 in population, a sample was drawn using a multi-stage sampling design. In the first stage, eleven communities were selected at random for a resident survey. Six of the eleven were chosen randomly for inclusion in this study. The names of these communities and their rates of cooperation follow.

The original goal was to obtain interviews with at least seventy-five business operators in each community. We again purchased lists of business names from American Business Lists. However, considering the very large number of businesses in urban communities, we purchased a random sample of names instead of the names of the whole population of businesses. American Business Lists was instructed to draw a random sample of seventy-five businesses plus fifteen extra from each town to account for refusals and closed businesses. Due to difficulties with American Business Lists (i.e. failure to delete non-business entries), and even after drawing two random samples, we were left with samples that varied in size for each town, but approximated fifty businesses each. Fortunately, sampled businesses were very cooperative, resulting in only a few who refused to participate. In all, 265 interviews were conducted with small city business operators, for an 84 percent cooperation rate.

Metropolitan Business Sample

For the study of businesses in metropolitan communities, four of Iowa's eight metropolitan communities were selected at random (again, the list of selected communities follows). The goal was to interview 450 metropolitan business owners and managers (or about 112 from each selected metropolitan community). American Business Lists had difficulty distinguishing between businesses located in the two metropolitan areas that are adjacent to each other—Iowa City and Cedar Rapids. As a result, they oversampled the Cedar Rapids businesses and undersampled the Iowa City businesses. Due to the high cooperation rate of contacted businesses, we believe the flaw in sampling does not threaten the validity of our findings. Over 400 metropolitan business operators were interviewed resulting in an 83 percent cooperation rate.

In order to evaluate the representativeness of our small-city and metropolitan samples, we compared the percentage of sample businesses in different industry categories to the industry distribution of all businesses in the sampled counties. The County Business Information is available in the 1997 County Business Data WebPages maintained by Oregon State University <http://govinfo.library. orst.edu>.

Because our sample was drawn from businesses in a community and the county business data is based on businesses in a whole county, we expected some differences between the sample and county data. However, since urban and metropolitan communities so dominate their county, the variation should be small. For this comparison we used Standard Industrial Classification categories.

As shown in Table A2 below, the sample for metropolitan businesses has more agriculture, manufacturing, transportation, wholesale, retail, and finance firms and fewer construction and service firms than the population of businesses in the counties. The urban sample has more agriculture, retail and finance firms and fewer manufacturing, transportation, wholesale, and service firms than the population of businesses in the counties. Given that we are comparing two slightly different groups of businesses, the variation is acceptable.

INTERVIEWING PROTOCOL

We contracted for the services of the Computer Assisted Telephone Interview (CATI) Laboratory at the Center for Family Research in Rural Mental Health at Iowa State University to conduct the interviews. The CATI Lab employs a pool of trained, experienced interviewers. We conducted briefing sessions with them to apprise them of the overall goals of the research, to work through phone protocols, and to confer on question phrasing.

Prior to all of the interviews, each selected business was mailed a letter explaining the purpose of the research and the expected length of the interview, assuring them of confidentiality, and providing them with a 1–800 number to call if they needed to contact the interviewers or research director. The local County Extension Education Director in each of the forty sample counties placed a press release in the community newspaper about the research, identifying the local community by name. When the business was contacted, interviewers specifically requested an interview with the owner, or if the owner was an absentee owner, with the manager in charge. If the owner was simply not available at that time, arrangements were made to call back and interview the owner. The interviews averaged thirty-five minutes for businesses in the rural communities. The number of questions were reduced for the urban and metropolitan study resulting in interviews averaging twenty minutes in length.

Table A2
Sample Businesses Compared to All Businesses in Selected Sample Counties*

| | Standard Industrial Code | | | | | | | |
	Agriculture	Construction	Manufacturing	Transportation & Communication	Wholesale	Retail	Finance, Insurance, and Real Estate	Services
METRO								
Percent of All Businesses	1.4	9.3	4.2	4.7	9.0	23.7	10.7	36.9
Percent of Sample Businesses	1.7	5.4	5.1	5.1	10.7	28.5	11.7	31.7
SMALL CITY								
Percent of All Businesses	1.4	9.4	6.0	6.4	8.7	26.1	9.4	32.6
Percent of Sample Businesses	2.3	9.4	5.7	3.0	6.8	29.1	12.1	31.7

*Two small cities in the sample are adjacent to metropolitan areas. The counties of the adjacent small cities were not included in the county business data shown in the table.

Rural Development Initiative – Business Survey (1997)
Telephone Interview Schedule

From Sample Records
County of business
City of business

From Census Data
1996 community population
      1 = Non-metro city with population of 10,000-15,000
      2 = Metro

Questions
1   *What is your position in the business?*
      1 = Owner
      2 = Manager *[GOTO 9]*
         9 = REFUSED
2   *Are you the sole owner?*
      1 = Yes *[GOTO 14]*
      2 = No
      9 = REFUSED
      How many other owners are there NOT including yourself?

3 thru **8** asked for the sex and racial category of the 3 most active owners.
      Sex: 1 = Male
      2 = Female
      9 = REFUSED
   Race: 1 = White
      2 = African American/Black
         3 = Asian/Pacific Islander
         4 = Hispanic
         5 = American Indian/Alaskan Native
         6 = Bi-racial/Mixed Race
         7 = Other
         8 = DON'T KNOW
         9 = REFUSED
9 thru **13b** were answered only if the manager was the respondent

9   *Are there other managers who have the same responsibility as you?*
      1 = Yes
      2 = No *[GO TO 14]*
      8 = DON'T KNOW *[GO TO 14]*
      9 = REFUSED *[GO TO 14]*
9a   *How many other managers with similar responsibilities work there?*
      88 = DON'T KNOW
      99 = REFUSED

10 thru **13b** asked for the identification of the gender and race of the managers.

        Sex: 1 = Male
                  2 = Female
                  9 = REFUSED
        Race: 1 = White
                  2 = African American/Black
                  3 = Asian/Pacific Islander
                  4 = Hispanic
                  5 = American Indian/Alaskan Native
                  6 = Bi-racial/ Mixed race
                  7 = Other
                  8 = DON'T KNOW
                  9 = REFUSED

14   *In what year did this business begin its current operation in this community?*
                  less than 5 years
                  8888 = DON'T KNOW

15   *Do you or the owner own or rent the space in which this business is located?*
                  1 = Own
                  2 = Rent
                  3 = Own and rent
                  8 = DON'T KNOW
                  9 = REFUSED

16   *Please briefly describe the major activity of this business (5 words or less):*

17   *Which of the following best describes the status of this business. Is it.....*
                  1 = An independent, single establishment firm (meaning this is the only
                      location of this business) *[GO TO 19]*
                  2 = Owned by another company *[GO TO 19]*
                  3 = Locally owned, but franchised to offer brand-name products or
                      services *[GO TO 19]*
                  4 = The owner of one or more branch establishments besides the one at
                      this location *[GO TO 19]*
                  5 = A franchiser which sells the right to use its concept to one or more
                      franchisees *[GO TO 19]*
                  8 = DON'T KNOW
                  9 = REFUSED

18   *Are the headquarters of your parent firm located*
                  1 = In the same county
                  2 = Elsewhere in Iowa
                  3 = Elsewhere in the U.S.
                  4 = Outside the U.S.
                  8 = DON'T KNOW
                  9 = REFUSED

The next group of questions concerns your experiences and background as the **owner** of this business.

19   **[IF Q1 = 2 GO TO 20]** *All together, how many years have you been in the line of work you are now in?*

The next group of questions concerns your experiences and background as the **manager** of this business.

20   *All together, how many years have you been in the line of work you are now in?*

21   *Prior to opening or joining this business, had you owned or operated another business?*
                1 = Yes
                2 = No
                8 = DON'T KNOW
                9 = REFUSED

22   *How did you get into this business? Did you....*
                1 = Start-up
                2 = Purchase
                3 = Inherit/purchase from family
                4 = Or get hired as or promoted to a manager
                8 = DON'T KNOW
                9 = REFUSED

23   *On the average, how many hours per week do you work at this business?*

This next section of questions deals with the different things businesses do to succeed. First we would like to know your attitudes about success.

24   *Please rate the following business strategies by their importance to the success of your present business on a scale of 1 to 5 with 1 being not important and 5 being extremely important. How would you rate....*

		NI				EI	NA	DK	REF
1.	Lowering prices	1	2	3	4	5	7	8	9
2.	Reducing operating costs	1	2	3	4	5	7	8	9
3.	Improving inventory control	1	2	3	4	5	7	8	9
4.	Offering quality products/services	1	2	3	4	5	7	8	9
5.	Providing wider choices, products/services	1	2	3	4	5	7	8	9
6.	Cooperating with other local businesses	1	2	3	4	5	7	8	9
7.	Customizing products/services to clients	1	2	3	4	5	7	8	9
8.	Utilizing effective marketing/advertising	1	2	3	4	5	7	8	9
9.	Serving people missed by other businesses	1	2	3	4	5	7	8	9
10.	Working to strengthen and improve the local community	1	2	3	4	5	7	8	9
11.	Offering distinctive goods/ services	1	2	3	4	5	7	8	9
12.	Offering more contemporary products or services	1	2	3	4	5	7	8	9

13.	Improving your image in the community	1	2	3	4	5	7	8	9
14.	Utilizing new/advanced technology	1	2	3	4	5	7	8	9
15.	Seeking advice from consultants	1	2	3	4	5	7	8	9
16.	Training employees	1	2	3	4	5	7	8	9
17.	Professional development as an owner or manager	1	2	3	4	5	7	8	9
18.	Networking with businesses outside the community for mutual benefit (e.g., lobbying, purchasing services, training,)	1	2	3	4	5	7	8	9

25 *Overall, would you strongly disagree, disagree, neither agree nor disagree, agree, or strongly agree with the following statement?*
"Showing a profit is the most important measure of business success." Do you...
1 = Strongly Disagree
2 = Disagree
3 = Neither Disagree nor Agree
4 = Agree
5 = Strongly Agree
8 = DON'T KNOW
9 = REFUSED

26 *What do you see for this business in the future?   Would you say it will.....*
1 = Expand
2 = Stay the same *[GOTO 32]*
3 = Or Get smaller *[GOTO 32]*
8 = DON'T KNOW *[GOTO 32]*
9 = REFUSED *[GOTO 32]*

27 *Does the expansion include adding a new product or service?*
1 = Yes
2 = No *[GOTO 29]*
8 = DON'T KNOW *[GOTO 29]*
9 = REFUSED *[GOTO 29]*

28 *Could you tell us about the new service or product?*

29 *Does the expansion include a growth in existing products or services?*
1 = Yes
2 = No *[GOTO 31]*
8 = DON'T KNOW *[GOTO 31]*
9 = REFUSED *[GOTO 31]*

30 *Could you tell us about the growth in existing services or products?*

31 *Does the expansion include adding employees?*
1 = Yes
2 = No
8 = DON'T KNOW
9 = REFUSED

32   *Please rate the success of your business (by your own definition of success) on a scale of 1 to 5 with 1 being very unsuccessful and 5 being very successful.*
            8 = DON'T KNOW
            9 = REFUSED

33   *The success of business depends heavily on external factors. We'd like to know how much of a threat to your business each of the following external factors are. Please rate each from 1 to 5 with 1 being not at all a threat to 5 being a severe threat.*

		NT				ST	NA	DK	REF
1.	Access to capital (financing)	1	2	3	4	5	7	8	9
2.	Cost of capital	1	2	3	4	5	7	8	9
3.	Cost of rent	1	2	3	4	5	7	8	9
4.	Cost of raw materials	1	2	3	4	5	7	8	9
5.	Labor costs	1	2	3	4	5	7	8	9
6.	Availability of labor	1	2	3	4	5	7	8	9
7.	Quality of labor force	1	2	3	4	5	7	8	9
8.	Competitors	1	2	3	4	5	7	8	9
9.	Availability and reliability of suppliers	1	2	3	4	5	7	8	9
10.	Demand for your products/services	1	2	3	4	5	7	8	9
11.	Federal/state taxes	1	2	3	4	5	7	8	9
12.	Local taxes	1	2	3	4	5	7	8	9
13.	Government regulations	1	2	3	4	5	7	8	9
14.	Trouble collecting debts owed you	1	2	3	4	5	7	8	9
15.	Crime-shoplifting/ vandalism	1	2	3	4	5	7	8	9

34   *Which of the factors I just mentioned do you think is the greatest threat to your business?*

35   *Which of the following best describes your firm's experience with financing for the past two years? Would you say your business.....*
        1 = had no need for outside financing
        2 = was usually able to obtain financing with desirable terms
        3 = was usually able to obtain financing on less favorable terms
        4 = was unable to obtain financing
        8 = DON'T KNOW
        9 = REFUSED

36   *What were your gross sales for 1996?*

37   *Now I'd like to ask you some questions about your employees. As we define it, there are three types of employees: full-time, part time, and temporary employees. Not including yourself, how many total workers does the business employ?*

PROBE: DO NOT INCLUDE CONTRACTED WORK. DO NOT INCLUDE ANY OWNERS. **DO INCLUDE** FAMILY MEMBERS WHO ARE EMPLOYEES

38   **[IF 37 = 0 GO TO 39]** *How many of these employees are members of your immediate family?*

39   *How frequently do members of your immediate family who are not considered employees "help out" at your business? Would you say...*
        1 = Very often
        2 = Often
        3 = Sometimes
        4 = Seldom *[GOTO 41]*
        5 = Never *[GOTO 41]*
        8 = DON'T KNOW *[GOTO 41]*
        9 = REFUSED *[GOTO 41]*

40   *All together, how many hours per month would you say your unpaid family members contribute to the business?*

41   *[If 37 = 0 GO TO 64]* *How many employees, including immediate family members, are permanent full-time employees?*

42   *How many employees, including immediate family members, are permanent part-time employees?*

43   *How many employees, including immediate family members, are temporary employees?*

44   *How many employees did your firm have five years ago?*

45   *.How many employees from neighboring towns commute to work at your business?*

How many, of your total work force are
46 *women?*

47 *African Americans?*

48 *Asians?*

49 *Hispanic?*

50 *American Indians?*

The following questions are about which benefits are available to your full-time (part-time) employees.

51 *Do your full-time (part-time) employees receive any benefits?*
1 = Yes
2 = No [GO TO 61]
8 = DON'T KNOW *[GOTO 61]*
9 = REFUSED *[GOTO 61]*

52 *Is paid vacation available to your full-time (part-time) employees?*
1 = Yes
2 = No
8 = DON'T KNOW
9 = REFUSED

53 *Is paid sick leave available to your full-time (part-time) employees?*
1 = Yes
2 = No
8 = DON'T KNOW
9 = REFUSED

54 *Are health and medical insurance's available to your full-time (part-time)employees?*
1 = Yes
2 = No
8 = DON'T KNOW
9 = REFUSED

55 *Is dental insurance available to your full-time (part-time) employees?*
1 = Yes
2 = No
8 = DON'T KNOW
9 = REFUSED

56 *Is life insurance available to your full-time (part-time) employees?*
1 = Yes
2 = No
8 = DON'T KNOW
9 = REFUSED

57 *Is a retirement plan available to your full-time (part-time) employees?*
1 = Yes
2 = No
8 = DON'T KNOW
9 = REFUSED

58   *Are bonuses available to your full-time (part-time) employees?*
          1 = Yes
          2 = No
          8 = DON'T KNOW
          9 = REFUSED

59   *Is a stock ownership plan available to your full-time (part-time) employees?*
          1 = Yes
          2 = No
          8 = DON'T KNOW
          9 = REFUSED

60   *Are flex hours available to your full-time (part-time) employees?*
          1 = Yes
          2 = No
          8 = DON'T KNOW
          9 = REFUSED

The following questions are about turnover of employees.

61   *Approximately how many permanent full-time workers quit their jobs at your business during the past 12 months?*

62   *Approximately how many permanent part-time workers quit their jobs at your business during the past 12 months?*

63   *Approximately how many temporary workers quit their jobs at your business during the past 12 months?*

64   *Have you participated in any training or professional development in the past 3 years?*
          1 = Yes
          2 = No [GOTO QPI15]
          8 = DON'T KNOW [GOTO QPI15]
          9 = REFUSED [GOTO QPI15]

65   *What have you participated in?*

66   *Can you think of any training needs for yourself or your employees which are not available?*
          1 = Yes
          2 = No [GOTO 68]
          8 = DON'T KNOW [GOTO QPI16]
          9 = REFUSED [GOTO QPI16]

67   *What training is not available?*

68   **[IF 37= 0 GO TO 70]** *Overall, how do you rate your employees with respect to their attitude toward work on a scale of 1 to 5 with <u>1 being very poor</u> and <u>5 being excellent</u>?*

69   *Overall, how do you rate your employees with respect to their skill level on a scale of 1 to 5 with <u>1 being very poor and 5 being excellent</u>?*

70   *Now I'd like to ask you some questions concerning your opinion about the local community. For the following items please answer if you strongly disagree, disagree, neither agree nor disagree, agree, or strongly agree.*

		SD	DA	NE	AG	SA	DK	REF
a.	Being a resident of [CITY] is like living with a group of close friends	1	2	3	4	5	8	9
b.	If you do not look out for yourself, no one else in [CITY] will	1	2	3	4	5	8	9
c.	When something needs to get done in [CITY], the whole community usually gets behind it	1	2	3	4	5	8	9
d.	Community clubs and organizations are interested in what is best for all residents	1	2	3	4	5	8	9

71   *Suppose for some reason you had to move away from [CITY]. How sorry or pleased would you be to leave? Would you be.....*
       1 = Very sorry to leave
       2 = Somewhat sorry to leave
       3 = It wouldn't make any difference one way or the other
       4 = Somewhat pleased to leave
       5 = Very pleased to leave
       6 = DO NOT LIVE THERE
       8 = DON'T KNOW
           9 = REFUSED

72   *In general, would you say you feel 'at home' in [CITY]?*
       1 = Yes, definitely
       2 = Yes, somewhat
       3 = No, not much
       4 = No, definitely not
       8 = DON'T KNOW
           9 = REFUSED

73   *About what proportion of the adults living in [CITY] would you say you know by name? Would you say......*
       1 = None or very few of them
       2 = Less than half of them
       3 = About half of them
       4 = Most of them
       5 = All of them
       8 = DON'T KNOW
           9 = REFUSED

74   *About what proportion of all your close personal adult friends live in [CITY]?*
       1 =   None of them live here
       2 =   Less than half of them live here
       3 =   About half of them live here
       4 =   Most of them live here
       5 =   All of them live here
       6 =   I REALLY HAVE NO CLOSE PERSONAL FRIENDS
       8 =   DON'T KNOW
           9 = REFUSED

75   *About what proportion of your adult relatives and in-laws, other than very distantly*
        related persons, live in [CITY]? Would you say.....
        1 = I have no living relatives or in-laws
        2 = None of them live here
        3 = Less than half of them live here
        4 = About half of them live here
        5 = Most of them live here
        6 = All of them live here
        8 = DON'T KNOW
                9 = REFUSED

76   *Please rate the friendliness of [CITY] on a scale of one to seven with 1 being very*
        unfriendly and 7 being very friendly.

77   *Would you say the failure of people to work together doesn't threaten, somewhat*
        threatens, or seriously threatens [CITY]?
        1 = Doesn't threaten
        2 = Somewhat threatens
        3 = Seriously threatens
        8 = DON'T KNOW
                9 = REFUSED

78   *How would you rate [CITY] on trust using a scale of 1 to 7 with 1 being 'trusting' and*
        7 'not trusting?

        Next, we would like to know how you have been involved in community affairs of [CITY]
        since you have become the owner/manager of your business. Please let us know
        whether any of the following statements are applicable to you.

79   *Since you have become the owner or manager of your business have you held an*
        elected office for your community?
                1 = Yes
                2 = No
                8 = DON'T KNOW
                9 = REFUSED

80   *Since you have become the owner or manager of your business, have you occupied*
        a leadership position in a civic organization or a church?
                1= Yes
                2 = No
                8 = DON'T KNOW
                9 = REFUSED

81   *Since you have become the owner or manager of your business, have you been*
        active in a civic organization or a church without holding any offices in the
        organization?
                1 = Yes
                2 = No
                8 = DON'T KNOW
                9 = REFUSED

82   *Have you been active in community activities that are not associated with any*
            organization?

            1 = Yes
            2 = No
            8 = DON'T KNOW
            9 = REFUSED

83   *Do you have the time to get involved in community affairs?*

            1 = Yes
            2 = No
            8 = DON'T KNOW
            9 = REFUSED

84   *Do you have the interest to get involved?*

            1 = Yes
            2 = No
            8 = DON'T KNOW
            9 = REFUSED

85   *Please indicate whether you strongly disagree, disagree, neither agree nor disagree,*
            agree, or strongly agree with the following statements about [CITY]?

		SD	DA	NE	AG	SA	DK	REF
a.	This business does not have much to gain by remaining in [CITY]	1	2	3	4	5	8	9
b.	Whenever possible, I purchase business supplies locally even when they cost more	1	2	3	4	5	8	9
c.	The people of [CITY] really care about the fate of this business	1	2	3	4	5	8	9
d.	If given the chance, I would brag about [CITY] as a good place to locate a business	1	2	3	4	5	8	9
e.	As a business owner/manager, I am willing to expend resources to help the Community	1	2	3	4	5	8	9
f.	In [CITY], residents do not go out of their way to support local businesses	1	2	3	4	5	8	9

86   *The following items are ways businesses support the community. How often has*
            your business assisted the local community? Would you say you have provided
            the following support never, seldom, sometimes, often, or very often:

		NV	SE	SO	OF	VO	NA	DK	REF
a.	Technical and financial assistance in community development and planning	1	2 .	3	4	5	7	8	9
b.	Support for local youth programs (Little League, Girl Scouts, etc.)	1	2	3	4	5	7	8	9
c.	Financial donations to local schools	1	2	3	4	5	7	8	9
d.	Support for local bond issues to finance community improvement projects	1	2	3	4	5	7	8	9

87   *Please rate how much [CITY] residents appreciate your business on a scale of 1 to
       5 with 1 meaning no appreciation and 5 meaning great appreciation.*

BACKGROUND INFORMATION

88   What was your age on your last birthday?

89   Is the respondent male or female?
       1 = Male
       2 = Female
       9 = REFUSED

90   What racial group do you consider yourself to be a member of?
       1 = White
       2 = African American/Black
       3 = Asian/Pacific Islander
       4 = Hispanic
       5 = American Indian/Alaskan Native
       6 = Bi-racial/ Mixed race
       7 = Other
       8 = DON'T KNOW   9 = REFUSED

91   What is your current marital status?
       1 = Married
       2 = Divorced/Separated [GOTO 94]
       3 = Never married [GOTO 94]
       4 = Widowed [GOTO 94]
       9 = REFUSED [GOTO 94]

92   What is your spouse's present employment status?
       1 = Employed or self-employed on a full-time basis
       2 = Employed or self-employed on a part-time basis
       3 = Retired [GOTO 94]
       4 = Full-time homemaker [GOTO 94]
       5 = Student [GOTO 94]
       6 = Unemployed [GOTO 94]
       7 = CO-OWNER IN THIS BUSINESS [GOTO 94]
       9 = REFUSED [GOTO 94]

93   What is his/her main occupation?

94   How many people, including yourself, live in your household:

95   [IF 94 = 1 GOTO 96] How many of the people living in your
       household are under 18 years of age?

96   How many years have you lived in [CITY]?

97   What is the highest level of education you have completed....
                1 = Less than 9th grade
                2 = 9 - 12th grade (no diploma)
                3 = High school graduate or equivalent
                4 = Some college, no degree
                5 = Associate degree
                6 = Graduate of Vocational or Technical School
                7 = Bachelor's degree
                8 = Some graduate work
                9 = Graduate or Professional degree
                88 = DON'T KNOW
                        99 = REFUSED

98   Considering all sources, was the combined income of all persons living in your
                household in 1996 above or below 25,000?
                1 = Above [GOTO 98b]
                2 = Below [GO TO 98a]
                8 = DON'T KNOW
                9 = REFUSED

                98a   1 = 20,000 to 25,000
                            2 = 15,000 to 20,000
                            3 = 10,000 to 15,000
                            4 = 5,000 to 10,000
                            5 = Below 5,000

                98b   10 = 25,000 to 35,000
                            11 = 35,000 to 45,000
                            12 = 45,000 to 55,000
                            13 = 55,000 to 75,000
                            14 = 75,000 or more

99   Is there anything else you can tell me that would help us understand the concerns
                and advantages of doing business in this city?

Appendix B: Case Study Phase

THE INTERVIEW PROTOCOL

Introduce self.

Explain the research background and goals.

Let me start by giving you some background to this study.

1. Rural Development Initiative community study in 1994.

2. Demise of small businesses seen as major threat to communities.

3. Next phase, relationship of businesses to communities. Telephone interviews in1995 and 1997 with almost 1700 business owners and managers in 40 Iowa communities.

4. However, telephone interviews are limited in the information they can provide. I think it's important to talk to business operators and community residents in person to understand their perspective. In 1999 follow up with interviews in 4 of original 40 communities to get perspective of business operators and residents.

5. There have been a number of reports and press releases containing information generated from the various phases of this research.

6. By next fall at this time, I hope to have finished a book about on this subject.

Community selection

> Of the original 40 communities, 5 were selected for more in depth study. Your community was selected for in depth interviews.

Interviewee selection

> You were recommended as someone who was very knowledgeable about how businesses and communities relate to each other. We will be talking to several other business operators in town, some selected at random and some recommended as being knowledgeable about the community.

Confidentiality assurance

With your permission, I would like to tape the interview.

I'd like to start by asking you a couple of background questions about yourself.

> Occupation

> How many years have you been in your current position?

> Type of business

> Length of residence in community

Now I'll turn to questions relating to your perspective about businesses and communities.

1. Do you think businesses have any obligation or responsibility to society? Please elaborate.

2. *If not specifically mentioned above.* . . . Do businesses have any responsibility to support the communities in which they operate? Could you elaborate?

3. If you were trying to explain to a new business person in town why a business should (or should not, depending upon how s/he answers question 2) support their community, what would you say?

4. As you think about all the varieties of businesses in (. . .), are there differences in the amount of community support or commitment that they provide? What features of the businesses might account for the different levels of community support they provide? Prompt . . . do you see any differences by kind of business, owner lives out of town, size of business, profitability.

5. Has the responsibility of businesses and communities changed over time? . . . if so how . . . and why? Can you give a specific example from (town)?

6. Overall, how supportive are local businesses of the community of (town)?

7. What is the reaction of local business people to a business operator who refuses to help out the community?

8. Think back to the first time you got involved in or provided support for the community. How did it happen? What motivated you to do it?

9. Do communities have a responsibility to businesses? Please elaborate. What is involved in the community's responsibility? What kinds of support might follow?

10. Example of community–business involvement

Business Operator

What was the last community/school improvement project that you supported through participation, leadership, technical assistance or financial assistance? Or the last community/school improvement project that you are aware of in which area businesses were involved?

Why did (didn't) you get involved?

Did you encourage (discourage) others to get involved? If yes, what did you do and how successful were your efforts?

If you were to do it again, what would you do differently?

Will you get involved in the same way again? (Are you likely to get involved in community projects in the future?)

Have you ever been involved in a community project (etc.) that was detrimental to you personally or to your business? Please explain.

Have you ever been involved in one that was rewarding for you personally or for your business?

Resident

What was the last community improvement/school/neighborhood project where you observed support in the form of leadership, participation, financial support, technical support, other kinds of support provided by a business operator?

Describe how the project got started and how it proceeded.

What impact did the project have on the community?

Did the project have any effect on the business or the business operators personally?

11. Now I'd like to ask you a couple of questions about the community spirit of the residents of (. . .).

Is (. . .) the kind of place where people usually get along with each other in spite of disagreements?

What is the lay of the land regarding the clubs and organizations in the community? Do they work together? Are clubs and organizations in (. . .) generally interested in what's best for all residents?

When something needs to get done in (. . .), will the whole community usually get behind it and work together? Can you give an example to illustrate

12. If you were to give advise to another community that wants to develop high community spirit among the business community, what would you say? How should they go about encouraging it?

13. Has (. . .) ever had a situation where there was a conflict of interest between the community welfare and business welfare? If so, please describe it. How was it resolved?

14. Is there anything else you can add that would help me understand how businesses and communities relate to each other?

Would it be okay with you if one of us came back at a later time to ask some follow up questions or to double check some of our conclusions with you?

If you have any additional comments you would like to share, please feel free to contact us at the phone numbers listed on the letter.

Thank you

November 3, 1999

INTERVIEWEES QUOTED IN THE TEXT

Name	Town	SIC* of Business
Avala, Doug	Socksberg	FIRE**
Barker, Vince	Manasis	Non-profit
Bassett, Denise	Gatlin City	Services
Black, Joseph	Gatlin City	Services
Blanchard, Lamont	Gatlin City	Non-profit
Bernstein, Christine	Caizan	Manufacturing
Borrus, Adam	Gatlin City	Services
Bromberg, Arne	Manasis	Retail
Butterfield, Lance	Socksberg	FIRE
Case, Larry	Manasis	Government
Crowell, John	Gatlin City	Manufacturing
De la Renta, Roger	Manasis	Retail
Deese, Ian	Manasis	Retail and Services
Eisenstadt, Mitch	Socksberg	Services
Ernst, Harriet	Socksberg	Retail
Ferro, Kerry	Gatlin City	Non-profit
Fowler, Earl	Gatlin City	Services
Gear, Bryant	Caizan	FIRE
Gerdes, Craig	Socksberg	Manufacturing
Grafton, Nick	Socksberg	FIRE
Haubrich, Hildeth	Pikeville	Non-profit
Henstin, Sarah	Caizan	FIRE
Heston, Ellen	Pikeville	Services
Klazowski, Walter	Gatlin City	Services
Komendras, Paul	Caizan	Services
Krivit, Wilford	Pikeville	FIRE
Lindsey, Steven	Socksberg	Government
Lotus, Rick	Manasis	Agriculture
Mannes, Bill	Pikeville	FIRE

Markus, Robert	Socksberg	Manufacturing
McCaffrey, Jeff	Manasis	Non-profit
McIntyre, Derek	Caizan	Retail
Mahoney, Sylvia	Gatlin City	Non-profit/city
Matsumoto, Al	Pikeville	FIRE
Nock, Maggie	Gatlin City	Retail
Opinski, Greg	Socksberg	Services
Oringer, Max	Caizan	Non-profit
Palmer, Michael	Caizan	Agriculture
Ragstad, Iris	Caizan	Government
Rebello, Elizabeth	Gatlin City	Retail
Rosenberg, Aaron	Gatlin City	Retail
Rossides, Jerome	Pikeville	FIRE
Runciman, Keith	Caizan	FIRE
Scherrick, Matthew	Caizan	Retail and Service
Schmidt, Reid	Pikeville	Non-profit
Sing, Nancy	Caizan	Retail
Slaughter, Jill	Manasis	FIRE
Sowinski, Ted	Manasis	Government
Thomas, Jim	Socksberg	FIRE
Timm, Melvin	Pikeville	Construction
Zander, Corey	Manasis	Services

* Standard Industrial Code
** Financial, Insurance, and Real Estate

CASE STUDY COMMUNITIES

Name	Population Category
Socksberg	500 to 9,999
Caizan	500 to 9,999
Manasis	10,000 to 49,999
Gatlin City	10,000 to 49,999
Pikeville	50,000 and above

Appendix C: Characteristics of the Participants in the Telephone Interviews

	Rural	Urban	Metropolitan
Business Characteristics			
Ownership			
Sole proprietorships (%)*		63.4	
Percent local	96.0	92.7	90.3
Average business age	25.6 years	20.3 years	21.2 years
Start in business			
started-up	49.8%	54.3%	56.6%
purchased	32.4%	23.9%	23.8%
inherited	12.8%	17.6%	13.1%
started as manager	5.0%	4.3%	6.6%
Respondent Characteristics			
Percent owners	78.0	71.3	59.4
Average years of age	47.8	46.5	45.9
Percent married	84.5	80.4	83.4
Years of experience*		19.7	
Years of residence*		27.0	
Percent female*		28.9	
Percent "white"	99.3	97.7	96.6
Average education			
(1=less than h.s., 2=9th-12th grade, 3= h.s. grad., 4=some college, no degree, 5=associate degree, 6=grd.voc/ tech school, 7=B.A, 8=some grad.work, 9=grad./prof. degree)	4.8	5.2	5.6
Average household income			
(1=<5,000, 2=5,000-10,000, 3=10,000-15,000, 4=15,000-20,000, 5=20,000-25,000, 6=25,000-35,000, 7=35,000-45,000, 8=45,000-55,000, 9=55,000-75,000, 10=< 75,000)	7.2	8.2	8.6

*If there is no statistically significant difference in the values by community size, the average of
the statistic for the three community sizes is shown.

Number of Employees per Firm by Size of Town

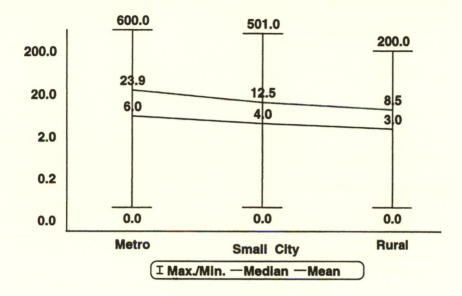

Gross Sales of Iowa Businesses by Size of Town (Percent of businesses)

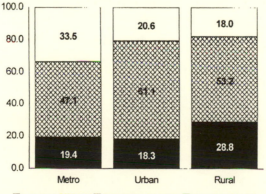

Appendix D: Statistics & Correlations of Firm Level Variables

Table D1
Rural Communities

	Mean	S.D.	1	2	3	4	5	6	7	8
1. Support	3.12	.95								
2. Involvement	1.53	.31	.52**							
3. Commitment	3.87	.60	.41**	.35**						
4. Education	4.85	2.01	.16**	.12**	.11**					
5. Owner/Mgr. (owner=1; mgr=0)	.78	.41	.04	.04	-.10**	.08*				
6. Live in town (yes=1; no=0)	.85	.35	.19**	.28**	.07*	-.06	.13**			
7. Local Owner (yes=1; no=0)	.96	.19	.09**	.10**	-.02	.02	.34**	.14**		
8. Log gross sales	5.38	.76	.28**	.24**	.24**	.04	-.38**	-.03	-.16**	
9. Log employees	.004	1.48	.20**	.14**	.20**	.03	-.23**	-.11**	-.07	.61**

* p < .05
** p < .01

198

Table D2
Urban Communities

	Mean	S.D.	1	2	3	4	5	6	7	8
1. Support	2.66	.91								
2. Involvement	1.42	.29	.43**							
3. Commitment	3.88	.64	.43**	.34**						
4. Education	5.16	2.12	.04	.19**	.10					
5. Owner/Mgr. (owner=1; mgr=0)	.71	.45	.07	.04	-.09	.12				
6. Live in town (yes=1; no=0)	.86	.34	.16**	.22**	.14*	-.07	.09			
7. Local Owner (yes=1; no=0)	.93	.26	.15*	.04	-.02	-.07	.42**	.11		
8. Log gross sales	5.62	.89	.29**	.21**	.17*	.07	-.31**	-.01	-.31**	
9. Log employees	.18	1.44	.14*	.00	.17**	.00	-.27**	.00	-.10	.56**

* p < .05
** p < .01

199

Table D3
Metro Communities

	Mean	S.D.	1	2	3	4	5	6	7	8
1. Support	2.59	.97								
2. Involvement	1.43	.30	.55**							
3. Commitment	3.89	.58	.33**	.28**						
4. Education	5.63	2.12	.16**	.24**	.08					
5. Owner/Mgr. (owner=1; mgr=0)	.59	.49	.15**	.22**	.01	.10				
6. Live in town (yes=1; no=0)	.88	.33	.16**	.13*	.17**	.09	.11*			
7. Local Owner (yes=1; no=0)	.90	.30	.14**	.14**	.08	.08	.39**	.18		
8. Log gross sales	5.73	.85	.16*	.06	.11	-.01	-.37**	-.09	-.25**	
9. Log employees	.42	1.40	.12*	.02	.13**	.09	-.38**	.00	-.14**	.60**

* p < .05
** p < .01

200

Author Index

Subject Index

About the Author

TERRY L. BESSER is Associate Professor of Sociology at Iowa State University. She is the author of *Team Toyota: Transplanting the Toyota Culture to the Camry Plant in Kentucky*.